Multi-Image Design and Production

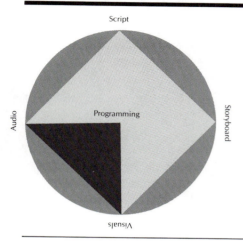

Multi-Image Design and Production

Phiz Mezey

Focal Press

Boston   London

Focal Press is an imprint of Butterworth–Heinemann

Line illustrations, unless otherwise noted, by
Carolyn Buck Reynolds

**Library of Congress Cataloging-in-Publication
Data**

Mezey, Phiz.
  Multi-image design and production.

  Bibliography: p.
  Includes index.
  1. Slides (Photography). 2. Audio-visual materials.
I. Title.
TR505.M49 1987   778   87-11804
ISBN 0-240-51740-7

British Library Cataloguing in Publication Data

Mezey, Phiz
  Multi-image design and production: an
  introduction.
  1. Magnetic recorders and recording
  2. Slides (Photography)
  I. Title
  621.389'32   TK7881.6

ISBN 0-240-51740-7

Butterworth–Heinemann
80 Montvale Avenue
Stoneham, MA 02180

10 9 8 7 6 5 4 3

Printed in the United States of America

Contents

Foreword

Our era is often referred to as the age of the specialist. As technological complexities and career-field sophistication expand, it becomes difficult to maintain an overall perspective. Some generalists do emerge, though, by melding related specialties, honing a cluster of skills to produce unique concepts or products. The multi-image producer is one such "superspecialist," combining the talents of conceiver, planner, writer, designer, photographer, graphic artist, sound engineer, and audiovisual choreographer (or programmer, in more mundane terms). While the individual producer might not be proficient in all these endeavors, he or she must have a working knowledge of them and many others as well—including sound design, narration direction, staging, and a host of necessary business and economic skills. As the size of a multi-image program (slide projector/ audiotape combinations) increases, the producer might delegate more and more of these tasks to other talented colleagues, akin to film and video production crews, but the producer of smaller shows often is required by budgetary constraints to be a one-person show, a "media wizard" of the highest caliber.

Multi-image is a mixed media art form— an electronic counterpart of cinema and opera—where many arts give equal support to a collaborative triumph. Yet despite the time and talent required to master writing, shooting, recording, and programming, multi-image is an accessible form of expression, a complex but manageable chal-lenge that can be conquered by individuals and small groups. As a result, multi-image productions from independent producers and small studios have survived and evolved in the past two decades, despite the fallout from the video explosion. Two-, three-, and four-projector shows used for community meetings, aesthetic expressions, classroom information, small group sales pitches, and many other purposes continue to find receptive audiences, even as large-format sales convention spectaculars are slowly dissolving away.

Small-format multi-image is a welcome entry port for many creators in the communication field. Armed with a few thousand dollars' worth of equipment (or less), they find complete project control is within their grasp. This leads to direct client interaction in all phases of the production, yielding a very interested, involved primary audience. The ease of transferring small shows to videotape for wider distribution is another advantage which enhances the size and style of the show.

Despite the attractions and proven success of small-format multi-image shows, there have been preciously few resources to help educate the emerging producers of these audiovisual statements. A sufficient number of magazine articles, seminars and workshops, and local presentations by groups such as the Association for Multi-Image International and San Francisco's Multi-Image Showcase have sustained several minigenerations of the continuing "new breed," but something more substantial was needed. Multi-image production texts are pitifully few, with the small-format producer virtually left out.

Into that breach steps Phiz Mezey, who has rectified past omissions with the publication of this book. Phiz—a "superspecialist" in her own right—has generously transformed a lifetime of experience into a written guide for the serious student, amateur, and small-format professional producer. Drawing on her own extensive career as a teacher (currently a professor of Educational Technology at San Francisco State University), writer (of numerous articles, scripts, and books), and award-winning photographer (with a solid history of exhibitions and national publications), Phiz has bequeathed her heritage of knowledge through a very complete, comprehensible book.

She establishes clear outlines for every major area of multi-image production, then fills in with enormous detail and illustration. As a teacher of multi-image, I welcome this book as a necessary resource tool for anyone seeking an accurate, practical

foundation in this unique medium. Phiz's undertaking presented an enormous task of organizing, simplifying, and documenting —all of which she has done admirably, just as any successful multi-image producer must when creating a bond with her or his audience. Every reader of this book should be grateful to Phiz for finding a way to synthesize the practical world into the written word.

Multi-image will continue to evolve, especially as more practitioners acquire higher skill levels and learn from each other's experiences. This book will be an invaluable tool in accelerating that progress, allowing a select group of Renaissance dwellers to thrive in a mass culture of increasing specialization.

Ken Burke, Ph.D.
Assistant Professor, Communications, Mills College, Oakland, California;
President, Northern California Chapter of the Association for Multi-Image International

Preface

When I began to teach multi-image production at San Francisco State University several years ago, I looked for a text to use with the course. I was surprised to find that few were available, and none seemed adequate to the task at hand. As the years passed, I kept looking. Meanwhile, I began to prepare my own materials, which eventually became the basis for this book.

I came to teaching directly from the field, where I had been working as a free-lance photographer, filmstrip and slide/sound producer, and sometimes scriptwriter since the late 1960s. I have always been concerned with some aspect of communication and how best to use each medium to reach others with substance, beauty, and clarity. I do not always achieve this goal, but I keep working at it.

One of my major concerns in multi-image production has been the overemphasis in the field on "special effects" at the expense of *substance*. I have also found that the very special craft and art of multi-image *photography* has been largely overlooked. The third oversight, it seems, has been the small production (up to three projectors) and the "small" producer. I have seen some exciting and innovative work in this area. Like repertory theater, it has its dedicated producers and followers. There is an untapped audience out there, and a definite market for small, challenging, and innovative presentations that can be used effectively in business, the community, education, and personal expression.

I have written this book for the small producer, for the individual just starting out in this multi-media field, and for the individual whose main thrust might be in another career area but who wants to produce a show for personal or professional application. I have tried to be clear and concise in my explanations and have organized the material so that chapters can be read sequentially or independently, depending on what the reader finds most useful. Although the book emphasizes the basics, it also tries to present the larger picture. I hope the reader/producer, if he or she so desires, can apply this information to the production of multiprojector wide-screen shows using more sophisticated equipment and effects.

My thanks for the help and support of members of the Multi-Image Showcase (MIS), a San Francisco-based organization of primarily small producers dedicated to the *art* of multi-image. Thanks also for the cooperation of the Association for Multi-Image (AMI), a national and international organization of professionals in the field. This is a starve-today/feast-tomorrow field. When we are busy, we are very busy. I appreciate the time given by those busy multi-imagists to search for slides and contribute suggestions for this book.

P. M.

Chapter 1

From Slide/Sound to Multi-Image: Introduction and Historical Background

As new technologies forge ahead, changing the way we work, live, and relate in our society, our desire for communication on a more personal level grows proportionately. The need to see, touch, feel, identify with, create, and communicate is a need within all of us that seeks expression in a more human climate. Today, the computer solves problems, performs complex operations, and does everything we can do—except create. Even a 35mm camera takes problem solving and decision making out of our hands; it reads light values, selects shutter speeds, and focuses the lens. All we have to do is point and press the shutter release. The motion picture screen, too, has reduced us to voyeur status. Through special effects that project fantastic picture worlds on the screen, we have become passive observers of a scenario too grandiose to contemplate in our own lives.

Technological advances have changed the world forever for us. But instead of longing for the good old days and indulging in nostalgia, there are more active ways in which we can express our individuality and creativity. By using some of the same technology that now seems so impersonal and overwhelming, we can communicate our own ideas through words, images, and music synchronized in a single expression. Multi-image production is one example of how we can organize and relate aural and visual media in a nonlinear presentation that can reach and teach audiences within minutes of viewer contact. Here, technology has given us the tools to reorganize time and space in a compact format that intensifies and enhances the perception of the viewer. In the process, the producer/creator meets challenges on many levels, involving mind and senses, relationships, organization and coordination, and technological savvy.

Through the process of multi-image production we not only touch other lives in a direct and personal way, but we also expand our own sensory, conceptual, and technical skills. The important ingredient here is that we are the initiators, in control of all the components, and we can make and reshape our production until we are satisfied that it communicates, in an original way, what we are trying to express.

Whether we choose to use one or several projectors, or address our presentation to a few or many people, we are tapping into a relatively new medium with a language all its own. That medium can deliver its message effectively in a fraction of the time it usually takes other audio visual media to reach the same point. It is the purpose of this book to guide the reader who wants to create satisfying, artistic, and professional presentations to a clearer understanding of the process of multi-image production.

MULTI-IMAGE: MORE THAN THE SUM OF ITS PARTS

Multi-image, formerly referred to as multi-media or slide/sound production, is unique in the audio visual field because it uses "still" photographs and graphics, rather than motion picture images, to build a story or present an idea. Yet it deviates from the tradition of still photography—"one picture is worth a thousand words"—because one image must build upon another sequentially and on multiple levels in order to develop an idea. Each slide might appear on the screen for a fraction of a second—just long enough to be "decoded" by the viewer; then the next slide appears. Or one slide can begin a slow fade up as another is slowly fading down, creating a third image in the process. This medium does not try to imitate motion picture's twenty-four-frames-per-second photography because the perceptive process is entirely different; the multi-image viewer participates in the process. In multi-image it is the viewer who must provide continuity and closure from his or her own perceptions and experience. This is why the audience is such an important consideration in the designing of a multi-image production.

In multi-image presentations, a great deal must be said in a very short time. This medium forces us to simplify, consolidate, selectively build one idea upon another, and choose our words carefully. The art, the poetry, and the music must be inherent. There are no lines to throw away, no embellishments. Perhaps it is the nature of the medium, but it is generally agreed that everything that has to be said can be presented in less than ten minutes—or the audience will begin to lose interest. Multi-image is a compact, condensed, idea-specific experience that intimately involves the viewer's senses of sight and hearing as well as thinking. Each slide has meaning and is connective. The sound track—narration, music, and sound effects — is carefully orchestrated to advance the story line without repeating what already has been stated by the visuals. No other audio visual experience is as concentrated or demanding.

When it all comes together—images, music, sound effects, narration, dissolves (programming)—multi-image becomes a total experience. That is why we say that the whole is greater than the sum of its parts. But there is little mystique to the medium. Multi-image is within the reach of most people who, with a little interest and patience, can put together a simple show for home viewing or more extensive application. One does not have to go to school to become a multi-imagist. Assuming we already have a camera, tape recorder, and one or two slide projectors, all we have to add is a synchronizer/dissolve or an AV sync recorder to enable us to program a complete one-projector or two-projector show (see Figure 1–1). The added cost would be somewhere between $200 and $600. Of course, we could buy more sophisticated equipment; we also could rent this equipment through the AV department of a camera shop or AV supplier. We could, if we planned for it carefully enough, build an entire system, from simple to complex, over a period of time.

I believe in starting simple, and that is what this book is about. First, we will find out what multi-image is, when and where it becomes an appropriate medium, and how it can be presented effectively. This book also will help us decide whether we have a feeling for this kind of production. There are many aspects of multi-image production. A person might become a producer, scriptwriter, graphic artist, sound engineer, multi-image photographer, composer, programmer, rephotographer, or any combination of the above in the process of learning about and practicing multi-image production.

WHAT THIS BOOK COVERS

This book addresses itself primarily to the small producer of educational, informational, and innovative programs, as well as to students interested in the field of multi-image production for commercial or artistic purposes. It examines multi-image planning and production primarily as a vehicle for creative communication and in the process covers all the technical information required to produce multi-projector productions. Since multi-image lends itself so well to artistic expression, as well as to the exploration of historical, social, informational, promotional, and educational concerns, the book covers these areas in depth.

Each chapter deals with a different area of design and production, including developing a concept and planning a show (Chapter 2); designing, scripting, and copyrights (Chapter 3); storyboarding the

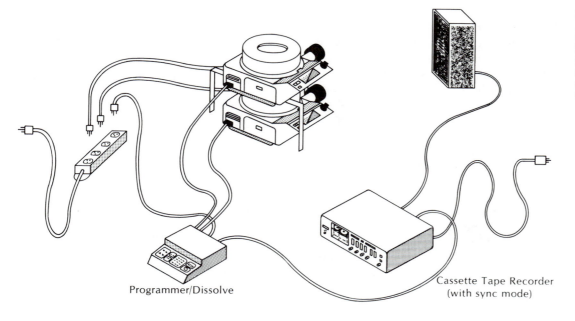

FIGURE 1-1
A simple two-projec-
tor setup today might
include two projec-
tors, a programmer/
dissolve, and a mon-
aural tape cassette re-
corder.

Programmer/Dissolve

Cassette Tape Recorder
(with sync mode)

show (Chapter 4); interviewing techniques (Chapter 5); photographing for multi-image (Chapter 6); selecting and integrating the music (Chapter 7); recording, editing, and mixing sound (Chapter 8); graphics: titles, formats, and masks (Chapter 9); editing the slides (Chapter 10); programming and special effects, and working with a computer (Chapter 11); and selecting appropriate equipment (Chapter 12).

Also included are planning diagrams, a sample proposal, the treatment, draft scripts, storyboards, photographic sequences, sample formats, and other related documents and visuals. At the end of each chapter is a glossary of terms used in the chapter. Appendixes, a bibliography, and a complete index appear at the end of the book.

HISTORICAL BEGINNINGS

The medium we now call multi-image is still evolving, and its potential has not yet been fully explored. It began at the 1900 Paris Exposition with a 360-degree, ten-projector exhibit that simulated a balloon ride across Europe. Hand-tinted 70mm motion picture film was used. That it evolved, ironically, into a slide/sound medium might have been a reaction to the limitations of early motion picture film. By using strips of motion picture film, projected a

frame at a time through a special projector, the first filmstrip was born.

The pioneer in the audio visual field was the Dukane Corporation, which in 1923 came up with the idea of developing filmstrips from motion picture film. Titles and commentary were incorporated in a series of still-frame visuals that were manually projected onto a screen, one frame at a time. By the forties filmstrip projection was being used for instruction in the military, but it did not reach the classroom until the sixties, through the support of government funding and special programs. Its value in giving short, specific instruction that can be paced at the convenience of the individual viewer (a precursor to programmed instruction) was quickly recognized as a classroom aid.

By then motion picture film had been replaced by 35mm stills, photographed with a half-frame camera that took seventy-two frames per roll. Audio (a turntable) and a built-in projection screen also were added. An audible signal on the sound track alerted the viewer when to advance the image on screen by rotating a knob by hand. Later, the filmstrip was advanced electronically, and a built-in cassette recorder replaced the bulky turntable.

Meanwhile, Kodak had come out with its Cavalcade Slide Projector, which it showed off at the 1939 World's Fair in New York. Using eleven slide projectors on a semicircular screen, Kodak presented two thousand slides in a "Cavalcade of Color." The sound track and control commands were carried on 16mm film, but there was no visual information on the film.

At a United States–Soviet Union exchange exhibition in the USSR in 1959, designers Ray and Charles Eames showed twenty-two hundred slides in "Glimpses of the USA." The slides had been transferred to 35mm film and were projected on seven TV-shaped screens, each 20 by 30 feet, with three screens on top and four on the bottom.

These examples are only are few of the many experimental efforts made by individuals and small groups in multi-media projection over the years, but multi-image did not reach the commercial and consumer marketplace until the late sixties and seventies.

EARLY SYNCHRONIZERS

With the popularization of the 35mm camera after World War II, film emulsions, including 35mm color transparency film, were vastly improved, and still-frame (slide) projectors reached the home market, along with mylar tape and stereo sound.

In the 1950s, "slides with sound" made its first commercial appearance, its first practical application being speaker support (the speaker advances the slides in a live presentation). Meanwhile, researchers were developing the first marketable synchronizing and dissolve devices.

Early attempts to synchronize sound and visuals employed pencil lead, aluminum foil, even the *absence* of sound to trigger the forward cycle of the projector tray. I remember transferring ¼-inch strips of aluminum foil to the back surface of a recorded audio tape. Every time the foil passed a contact post which we had mounted on the tape recorder, the tray in the projector would cycle forward.

Kodak did produce a tone-generating device in the early sixties that connected with its Cavalcade Projector, creating an audible beep on an open-reel audio tape. When the first Carousel Projector (model 500) came out, Kodak made a sound synchronizer (Figure 1–2), a small electrical circuit device the size of its remote control switch that interfaced with a projector and tape recorder. By pushing a button, the operator

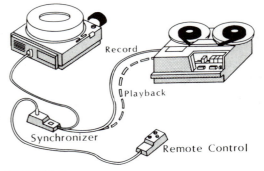

FIGURE 1–2
A 1960s synchronizer device connected to the remote control switch of the programmer. Every time the remote button was pressed, it recorded a high-frequency signal on the tape, which on playback advanced a single projector.

could generate an *inaudible* 1,000-Hz frequency signal on the audio tape (next to the sound track), which, on playback, triggered the closing of a relay in the projector (like a remote control), advancing the projector tray. This made possible images with narration and music in what we then called a slide/sound presentation.

THE DISSOLVE CONTROL

At this time, experimenters were already working to create smoother transitions between images, through the manipulation of the lamps of two projectors working alternately. Kodak came out with the Kodak Dissolve Control (Figure 1–3), a black box with one dissolve rate that controlled the lamps of two projectors through rheostats. The principle of the dissolve action is much like two dimmer switches operating through a single shaft. A knob is rotated, and one projector becomes brighter while the other fades to dark, providing smooth transitions between images. If we wanted a two-second dissolve, we would rotate the knob in two seconds, causing one projector to go from bright to dark while the other went from dark to bright. By adding electrical circuits to this dissolve unit, a continuous electronic tone could be recorded on tape with each rotation. This became known as an analog signal. Later dissolve control modules had the synchronizer built in. But it took another ten years for the hardware to catch up with the demand for slide/sound equipment.

Early commercial dissolvers were made with knobs or sliders, and some inexpen-

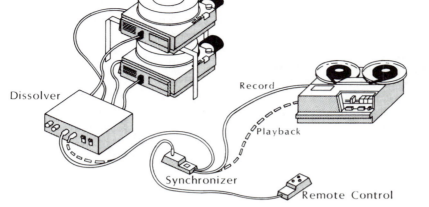

FIGURE 1–3
A dissolver was added to the synchronizer in Figure 1–2 for two-projector control. Note that the synchronizer is still external to the dissolver.

sive units today still use this technique (Figure 1–4). It was difficult to time a dissolve precisely. We had to keep our eye on a stopwatch, listen to the music, watch the screen, and manipulate the knob or slider, all in a matter of seconds. But many a successful show was and is still being made that way.

By the mid-1950s a company called TeleMation was marketing twelve-device paper tape programs, used mostly in military and government installations and displays. Dukane pioneered the first commercially marketed programmer in 1963, using 8-channel perforated paper tape to control up to eight projectors and capable of controlling up to twenty-four projectors (Figure 1-5). But it took another ten years before slide/sound, or multi-media as it was then being called, came into its own. In the mid-sixties, producing a show was only

part of the task. We usually had to travel with our presentations, carrying and setting up our own equipment, because no two manufacturers made compatible hardware and few clients were willing to invest in equipment, let alone deal with the problems of setup. There were too many patch cords, too many connections, and too many things that could go wrong during a presentation.

In frustration one day I asked the AV specialist at San Francisco State College, where I was then employed as the media specialist, if there was any way to simplify the packaging and distribution of our slide/sound productions. In response to our particular need Joe Spurgeon came up with the first fully integrated circuit programming device. It was called the Pulsamatic Synchronizer, a lightweight box that could fit in your palm. It ran on a 9-volt battery,

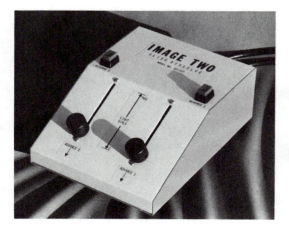

FIGURE 1–4
These two simple dissolvers using sliders and knobs are still in use today. The synchronizer is built in.

generating a tone on stereo tape that could be played back on any open-reel stereo tape recorder. Now, in one compact package, we could deliver to our educator/clients the slide tray, tape, and Pulsamatic Synchronizer, complete with instructions.

In 1969 Spindler-Sauppé (now Sauppé Media) developed a two-projector dissolve unit and the following year came out with a manual paper (mylar, surrounded by paper on both sides) punch tape with a sophisticated 1,000-Hz sync pulse time built in. It was called Media Mix and had six functions and nine auxiliary channels, capable of programming up to twenty-seven shows. These paper tape programmers were the forerunners of our memory programmers today. (See Figures 1–5 and 1–6.)

The light shows of the late sixties raised the audio visual experience to expressive heights. This new entertainment was called multi-media because it combined music, sound effects, graphics, photography, and colored gels in one mind-blowing presentation. With the popularization of light shows and experimental multi-media productions such as The San Francisco Experience in 1971, slide/sound began to attract widespread attention. The new media experience was the projection of multiple images on a wide screen, panoramically, in rapid succession, bombarding the audience with imagery and sound. One just sat back in awe and watched it all happen. Multiple slide projectors and motion picture projectors kept image upon image tumbling on the screen, while state-of-the-art audio tracks filled the auditorium with sound. The emphasis was on the word *multi,* and the purpose was to present a cornucopia of color, images, and sound to a paying audience. The San Francisco Experience show is still around, now in its fourth revision.

By the early seventies multi-media had become a viable commercial vehicle. Business and industry began to see it as an alternative to the more costly film and video production. It proved to be an excellent medium for client contact and sophisticated promotions, sales, and in-house training. Commercial popularity accelerated the demand for more sophisticated equipment, and audio visual manufacturers began to turn out state-of-the-art hardware—dissolver/programmers that combined variable dissolve rates, special effects, and sync pulse capabilities in one machine. This is discussed in greater detail in Chapters 11 and 12 on programming and equipment. Suffice to say that with the advent of the microcomputer, analog signals gave way to digital signals (a short "burst" of numbers or a code when the operator presses the appropriate button).

DEFINITION OF MULTI-IMAGE

The term *multi-image* was born in the mid-seventies. The new designation was meant to place the emphasis on the number of different images being projected at any one time and implied the use of multiple projectors, thus breaking from the earlier term multi-media, which acknowledged the different kinds of media involved. The term

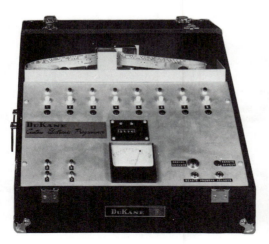

FIGURE 1–5
Dukane's prototype eight-channel paper tape dissolve control, circa 1965. (© Richard Schreul)

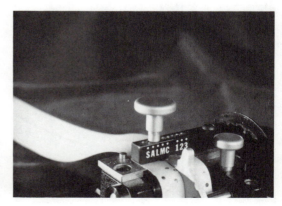

FIGURE 1–6
Close-up of the Spindler-Sauppé Paper Punch Control, 1960s.

FIGURE 1–7
Two-projector home setup today, using programmer, inexpensive stereo cassette tape recorder with built-in mixer, and two speakers. (Impact Communications, Inc.)

multi-image has not caught on with the general public, however, nor is it precisely defined. Perhaps multi-projector would have been a better term, since most producers argue that multi-image implies the use of two or more projectors in a presentation. Since the term multi-image actually means many images, one could argue that a single-projector production should be included in this designation because several images can be incorporated in a sandwich, or through masks, in a single-slide, single-projector presentation. I use the term multi-image throughout this book when referring to productions using two or more projectors, as well as those using a single projector.

Commercial use of multi-image productions continues in the eighties, although lower costs of video and computer equipment, and the advent of the videodisc, have opened new possibilities in the interactive media field. Multi-image production has now caught on as an easily accessible me-

dium for community outreach programs, as an educational tool, an informational and documentary medium, and an art form. Today, although large companies might still vie for nine-, sixteen-, and twenty-four-projector productions, many independent producers, whether for professional or personal reasons, are rediscovering and exploring the potential of two- and three-projector presentations. It is to these smaller producers that this book is addressed.

Almost anyone with interest in the medium can learn to master all the steps in the process of multi-image production. This is a field where one can choose to work alone, as a team, or in conjunction with experts in specific areas. Whatever direction we choose, we should be aware at the outset that it will take time and patience, planning and organization, a little imagination and losts of enthusiasm. As anyone who has completed a multi-image presentation can tell us, each step in the process is a challenge, and the final product is an

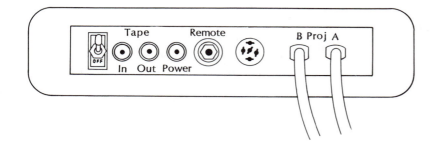

FIGURE 1–8
Rear view of a two-projector programmer/dissolve. It is lightweight and easy to connect. (Richard Weinberger)

FIGURE 1–9
This cassette tape deck is a four-track, three-channel machine. With this unit we can produce a master control tape with stereo sound and sync, then play back the show. It also has a built-in 25-Hz tone generator on the cue track that automatically stops and restarts the slide show as needed during live speaker support presentations. It is compatible with most external programmers. (© Phiz Mezey)

accomplishment. But the total experience is one of learning, growing, understanding, achieving, and communicating in a world that is becoming increasingly splintered and complex.

GLOSSARY

Analog signal Represents the actual change in a frequency. It duplicates (reproduces) both the volume (amplitude) and the change in frequency, in a continuous but varying tone.

Audio visual (AV) To hear, to see. The general term used to describe television, video, and multi-image production.

Channel A distinct path within an electronic system that carries a signal or conveys information.

Circuit An electronic path between two or more points; for example, the conduction of electrical energy through a given path in the interconnection of two or more pieces of equipment.

Digital signal Information transmitted in a sequence of discrete on/off pulses or signals representing numbers and having a given amplitude and predetermined tenure. More reliable than an analog signal because it is immune to electrical interference and has an increased dynamic range. Cf Analog signal.

Dissolver A device that controls the illumination from one or more projectors in such a way that the images fade from one into another at a fixed or variable rate.

Filmstrip A continuous strip of film in which the frames are a connected series of still images to be projected on a screen by a special filmstrip projector. The images can be advanced at the whim of the viewer, who controls the advance mechanism.

Frame One unit of image space of predetermined size (such as 35mm, 16mm) on a strip of film.

Leisure time A noun that describes a method of programming a show using computer memory to hold changeable cues until the show is programmed to the operator's satisfaction. As contrasted with programming in real time.

Light show A form of visual entertainment popular in the 1960s accompanying rock music shows in which a series of colored lights and other special effects are projected onto a screen or wall surface in concert with the music.

Medium An intervening agency through which something (written, heard, or seen) is transmitted.

Memory programmer Also called *leisure-time programmer*. A device used with its own built-in storage system to perform certain predetermined functions. In addition to controlling slide projectors and dissolvers, it can be programmed to perform other functions, often via interfaces, such as operating other AV equipment or controlling room lights. Cf Programmer/dissolve, Leisure time, Real-time programming.

Multi-image A visual medium in which two or more images are projected on one or more screens.

Multi-media The coordinated use of several media, such as narration, still photographs, motion picture film, and music, in a single presentation.

Panoramic A wide-screen effect created by combining two or more images in projection. Seamless masks are used to create the appearance of a single continuous image.

Programmer Either the equipment that programs or the person who programs using such equipment. When referring to the equipment, the programmer is either a real-time or leisure-time unit. The person using this equipment programs a show, bringing together all the elements through pacing of the dissolve rates, fade times, superimpositions, special effects, and so on.

Programmer/dissolve A device (either real-time or leisure-time) that combines the functions of a programmer, dissolve control, and synchronizer in one unit. Cf Memory programmer, Real-time programming.

Prototype A trial model that is tested and refined to produce a more sophisticated version.

Real-time programming Programming visual effects live, in the exact time they are happening. Cf Leisure time, Memory programmer.

Remote control A device that allows for the control and operation of equipment from a remote location.

Rheostat A resistor (impedes the flow of current) that allows for the continuously variable dimming of lights or amplification of sound.

State of the art The term used to refer to equipment and media that represent the latest and most advanced technology. It also implies excellence.

Still photography Opposite of motion picture photography. The term refers to the creation of single-frame images that are intended for viewing as prints, filmstrips, or slides in a one-at-a-time or sequential presentation.

Sync pulse An electronic signal generated by a synchronizer that controls the operation of one or more pieces of equipment. The pulse contains operation commands that have been transformed into a code that can be easily transmitted or recorded. The pulse may be either analog or digital.

Sync recorder A tape recorder that also has a built-in synchronizer. The recorder is usually a cassette player with the Philips ANSI head configuration/tape format.

Synchronizer A device that generates and decodes sync pulses in order to control the operation of other equipment. In this reference, it matches sound with visuals through a prerecorded sound track. When used with a tape recorder, the sync pulses are generated and recorded onto a separate channel in conjunction with an audio source that has been recorded onto the other channels. During playback, the synchronizer translates the pulses back into control commands that signal a slide change. The synchronizer is usually built into a dissolver, programmer, or recorder.

System A combination of components or modules, each performing a specific function and designed to work together as a complete unit.

Technology The entire body of methods and materials used to achieve the advancement of mechanical and applied science in industrial and commercial ventures.

Tone generator A device that generates variable frequency signals.

Chapter 2

From Idea to Production Master Plan

All creative work begins with an idea. But it is a long way from an idea to a finished presentation. We might have the best intentions of successfully communicating our ideas or visions to others, but without a plan we could bog down in unresolved detail somewhere along the line, or even lose sight of our direction because there are too many pieces to juggle. What might seem easy for others can be complicated when *we* attempt it.

Most creative ventures, as we know, are a combination of inspiration and perspiration. Ideas might come easily, but putting those ideas into an expressive form that communicates what we are trying to express can be work. One just does not scatter ideas like so many seeds in the wind, to fall wherever they may. An idea needs to germinate; it needs to be connected to other ideas to form some kind of coherence. Thoughtful planning, a "thinking through" of our project, helps us develop a place that can take us where we want to go once we know what we want to do and why we want to go there. This plan can free us from ambiguity and vagueness. It does not mean we are locked into a fixed idea, but it does eliminate a lot of directionless meandering.

Let's start with a simple idea: designing a show around a vacation trip. Even if the photographs already have been taken, we still have to plan the show. First, we can decide how (in what order or arrangement) we want to present our slides. Or we might find a central theme around which we can group our images. Or we might decide to focus on something unique about each area we visited: the statuary, the architecture, the indigenous people, the character of the streets. *Grouping images* and *planning sequences* around a *central theme* are key designing tools for a successful presentation.

We might even research some background material to expand on our subject and implement our slides by copying relevant historic or artistic scenes from available postcards or books on the subject. (Of course, if we are planning to show our slides outside the home or professionally, we should get written permission to duplicate these images. See Chapter 3 on copyright.) The point is, once we have decided on our theme, our next step is to develop a visual story line, or a series of sequences that will hold our viewers' interest and involve them more actively in our production. We would like them to come away from it with something more than when they arrived. It is one thing for our guests to acknowledge that their hosts are good photographers; it is quite another for them to say, "I never knew that before" or "Seeing that show was an experience!"

WHAT DO I WANT TO SAY?

One of the first questions we must ask ourselves is What do I want to say? Can I sum it up in a sentence? Can I express it as a statement? That is the hardest part of the task. But once we have clarified exactly *what* it is we want to say, the rest starts to fall into place. The following are some bare-bones statements that describe actual slide/sound productions that have been produced. I usually begin, on paper, with "I want to show that . . ." and follow it with the number of things I would like to express through my multi-image production. Once I rearrange these ideas in their order of importance, I can blend them into an all-inclusive statement. Even abstractions express ideas that the artist can use in a statement. The following are examples of statements from actual productions:

Statement 1
Skating in the park on Sunday is fun for everyone—old and young, families, people of color, people from different communities. Even a bad fall can't dampen the enthusiasm.

Statement 2
Five days with the Lacandon indigenous people deep in the jungle of southern Mexico gave us insights into a culture from another age, but three years later after the first road came through, the culture was all but gone.

Statement 3
Crime prevention is everybody's business; a concerned, informed, alert citizenry is the best antidote to crime.

Statement 4
Shapes and colors abstracted from nature, supported by music and sound effects, can create an intense sensory experience. Through creative use of masks, slow dissolves, and rephotography we will create, in increasing complexity, a feast of imagery and sound, providing a deeply personal experience for the viewer.

What we have accomplished, through our statement, is a clarification of our intentions. This opens a path that we can follow from introduction to conclusion of our audio visual presentation.

THE IMPORTANCE OF AUDIENCE

Knowledge of the audience is important because it will help set the tone, the pace, and the internal structure of our presentation. To define one's audience as just *anybody* is unrealistic, because we would not design material for a group of six-year-olds in the same way we would design for adults. And we know that friends sitting in our living room would not necessarily have the same interests as students taking a course in cultural anthropology. Subject matter, language, pace, tone, even the choice of images take their cue from the audience we wish to reach with our message. The more we know about them, the more successfully we can shape our material.

Let's look more closely at statement 3: "Crime prevention is everybody's business; a concerned, informed, alert citizenry is the best antidote to crime." (See Figure 2–1, page 12.) To whom are we addressing ourselves? In this instance, the appeal is to the residents of the city, the people of the neighborhoods. The purpose is to encourage them to form neighborhood alert groups and with the help of trained crime prevention experts to work out their own crime prevention programs. Upon further investigation we learn that this audience is culturally and economically diverse, including young working professionals, multiethnic minorities, and elderly retired people. Obviously, our images must reflect all these groups; our script must be simple and direct, not patronizing. The music should be neither classical nor punk rock. Upbeat seems reasonable. As we define our audience, some decisions are being made. Not all audiences need to be this specifically defined, but this example illustrates the importance of knowing not only what we want to say but to whom we are addressing ourselves. It is one of the most important considerations in a multi-image production.

CLARIFYING OBJECTIVES

We know what we want to say and to whom we want to say it. But what is the audience going to get out of it? We might say, "I just want them to be entertained." Really? Do we really want them to be passive observers and walk away with nothing more than ten minutes spent in mild amusement? They can get all that in a soap opera. We want our audience to have more. At the very least, we want them to be responsive to the imagery and sound and to remember what we had to say and how we said it. We might even want them to learn something, feel differently, behave differently, or take some kind of action as a result of our presentation.

Setting objectives for our audience will

FIGURE 2–1
Sequence of slides
from "SAFE in the
City," a two-projector
show on building
neighborhood alert
groups in the commu-
nity. (© Phiz Mezey)

help keep us focused in our presentation. If we want to foster an awareness of a problem, our material will be geared toward developing that awareness. If it is an action we wish them to take, we will create a mood or desire for this action. If we want them to gain some specific factual knowledge, we will pay attention to exposition, clarity, and pacing, and we might repeat these facts at appropriate intervals or review them in summation at the end of the presentation.

We might have multiple objectives in mind. We should identify them at the outset and pay attention to their implementation throughout our work. Whether we want to make a point, change an attitude, give important information, persuade the viewers to our point of view, or make them want to buy or take a trip, we should establish these objectives at the outset. Afterward we can ask ourselves, "Did I meet those objectives?" If the answer is no, not really, we might go over our material and find out why it did not work, then refine those areas.

Let's look at our "Skating in the Park" production, as described in statement 1: "Skating in the park on Sunday is fun for everyone—old and young, families, people of color, people from different communities. Even a bad fall can't dampen the enthusiasm."

How can we express our objectives here? First, we can start with what we would like the audience to feel, think, do, remember, and appreciate after they have seen this production. We can start with a general list headed by "I would like the audience to:

enjoy the upbeat mood and pace of the production."

appreciate the fact that skating in the park is a family activity."

be aware that it's a multiethnic activity."

be aware that it can be enjoyed by people of all ages."

see it as one of the positive aspects of city living."

be aware of some of the hazards in skating."

enjoy the upbeat music and colorful action of this presentation."

Now we have a focus and a direction for our production. Add a working title, "Sunday in the Park," which of course can be changed later, and we are ready to go ahead with a proposal, treatment, and storyboard. (One of our early realizations was that the images and music would be strong enough to carry the message *without narration*.)

WORKING WITH A CLIENT: ASSESSING THE CLIENT'S NEEDS

If we are working with a client, we should ask him or her many of the questions we have been asking ourselves. We might prepare a questionnaire to be filled out in writing by the client, or better still, ask these questions directly.

Needs Assessment Questionnaire (Partial List)

What is the general subject matter of the presentation?

Who is the intended primary audience?

How will this production be used?

What do you want to say? Or . . .

What are the primary goals and objectives?

Where will it be shown? (What facilities are available?)

How will it be projected? One screen, two screens, wide screen? One projector, two projectors, three projectors?

What resources or equipment are available?

What kind of budget will we be working with?

What is the time line for the production?

See a complete needs assessment questionnaire in Appendix A.

After this interview, we will have a better idea of what the client wants and can assess it before preparing a proposal. A *proposal* is a statement of the what, where, why, when, and how of our production, based on an assessment of the client's needs and our own recommendations as to how best to achieve them. The proposal covers what we plan to do and how we plan to go about it. Questions we might ask ourselves before

we write the proposal should include the following:

Is multi-image the best medium for this presentation?

Can we, based on client expectations, deliver what the client envisions?

Can the client personnel handle the equipment and set up the production after it is delivered? Or . . .

Should we make a one-projector show instead? Or . . .

Should we design a show for transfer to video tape?

Is the client aware of and prepared to meet the costs of production? (See Figure 2–2.)

PLANNING REALISTICALLY

Planning also includes a realistic approach to the problem of equipment and costs. How and where the production will be shown is an important consideration when designing a presentation. If it is the client's intent to show the production in as many homes as possible, we would not be thinking of a three-projector production with four-track open-reel playback. We probably would be planning a one-screen, one-projector production that could be packaged compactly to be easily set up and operated by one person. Or we might be thinking of a two-projector, single-screen production to be transferred to video tape for more convenient viewing. If we design our show for video tape, the client should be made aware that the images will lose their sharpness and color fidelity in the transfer and will be projected on a smaller screen with a different image-to-screen ratio (3:4) than the 35mm image ratio (2:3). If we design for inclusion of varying slide formats, we will want to plan for multiple projections and perhaps a two-screen butt overlap. (See Figure 2–3.)

What equipment is available; how feasible is it to rent or buy equipment for the presentation; how much money has been budgeted for film, processing, graphics, sound, and other production costs—these are questions that should be answered be-

FIGURE 2–2
Flowchart on plan-
ning stages prior to
production of a
multi-image show.
(Design courtesy Phiz
Mezey)

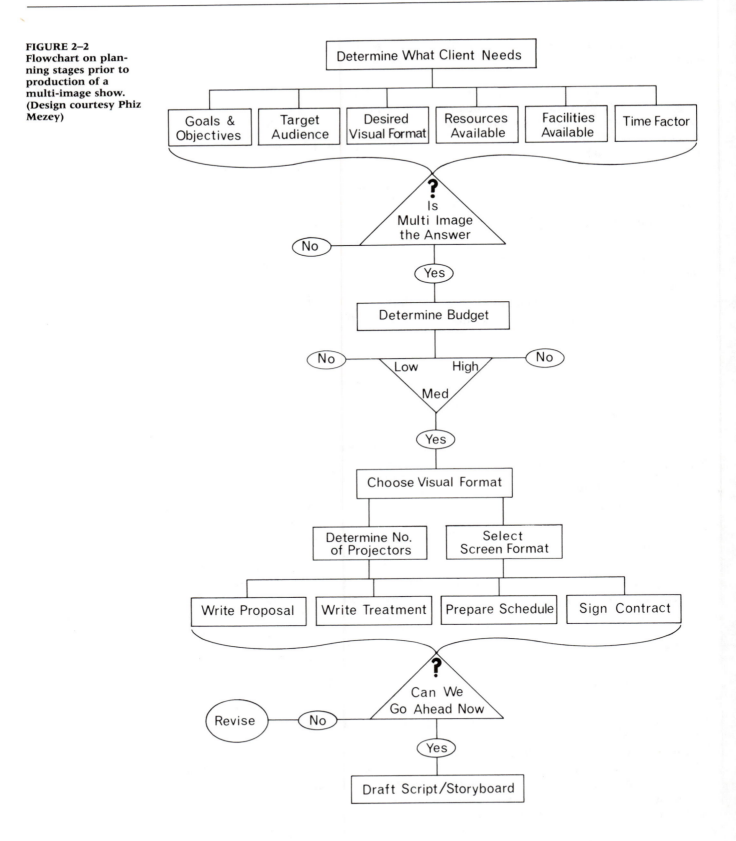

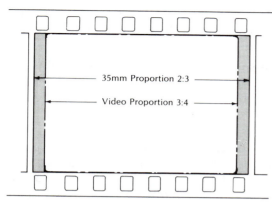

FIGURE 2–3
The ratio of a 35mm slide, height to width, is 2:3. The ratio of a television screen, height to width, is 3:4. If we know beforehand that our slide production will be transferred to video tape, we should make allowance for this difference when we photograph the show.

fore the production is designed. We also should be thinking about how long we want the show to be, approximately how many slides we want to include, and what the ratio of actual photographing to final selection of slides will be—5:1? 3:1? If it is 5:1 (for every five images photographed, *one* will be selected for the show) and we expect to use approximately 120 slides in a two-projector show, we are talking about photographing 600 slides, or around sixteen or seventeen rolls of film.

Are we planning to do our own sound track? With our own equipment? Or will we rent studio time? Will we need a sound engineer's time as well? Will we prepare our own graphics? Or hire a graphic artist? Will we do our own rephotography or send it out to be handled commercially? All these are early considerations that must be at least partially resolved before we get too involved in production, because costs play a large part in some of the design decisions we will be making.

RESEARCHING THE MATERIAL

Research involves all the above planning considerations, as well as searching out background information in preparation for the script. Before we design the final product, we should find out as much as we can about the subject from books, publications and archives, the people who are involved, and subject matter experts (people who are

knowledgeable in the field). We will need this information in preparing our script, and in some instances we might even conduct taped interviews to gain a better understanding of our subject matter.

THE PRODUCER AS ORCHESTRATOR

Timing and pacing will play a critical role in our production. It is generally agreed that an effective multi-image presentation will last from six to ten minutes; after that, audience attention tends to dissipate. That is why each image must advance the story line; that is also why the script, music, and pacing of the dissolves should heighten audience awareness and receptivity. A slide held too long on the screen, images that disappear too soon, or a sync pulse that is too early or too late can mar an otherwise exciting presentation. Multi-image is an orchestration of all these diverse elements. The producer is the maestro who shapes and molds these components so that they merge into a single, unified, cohesive aural and visual experience. (See Figure 2–4.)

REVIEW OF STEPS IN PLANNING

Thus far we have described our statement of intent, identified our audience, and clarified our objectives based on what we hope the audience will get from our project. We also have decided on the format (number of projectors and screens) and the desired

FIGURE 2–4
Flowchart showing the circular relationship between script, storyboard, visuals, audio, and programming. (Designed by Phiz Mezey)

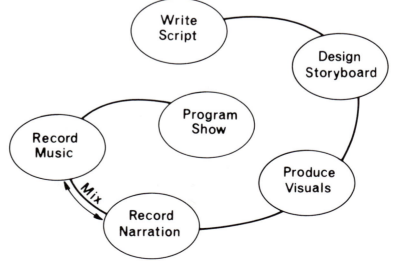

length of the production. And we have begun to think about what equipment is needed, whether to rent or purchase the hardware, the costs of materials, and the time (schedule) required to complete the production. We are now ready to work on the narrative design.

It is important that we understand how big or small the production can be, and that we plan realistically to bring it to fruition. Although it is the intent of this book to enable readers to undertake all the tasks of production themselves, once we know how to do it and have experienced working with all the components on our own, we might decide that we do certain tasks better than others. We might involve other people who are better trained or better equipped to handle the tasks that we would rather not handle. Knowing our own limits is an important factor in planning a production. (See Figure 2–5; see also the standard production agreement in Appendix B.)

GLOSSARY

Audience   The individuals or specific group for whom the production is designed.

Client   The person or organization that contracts for the production.

Design   A structural and aesthetic plan for the integration and balance of all the components in any medium. In a multi-image production, it also refers to the conceptual or structural integration of all the parts, including production format, narrative line, visual and aural balance, pacing, and programming.

Flowchart   A visual representation that depicts the logical flow of all aspects of a production.

Master plan   A chart or table that provides a timetable of what and when the elements of a production should be executed.

Needs assessment   The process by which data are collected from individuals or groups involved in a particular situation to determine the nature of the problem and to analyze and evaluate the avenues toward solution or resolution of same.

Objectives   The specific goals, usually observable and stated in behavioral terms, that indicate the desired outcome of an intervention.

Producer   The person or organization that directs, coordinates, and takes full responsibility for all stages of the production, from proposal, budget, and schedule, through preparation of script, storyboard, art, photography, music, sound mixing, editing, and programming.

Programming   The planning and execution of various control commands, using a dissolve device, programmer, and/or computer to control and pace the fade rates of various projectors in a multi-image production.

Ratio   The relative size of two quantities expressed as the quotient of one divided by the other. 35mm slide ratio is 2:3; video screen ratio is 3:4.

Rephotography   The process of duplicating film transparencies using special equipment. In rephotography the full image or only part of an image might be duplicated; exposures can be adjusted; color balance can be corrected; format ratios can be changed.

Screens   Multi-image productions can be designed for single-screen projection, although some designers might choose to project images on two or more separate screens. Slide format versatility is further increased by the use of two-screen butt overlaps (continuous) or a wide screen that can accommodate smooth-edged panoramics.

Statement   A clear exposition of the purpose and intent of a production.

Story line   Also called *narrative line,* it is the connective thread of a production that ties the ideas or theme together in some logical order. There may be other ideas or cross-threads interwoven in the fabric, but the story line carries the dominant thought or theme throughout.

PROPOSAL

LEGAL MODELS, THE LAWYER'S AID

STATEMENT OF PURPOSE: We would like to educate attorneys on the benefits of using legal models in courtroom trials to make their point quickly and clearly. To accomplish this, we will show how a model can be a visual aid to the comprehension of the elements of a case. We will show that a model, which appears real, allows the same setting to be seen by everyone: the judge, the jury, the witnesses and the attorneys. We will also demonstrate how the models of crime locations are made.

RATIONALE: Legal professionals need to know how the outcome of trials can be aided by scale models of the crime scene.

AUDIENCE: Practicing attorneys.

OBJECTIVES (desired outcomes): Attorneys will have models constructed for their clients in order to increase the chances of winning their trials. They will know how to use a legal model in court to help the jury picture the crime more accurately.

PROJECT OUTLINE:
    A. Dramatization of Chol Soo Lee case
        1. Police photos, mug shots, exhibit tag

    B. Research and preparation
        2. Interviews, drawings and plans, measurements

    C. Steps in construction

    D. Attorney using model to make points more clearly

PRODUCTION DESIGN AND TREATMENT: This will be a two projector, single screen, multi-image show, five to seven minutes in length. It will be predominantly visual with voice-over narration. Music at the beginning and end only.

EVALUATION: Questionnaire for lawyers who have seen this production.

RESEARCH SOURCES, RESOURCES: Police reports, lawyers' files, photos of sites, drawings, actual models.

PRODUCTION SCHEDULE:
  Script by _____   Narration by _____
  Storyboard by _____   Soundtrack by _____
  Photography by _____ Slide edit by _____
                            Cueing and programming _____

PROJECTED BUDGET:
  Producer $_____   Materials, film and processing $_____
  Script writer   _____   Additional expenses
  Graphic artist   _____   Travel   _____
  Photographer   _____   Video Transfer   _____
  Sound track   _____   PROJECTED TOTAL   _____

FIGURE 2–5
Example of a proposal and budget for a six-minute presentation proposing the use of legal scale models in a courtroom. Attorneys are the targeted audience. The writer/producer is Fredda Kaplan Robles.

Chapter 3

Narrative Structure, Preparation of the Script, and Copyright Law

Most multi-image productions start with a script. The script presents a story line and creates a structure in which the visual and aural elements can take shape. But not all multi-image productions begin with a formal script. Some shows tell their story entirely through visuals, with music as a background. In this instance, a storyboard—a frame-by-frame depiction of the visuals—will replace the script. But even a storyboard has a narrative line and a structure. In still other productions, the producer might record live interviews or personal commentary first, before incorporating the edited, recorded commentary in the script format. But with or without a formal script, all multi-image productions require a narrative structure, the conceptual framework on which the content will hang. It is this structure that will determine how the visual and aural strands will be interwoven to create an aesthetic whole. If our narrative structure is weak, our whole production stumbles, no matter how good the music score, how poetic the script, or how cleverly we use special effects.

The script, storyboard, and sound must be seen as an integrated whole, not as separate and distinct components. Each contributes to the building of the story. When we talk about the design of the production, we mean the master plan, including all its parts, as envisioned by its creator. It is important to the integrity of this conceptualization that the writer becomes a visualist, the artist becomes familiar with the narrative structure, and the composer reads the script and keeps the images in mind. (See Figure 3–1.)

BALANCE, STYLE, AND TONE: ELEMENTS IN NARRATIVE DESIGN

As producers we will be making several preliminary decisions. Will our production be predominantly visual, with the narration as counterpoint to expand or reinforce the visual information? Will the visuals be self-explanatory, requiring only the music to emphasize and expand the experience? Or will there be strong verbal content, with images projected to enhance the script? It is important that we know at the outset what the balance will be between the three media—which will dominate and which will support. This also is an important element in the narrative structure.

What will be the most appropriate style for our presentation? Dramatic? Documentary? Instructional? Comedic? What kind of visual will best lend itself to each of these styles? Photographs? Graphics? Animation? Can we combine different visual media in this production? What image format lends itself best to the tone of the production? Will our approach be light, mysterious, humorous, formal, or informal? Will we use a narrator, live commentary by different voices, poetry, dialogue? And what kind of music will best fit the mood and tone of this production? Classical, rock,

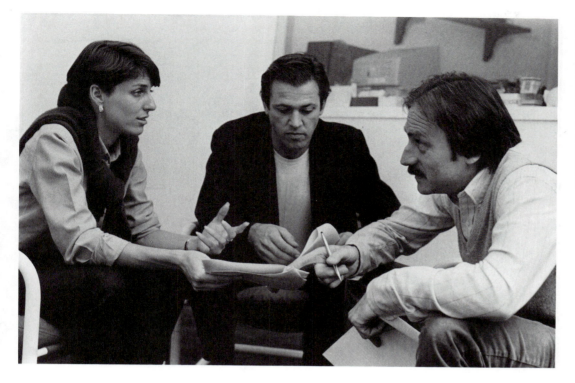

FIGURE 3–1
It is a good idea to bring the producer, writer, and other media personnel together in the pre-production phase to facilitate the flow and balance of the media components in a production. This photograph was taken at the studio of Rainbow Productions. (© Phiz Mezey)

electronic, popular? Will the music be original, live, or canned?

Along with these decisions about the design of our production are the proposed length of the show, the audience to whom it is directed, the size of the room or theater in which it will be presented, and the number of projectors and screens we plan to use. A description of our overall plan—all the considerations covered in the above two paragraphs—should be included in the formal proposal, which, when translated descriptively, will become the substance of our written treatment.

THE TREATMENT

A treatment is a short narrative description of what the audience will see and hear in this production. It is written primarily for the client who might not have the technical or professional background, the time, or the interest to go over the details of our proposal and production plans. In a few paragraphs, the treatment describes the content and format of a show. It sets forth the purpose, intended audience, narrative structure, and production format of our presentation, then describes what will be seen and the essence of what will be heard in each

major segment of the production. It is the whole show in a capsule. The treatment can be a helpful reference for the scriptwriter, photographer, and graphic artist because it puts the production in perspective, reminding us where we want to go and how we plan to get there. Sometimes an artistically realized storyboard can support and enhance the treatment (see Figure 3–2).

THE SCRIPT

Most often, the script is the first step in the production process and becomes the framework for the entire performance. If the images alone tell the story, then the storyboard takes the place of the script, and the narrative design is made clear through the images. In this chapter we will discuss the writing of a script, which in multi-image production sets the tone of the presentation, establishes the kind of imagery that fits best, suggests the tempo and style of the music, and determines the pace and approximate length of the show.

The printed page is something concrete to which a client or board of directors can relate. Once the script and storyboard have been approved, the producer usually is free to work on the rest of the production un-

FIGURE 3–2
Example of a treat-
ment. Robles takes
her cue from the
project proposal and
describes her produc-
tion for the client's
board of directors.
The treatment can
vary in length and de-
tail, depending on the
situation. (Fredda Ka-
plan Robles, "Legal
Models")

```
                          TREATMENT

                 LEGAL MODELS, THE LAWYER'S AID


This production will be a two projector, single screen, multi-image

show which will educate attorneys on the benefits of using scale

models of crime scenes in jury trials.  It will show how these legal

models are constructed and how to use a model to win a case by

helping the jury to picture the crime more accurately and vividly.

The production will be approximately six minutes in length.


This presentation will be divided into three parts with voice-over

narration.  It will open with the dramatization of a crime using a

model as the set and magnetized painted plastic people as the

participants.  Police photographs taken at the scene of the crime

will show how accurate the details of the model are.  It will raise

questions about what the witness could see from his vantage point

and whether he would be able to identify the face of the suspect

from that distance.


The production will show drawings and plans and the step by step

growth of a model.  It will show an attorney using another model to

make his point quickly.  Music and graphic titles will be used at

the beginning and end of the show.
```

hindered, as long as the client understands that, although the preproduction script will not change in substance, of necessity it will go through many modifications and re-writes before it is combined with imagery and sound.

• First Steps

As writers, it is important that we know exactly what the client wants to communicate, and it is helpful to jot down main ideas and subsidiary ideas in outline form, then work them into our story line. The project proposal, or treatment, can be helpful to the scriptwriter, and the producer can give an excellent overview of the project, including ideas relevant to the tone and feeling of the script, music, and images. Although there are no specific rules of multi-image scriptwriting, here are some suggestions for consideration.

Scriptwriting for multi-image is different from scripting for motion pictures. In film, twenty-four frames per second create the illusion of a visual continuum, and sound is synchronized with the lips of the persons speaking. Not so in multi-image. Multi-image almost always entails a voice-over because we are working with stills. This means that the viewer must put voice and images together in his or her own mind. That is why it is so important that the sound track and images relate contextually. Most of us have experienced the multi-image production where, as a result of mechanical misfunction, sound and imagery suddenly go out of sync. The result is confusion, frustration, and ultimately the desire to tune out and turn off.

We also have experienced another frustration—the image that just sits on the screen while the narrator indulges in an endless monologue, creating audience boredom and impatience. That is why multi-image scriptwriting is so demanding and time-consuming. The script should establish the pacing of the show; suggest the number of images that can be shown within a given period of time; and pare down the monologue by eliminating unnecessary metaphors and trying to convey ideas in simple, direct, concrete conversational form.

The multi-image scriptwriter must write for the eye and ear. Some phrases defy visualization. We must be able to see the images in our mind's eye as we write. The written phrase should suggest a series of images—not illustrations, but images that complement and extend the meaning. We also should listen to the sound of our words as we write. The spoken word is much less formal than the written one.

• Writing the Introduction

The function of an introduction is not just to grab the attention of the audience but also to set the stage for what we are about to see, like the overture to an opera. The body of the production follows, developing one idea or thread at a time and connecting these threads through exposition. Finally, the conclusion ties up all the loose ends, lest the entire piece unravel. It sometimes includes a review of ideas presented and almost always refers back to the opening statement.

Not all productions follow a formula, but successful narrative design is a continual interweaving of visual and aural components that create a perceptual whole, involving not only the senses but the mind

as well. Without the shape of content, without context, the audience might react indiscriminately to visual and aural stimuli, leaving a feeling of confusion. As we said, there are exceptions, but after viewing hundreds of multi-image presentations, I have come to the conclusion that too many of them get caught up in the sound track and special effects and forget what they started out to say or where they were going. Too often we wind up with great color and sound but little substance. (See Figure 3–3.)

• Simplify

Brevity and direct language are the dictums for the multi-image writer. The words should be simple and to the point; let the images on the screen be the adjectives. How much can one say in a fraction of a second? Or even two seconds? Just as the images must deal with one idea at a time, so must the script. Assuming that we speak normally 125 to 150 words a minute and our production is six minutes long, our entire production cannot contain more than 750 to 900 words. But we do not want continuous narration; there should be some quiet spaces for the viewer to contemplate the images.

Since we cannot view and listen simultaneously (to concentrate fully, hearing and seeing must offset each other slightly) and since the projector requires a 1.2-second wait for each slide change (in addition to the time the image is on the screen), we are even more limited in the length of our script. (With more projectors, of course, the slide-change time is minimized). Extraneous verbiage always slows down the action and interferes with the development of the material. There is no room for superfluous words in a multi-image production. (See Figure 3–4.)

Admittedly, some clients demand that everything but the kitchen sink be included. It is the producer's and the writer's job to discourage this, as it can detract from the effectiveness of the medium. Limit the number of ideas or concepts introduced, or at least combine them in such a way as to keep the essentials without risking the loss of the viewer's attention. If the verbal aspect becomes more complex, the visuals should become more simplified and supportive, more like a music background al-

FIGURE 3–3
Two examples of show introductions. In a few words and images, the script-writers capture viewer attention, introduce the subject, establish the tone and pace of the production, and set the stage for what is to follow. (Introduction A, ©Phiz Mezey, "SAFE in the City." Introduction B, © John Harrison, "A Gift Among Friends")

INTRODUCTION: Safe In The City

MUSIC Up,

and Under...

NARRATOR: San Francisco is a beautiful city.

We pride ourselves in our friendliness,

our individuality, our outlook,

and value the privacy of our homes.

So when this vision of ourselves

and our community is disrupted--

when a burglar breaks into our homes,

or a neighbor is mugged--

we react with pain and outrage.

Something should be done about it!

Well, something is being done.

All over the city people are organizing--

on their blocks, in their homes,

to prevent break-ins,

to keep violence off their streets...

A

lowing the audience to concentrate on the narration. At times this change in emphasis might be justified, but it limits the potential of the medium.

• **Writing Is a Visual Experience**
Writing for multi-image is a discipline that requires visual awareness as well as the ability to take complex ideas and put them into simple, clear, direct, unembellished sentences. The multi-image writer is a visualist who, as he or she writes, can project images or visual concepts that will work with the words. This is not as easy as it sounds. Many good writers think "liter-

ally," and they choose words that do not lend themselves to visual interpretation. It takes practice, and some experience with a camera or an art class, to develop a visual awareness that can be used in conjunction with writing expertise. Following are two examples of fairly straightforward statements that lend themselves to visual interpretation:

1. "Technological advances have changed the world forever for us."

   Can you write down ideas for a sequence of images that can effectively carry out this thought?

INTRODUCTION: A Gift Among Friends

MAN'S VOICE: The waiting is the hardest part.

SFX: PHONE RINGS

And every phone call makes your heart
beat even faster. (chuckles) They say that's
not too good for a guy with a bum ticker.
You wonder if this is the call you've been
waiting for.

FRANK: (Excitedly) Hello! (Then suppressed)
Oh, hi. No. Nothing yet.....

NARRATOR: Frank MacCrae has been living next
to a telephone and a beeper for over three
months. It's costing him about two thousand
a month to live just 10 minutes from Stanford
Hospital...

B

2. "All over the city people are organizing,
   on their blocks,
   in their homes,
   to prevent break-ins,
   to keep violence off their streets."

What images would you select to enhance these words? (See Figure 3–5.)

With the possible exception of instructional packages, visuals should never be illustrations of the spoken word, nor should the narrator describe what is already obvious on the screen. Since both are symbolic codes, each must enhance the other rather than duplicate it. Together they tell a story, each medium extending the idea suggested in the other.

• **Page Format**

There are different formats for writing multi-image scripts, but I like the split page where the right two-thirds of the page is designated for the script and the left one-third is for the visuals. (See Figure 3–6.) As I think of relevant visual concepts, I jot them down alongside the text. When one person is producer/photographer/writer, this technique can be enormously helpful. More often, the photographer and scriptwriter are different people, and there is no

IMAGES OF INDIA

India has many languages and religions, but Hinduism is the major faith in India. Hinduism is a religion with many gods and goddesses, but all are manifestations of one supreme principle, known as Brahman.

God, in Hindu religion, can be approached in many ways...as father, mother, lover, child, or even in animal form. Of all the Hindu gods, the three most popularly worshipped are Vishnu, the preserver of the universe; Devi, the Great Goddess; and Shiva, the Great God.

SFX: FLUTE

Who is Shiva? To his devotees, Shiva is everything--motion and calm, male and female, light and dark, ascetic and lover, everything and its opposite. He is known by more than a thousand names. Images of Shiva have been created to help his devotees approach him...

guarantee that the photographer will appreciate someone else's visual ideas, but it does help to keep communication open. Scriptwriter and photographer should be in early contact, although some producers find this unnecessary. The producer, of course, will coordinate all the activities. Often visual concepts will come from the producer as he or she discusses the script plan. I jot down these ideas, as I find them useful guides in my writing.

The initial script is going to be the first of many drafts before actual production. Ultimately, it will include, besides the narration, recording cues for the narrator and descriptors of the images opposite the words with which they are to appear. (See Figure 3–6.) It is from this final version that we usually record the narration and edit the sound track. The final script also might include sync cues, although in more complex productions, the sync cue sheets might be separate. See Appendixes D and E for examples of complete scripts.

• Writing Is an Aural Experience

As we develop each scene, always mindful of where we are heading, we should speak the words aloud and listen to the way they sound. Remember, we are not writing for print but for the ear. Rhetoric, a sophisticated vocabulary, and most adjectives are out. (Images generally replace adjectives.) We might not be creating immortal prose, but the combined effect of narrative, visuals, and music might very well be poetic.

• Scripting Live Interviews

Some productions call for personal remarks or reminiscences that must be taped live. How do we script a live interview? When we plan to include personal remarks in our show, we probably have some expectations of what the person will say or have prepared questions to guide the responses. In our first draft script we can project the substance of those remarks—for instance, "Jackie, age about seventy, joined a crime prevention block club after a neighbor of hers was mugged. She describes (in seventy-five words or less) her first experience with the group, and the culminating block party they had last week." After the actual interview has been taped and edited, Jackie's exact words can be typed into the script, replacing the above description. This

FIGURE 3–5
Slide sequence from "SAFE in the City," a Mezey production. (© Phiz Mezey)

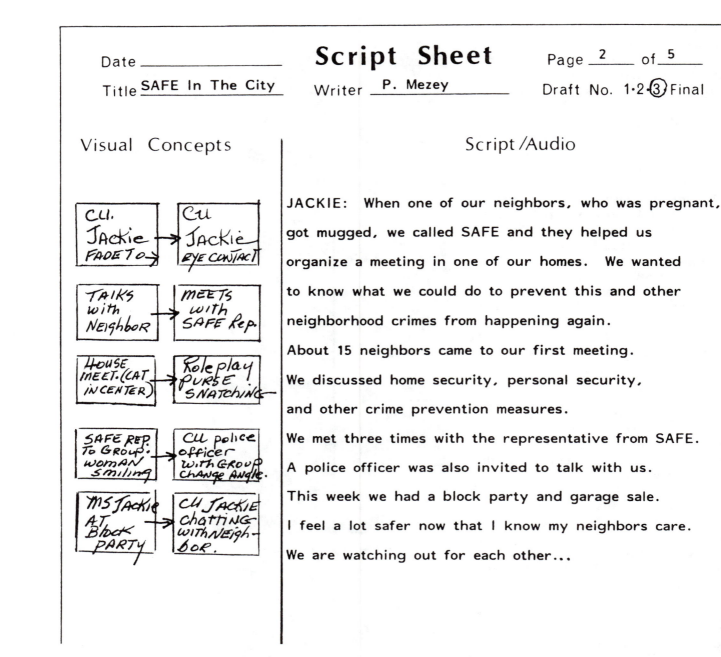

Script Sheet

Date _____   Page __2__ of __5__

Title SAFE In The City   Writer P. Mezey   Draft No. 1·2·③·Final

Visual Concepts

CU. Jackie FADE TO→	CU Jackie EYE CONTACT
TALKS with NEIGHBOR →	MEETS with SAFE Rep.
HOUSE MEET.(CAT IN CENTER) →	Roleplay! PURSE SNATCHING
SAFE REP. To GROUP. WOMAN smiling →	CU police officer With GROUP Change ANGle.
MS JACKIE AT Block PARTY →	CU JACKIE chatting with Neighbor.

Script/Audio

JACKIE: When one of our neighbors, who was pregnant, got mugged, we called SAFE and they helped us organize a meeting in one of our homes. We wanted to know what we could do to prevent this and other neighborhood crimes from happening again.

About 15 neighbors came to our first meeting.

We discussed home security, personal security, and other crime prevention measures.

We met three times with the representative from SAFE.

A police officer was also invited to talk with us.

This week we had a block party and garage sale.

I feel a lot safer now that I know my neighbors care.

We are watching out for each other...

FIGURE 3–6
Visuals, sketchy or concrete, can appear opposite the script. Here the scriptwriter/ photographer previsualizes the sequence. Final images might vary considerably from this early conception. (© Mezey Productions)

is useful for recording and later cueing the script. (See Chapter 5 on interviewing techniques.)

MULTI-IMAGE AND COPYRIGHT LAWS

I will address two areas here because they affect some of the decisions we will be making during this production.

1. What rights does the multi-image producer have in using the published or recorded work of other writers, photographers, composers, music arrangers, etc.?

2. How does a producer or organization copyright a completed multi-image presentation that includes the creative work of several people?

Any work that has been copyrighted (registered with the U.S. Copyright Office), before or after publication, is copy-protected by law. Since January 1, 1978, this has been extended to cover the life of the author, plus fifty years. Any infringement of these exclusive rights is answerable under the law.

• Fair Use

Written permission by author, artist, or composer/arranger of existing copyrighted work is always required before any of this material can be incorporated in a new production, unless the *Fair Use* definition applies.

Fair Use is defined as unauthorized copying of part of a work, or an entire work, that does not interfere with its "normal commercial exploitation." Fair Use assesses the needs of the unauthorized party in the use of the material (such as in education, research, or criticism). When determining fair use, the court considers the following points:

1. Purpose of use—commercial or non-profit?
2. Nature of material—type of work.
3. Amount of or portion of a work in relation to the whole—were some quotes (a portion of the work) or entire tracts used?
4. Effect of the work on the potential market—will the original author sustain financial loss due to this use? The many possible direct or derivative uses of published or audio visual media for either nonprofit or educational and training uses still remains a confused and controversial issue. It seems reasonable to assume that copying a limited portion of a work, for the purpose of personal use in the home or educational use in a classroom, is not an infringement of copyright. Yet a publisher might argue that such use interferes with the sale of books, records, and so on. Even if our multi-image production meets all the criteria listed above, we should still keep a healthy respect for the original (or published) work of any copyrighted author or artist, including visual artists, musicians, music arrangers, and so on.

Whenever there is the slightest doubt of our right to use this material, we should check with the composer, music arranger, author, artist, or publisher, requesting permission to use said material in our production. This can be time-consuming and costly, but there are agencies that can help us in this search. Some librarians will make a copyright search for us. There are music clearance sources such as the Mary Williams Music Clearance Corporation in Hollywood, California, or the Harry Fox Agency in New York City. In San Francisco the Bay Area Lawyers for the Arts can give helpful suggestions.

Many multi-image producers, however, prefer to save the time and expense of such a search. Instead, they use *library music* sound tracks composed especially for this kind of use and made available through commercial music libraries. Producers pay a library fee to listen to and select the appropriate music and a "needle-drop" fee when the music is incorporated in a production. The library takes care of all the clearances. This is a quick and inexpensive way to bypass the copyright search.

We also can buy *clip art* books. Here, the editor has done the copyright research for us and has duplicated artwork on which the copyright law no longer applies. For the price of a book, we can clip and copy any of the images in these books.

When using copyrighted material, with permission or under the fair use section of the copyright code, always give the author full credit by providing all pertinent information about the work quoted or used.

A third choice, of course, is to hire composers, artists, writers, and photographers to produce *original work* for the production, making unnecessary all or most of the above clearances. In this instance, an agreement should be drawn up with the artists involved, clearly defining their relationship to the production.

• The Copyright Law of January 1978

Under today's copyright law, passed in 1978, original art, music, photographs, and productions are copy-protected for the life of the author plus fifty years. Technically, we cannot copyright a book or a video tape. We copyright the literary, musical, artistic, and dramatic work embodied in the book, video, or multi-image production.

In the past each component in the show—script, music, artwork, photographs—had to be registered separately. With the Copyright Law of January 1, 1978, a new class was established. We can now register an entire "kit" of different components, such as an audio visual production, in Classification PA (Performing Arts), provided that the same firm or person owns all the components covered by the registration. For multi-image registration, a cassette tape (with the complete sound track) and a duplicate set of slides will meet the requirements for registration.

Of course, if the music had an earlier copyright date, the first date would take precedence—for the music portion. But the show, as a whole, would still by copy-protected.

The Copyright Office in Washington, D.C., will send applications and information on request. Write to the U.S. Copyright Office, Library of Congress, Washington, D.C. 20559. Or call their twenty-four-hour hotline, (202) 287–9100, for the forms desired. If more information is needed, call the Copyright Specialists at (202) 287–7700.

GLOSSARY

Aural Received through the ear or the sense of hearing.

Client The person or organization that contracts for the production.

Copyright The exclusive right to the publication, production, or sale of the rights of a literary, dramatic, musical, or artistic work, granted by law for a definite period of years to an author, composer, artist, distributor, etc.

Format (1) A plan for the organization and arrangement of a specified production. (2) The shape, size, and layout of a particular page, slide, screen, book, or magazine.

Library music Recorded music that is licensed for use in a production or is available for purchase. Once the fee is paid, the producer may use the recording without having to pay royalties each time the production is played. Cf Needle drop.

Live Voice, music, and signals in the actual performance. Or the part of a production that does not originate from a recorded source. Many multi-media productions contain both recorded and live components.

Narrative structure A basic structural design that underlies the writing of a script. It defines the shape of the content, including the story line, visual and aural formats, pacing, and cueing. This design may be modified, or changed, but it is generally the prelude to a production.

Needle drop When a producer selects the sound components from a music library, he or she will be charged for each selection used in production or each time part of a selection is used in production, hence the term *needle-drop charge*.

Rhetoric The art of literary composition, including the use of figures of speech, used to influence or persuade the reader. Rhetorical writing is antithetical to multi-image scriptwriting.

SFX Also known as *sound effects*. The recording of sounds other than music and narration.

Treatment An informal description of a production that tells in sentence form what will be seen and the essence of what will be heard in the presentation. It includes information relevant to number of projectors, screen format, duration, and intended audience.

Voice-over (Voice over image.) The projection of an image or images in conjunction with the narration from a separate source; not synced with lip movement.

Chapter 4

Storyboarding: The Visual Backbone of a Presentation

The word *storyboard* defines itself. Storyboarding is our visual projection, on paper, of the flow of imagery as we envision it in our production. Of course, it may be just an approximation of the story line or narrative flow of our show, yet rough sketches can indicate the relationship of images from frame to frame, as well as size, direction, color, and continuity of subject matter. Thus, before we get involved with the expense and time of photographing, animating, or graphically illustrating our show, the storyboard can help us organize our visual thinking in much the same way the script organizes our ideas on the verbal level. A storyboard is the photographer's and graphic artist's "script" and can be a valuable organizing tool for the producer as well. Storyboards also help the client conceptualize the production. If the script gives structure to the presentation, it is the storyboard that fleshes it out and adds the visual dimension.

There are two kinds of storyboards. One is specific and detailed, giving the client a visual preview of the production; it virtually sells the idea. The other is less detailed (it can be a series of imperfect sketches) and is used as a planning tool for the producer, graphic artist, photographer, and programmer. There are different formats used for storyboarding: (1) printed or photocopied frames in the same 2:3 ratio as 35mm film frames, grouped sequentially on a sheet of 8½-by-11-inch paper; (2) 3-by-5 unlined file cards, each representing a single frame. Sometimes an illustrator is called in to create a storyboard of larger dimensions to "sell" the idea to the client.

When we storyboard for production purposes, we usually draw rough projections, indicating subject continuity, relationship, direction, spacing, relative size, and so on. Below each sketch is space to include brief descriptors, which sometimes carry graphic instructions or paraphrase the script idea that accompanies the image. (See Figures 4–1, 4–2, 4–3.)

STORYBOARDING AS A PLANNING TOOL

After visualizing what we hope to show in our production, we will change our minds many times. That is why some multi-image designers prefer to use 3-by-5 unlined file cards. This permits the frame content to be moved around on a surface until a preferable sequence or relationship is found. Each card can be numbered sequentially in pencil pending further changes. Cards, however, require a great deal of wall space or table space when spread out. Some designers prefer a smaller format—several printed frames grouped in tandem on a single 8½-by-11-inch page—so that images and relationships can be seen immediately. Under the frames on most printed layout sheets, there is adequate space to add visual descriptors or corresponding phrases from the script. In either format, the materials are readily available. The file card storyboard can be tacked to corkboard, or a wall

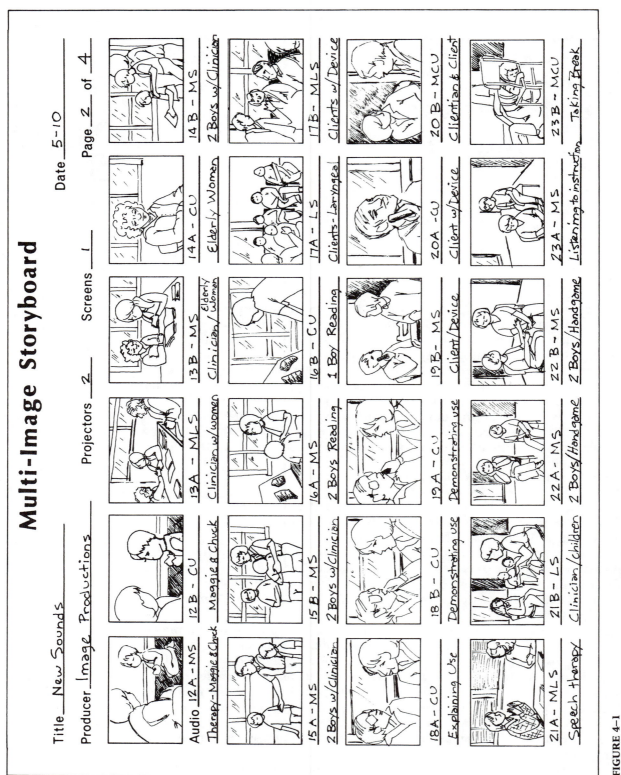

FIGURE 4–1
Storyboard for a two-projector production (video transfer) to attract students for a training program in the field of communicative disorders. (Image Productions; Suzanne Haile, artist)

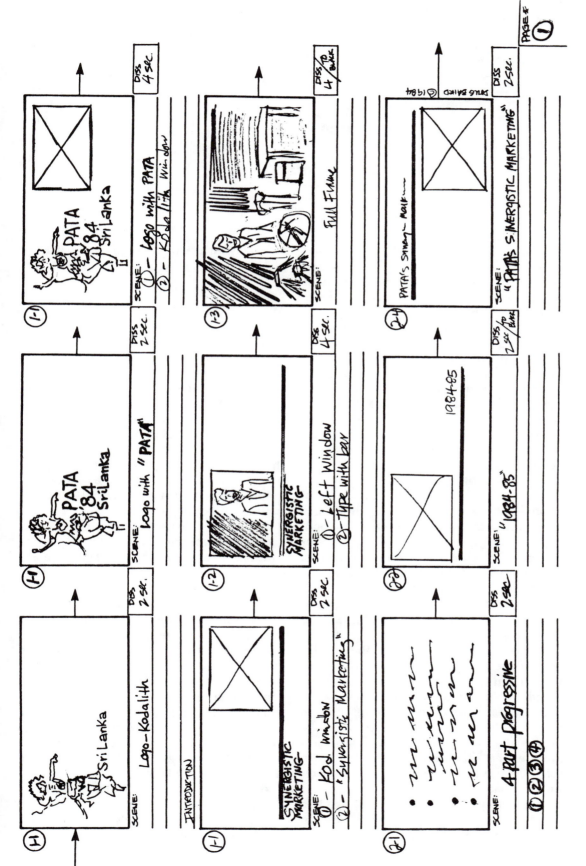

FIGURE 4-2
This storyboard for a three-projector speaker-support series is a preliminary sketch showing different possible introductions for the series. The windows with the Xs show where a photograph (not yet selected) will appear. Each producer creates his or her own storyboard system, and thus no two are exactly the same. (Doug Baird Productions)

FIGURE 4–3
Three-by-five file cards are another way to prepare a storyboard. Individual cards offer the convenience of changing the arrangement without having to redo the whole storyboard. Also, old cards can be discarded and new ones inserted as the work progresses.

planning board can be purchased in an AV, stationery, or school supply store. Television or multi-image layout pads or single sheets also can be purchased with the frames preprinted. Or we can design our own storyboard format to meet the needs of a specific production.

Although the script usually is written before the storyboard, there are instances where the storyboard is designed first or where there is no script at all and the storyboard replaces the script. Usually the storyboard, at least in rough form, is completed before the photographer or artist begins his or her work. Sometimes it is not completed until after most of the photographs have been taken, as in the case of photographs selected from existing files.

Why, we may ask, is there a need for both a multi-image script, which already includes in its format a column for visuals, and a storyboard? They serve different purposes. The storyboard emphasizes the visual continuity, with a few descriptive lines from the script. The script emphasizes the verbal continuity, with brief descriptors of the accompanying visuals. At the conclusion of the production stage, visual information can be transferred from the storyboard to the visual column in the script (usually as abbreviated descriptions) to help coordinate the audio track with the visuals and as a guide in the final programming of the show. Since I write my own scripts, I use the visual column as my preliminary storyboard so that I can project visual concepts while I am writing. If a client is involved, I hire a graphic artist to transcribe these concepts to a more artistic

visual layout when the script has been completed.

MANY WAYS TO STORYBOARD

Like everything else in multi-image production, there is no absolute about storyboarding. It is a creative process. Depending on the complexity of the subject matter and the situation, the type of script and storyboard is the producer's choice. Each producer sets up his or her own system and time frame. The important point is that there should be a system for pulling as much of this material together as is possible before production starts; otherwise the situation can become chaotic.

I know a documentary imagist who scripts and storyboards in her head. She is fortunate to have such an excellent memory, as well as an understanding client. The secret of her success (or failure), however, is that she always follows the same formula. There is no innovation. What worked once will work again, and again. Maybe.

Some creative multi-imagists do not storyboard at all. This approach leads the photographer to a tendency to overshoot in order to cover all the possibilities. Unfortunately, there will inevitably be gaps in these sequences when they are pieced together on the light table during the editing phase. And this means reshooting at a later date to fill in the blanks. My own experience in multi-image indicates that storyboarding helps the inexperienced designer visualize the flow of images and words, can save money in production time and materials, and will shave hours off the editing phase of production.

STORYBOARDING FROM FILE

If we have the slides already in file, the storyboard can be created after we have pulled some of these images together into possible sequences. We can place these slides in plastic pages (twenty slides per page) and make a color photocopy of the entire page at a local copy shop. Then we can cut the photocopied frames apart and make a storyboard pasteup of selected frames to be shown to the client. Having such a layout gives us greater freedom in playing with individual slides on the light table. Thus, we can try out different arrangements in the editing stage, while still being able to return to the storyboard layout for comparison.

CREATING A SHOT LIST

Some producers use the storyboard to create a shot list (Figure 4–4) for the photographers, grouping the images by physical location even though they may be out of sequence. This can be an enormous time saver for the photographer who must shoot in several locations. It is important, however, that the photographer refers to the storyboard so that he or she can keep mood, relationship, color, size, and continuity consistent. I always check out the storyboard and the script before and while I am working from a shot list. Later, when the pictures have been taken and laid out in a first edit on the light table, we can rearrange them to conform to the original storyboard. Sometimes the arrangement of the actual slides laid out on the light table might be preferable to, and deviate from, the original storyboard. That is fine: The storyboard has done its job.

MATCHING FRAMES ON THE STORYBOARD

We have talked at great length about the importance of content and narrative design for the successful communication of our objectives in a multi-image presentation. But we have said little about the medium of multi-image and how, through its unique syntax, the medium itself can challenge our perceptions in ways not experienced before. To utilize its potential fully we must consider how it is different from other media.

In multi-image we use still images, projected sequentially, but there is never the illusion of motion as there is in film. The success of multi-image projection is dependent on movement of another kind. In motion picture film we view twenty-four frames per second. In still photographs one image might be contemplated for as long as the viewer desires. Neither situation is possible in multi-image. The images appear on the screen as single frames but might not be held in view more than a fraction of a second before dissolving into other images. In that brief time the viewer must grasp the idea, or hold the image in the mind's eye, and anticipate the next frame, drawing on her or his own perceptions. In multi-image we are relating to both a linear flow and a layering of ideas. The viewer becomes an active participant in that process. That is why each frame at best can represent essentially only one idea at a time. Each slide becomes a building block in a sequence of images that unfold in narrative or conceptual progression.

Relating slides by content, for continuity, physical direction, color balance, and relative size, is very important in this process and should be a prime consideration in the storyboard phase. In single-projector productions, the projector lamp fades out between each slide, and whether the image is frozen on the screen or cut, we will always have that awkward moment of black between images. With two or more projectors, one image dissolves into another. The dissolve function creates more options, particularly in a slow dissolve. Here, as one image fades out, another is emerging, creating a third image that seems to grow out of them. This is where the art of matching slides comes in. In planning our storyboard, we should be thinking not only of the story line, but also of how the placement of the visuals can implement and advance it. (See Figure 4–5.) Although relative size, shape, color, placement, and

FIGURE 4-4
Another convenience is the shot list, pulled together from the storyboard. This is a valuable work sheet for the photographer, allowing him or her to group the photographs in one location at a time. The photographer should always have access to the storyboard and the script for reference on relationships and continuity.
(© Mezey Productions)

Shot Sheet

Production/Project ___SAFE In The City___   Page ___1___ of ___2___

Producer___P. Mezey___   Date_____

Slide No.	Sequence	LS MS CU	Description
	7	MS/	Safety Specialist with homeowner or
		CU	rentor, showing SAFEty (burglary) haz-
			ards in home. (Several shots, different
			check-points for 5-slide sequence.)
			Incl. Safety Specialist writing notes
			on pad as she's checking.
	7	CU	Identification Process, using tool to
			engrave ID.
	1	MS	Police Officer with concerned citi-
			zens; homes in bkgnd.
		CU	Same group, citizens' faces.
	5	MLS/	SAFE staff in meeting, sharing ideas,
		MS	etc. Keep this informal.
		MS/CU	Two staff memb. in animated discussion
	4	CU	Homeowner/rentor discussing (with aud-
			ience) the crime that didn't happen
			because of neighborhood vigilance.
			Get dynamic shot.
	4	LS/MS/	House meeting, daylight. Take group
		CU	interaction, for 5-slide sequence.
			CU faces, also MS two/three-person
			conversation.
	4/6	LS/MS	A different house meeting, same treat-
		CU	ment. Show ethnic/cultural variation.
	10		Photos of Mayor, at desk, talking. At
			meeting, speaking. Get her CU, as if
			talking to audience.

direction of the subject matter are important in single-projector productions, these elements become critical in two- and three-projector productions. An early knowledge of the story line and script, as well as an understanding of how images can be paired and juxtaposed, is an asset to the photographer or graphic artist involved in multi-image production. Just as it is important for a multi-image writer to have a visual orientation, it is equally important for a photographer to be able to think conceptually and sequentially.

RE-CAPTURING THE ORIGINAL IMPACT

Here is a descriptive example of what I mean. We all have experienced nature's changing colors, shapes, and forms. Many of us have photographed these moments, only to be disappointed by the two-dimensional result, which never seems to do justice to our original experience. Multi-image is a medium that allows us to re-create the emotional impact of that experience.

Let's take a morning scene of mountains and lake, the mist sitting low on the lake. We could take several color transparencies of the lake's early morning dark blues and purples, the low mist, even the spot of red on the horizon. We could show the scene brightening, red turning to yellow, yellow fading finally to white hot light. Verbally it works; visually it becomes tedious after three slides. The dissolves of one image into another would give us a nice progression of color but little else. Everything is chronological and predictable—not very exciting. As multi-image photographers, we have the opportunity to work on many levels, to move back and forth within the planes of the scene, and even to take some liberties with time.

Just as a writer shapes and bends reality to get closer to the truth, so can a photographer shape and bend the truth of what he or she sees to re-create the original impact of a scene. At different focal lengths, our lens might explore the mountain range—at a distance, at middle distance, and close up—while the aforementioned color changes are taking place. We might photograph a log poking out of the watery mist, then take several frames of moisture

A

B

C

D

E

FIGURE 4–5
This outdoor sequence can be re-arranged several different ways, depending on what the multi-imagist wants to say. We could open with slide *B* and end with slide *E*. Editing, in the context of the whole, is covered in Chapter 10. (© Phiz Mezey)

droplets on a twig, the sun through a leaf, a small bird on a branch, and a person filling a pan with water at lakeside, all with the mountains in the background.

Later, by creatively relating and sequencing these transparencies, both in a forward progression and as a layered composite, we can bring our viewers far closer to the truth of our experience than a straight documentation of that morning's sunrise could have done. Exploring the entire scene from distant range to smallest detail—light and shadow, sunshine and mist, blues and yellows—is what multi-image is all about. Being able to conceptualize the sense of this scene (not the chronology in this instance) is what storyboarding is all about. Let the photographer fill in the subtleties. The photographer might be presented with only the bare-bones concept, but if we have done our homework, the results probably will meet our expectations.

GLOSSARY

Color balance Color temperature is measured in degrees Kelvin; the higher the temperature of the light, the bluer it appears. (The expression *white heat* refers to the color of intense heat.) Conversely, the lower the temperature, the redder it is. Since film emulsions are balanced for different light sources, we purchase daylight film for exposure outdoors (approximately 5500 degrees Kelvin) and tungsten film for indoors (3200 or 3400 degrees Kelvin). We also can achieve balance with the addition of color correction filters in front of the camera lens (for example, an 85A filter applied to daylight film shot indoors takes out the yellow/red and balances the light for 3200 degrees Kelvin). Since fluorescent lamps emit green and blue, we balance them with the addition of magenta and yellow correction filters in the proper proportion. We also can balance the color during rephotography by increasing or decreasing filtration.

Continuity In a script, the smooth and logical transition from one scene to another; in a storyboard, the transition from one visual sequence to another. Cf Storyboard.

CU Close-up. The subject's head occupies the full screen.

Light table A table constructed so that one or more fluorescent lamps are placed underneath translucent glass or plastic permitting the even illumination of transparencies for the purpose of organizing and editing.

LS Long shot. The subject is viewed full length, or at a distance.

MS Medium shot. The subject is seen at a middle distance.

Storyboard A series of sketches or images that visually represent what the producer intends to portray. It shows the composition of each frame in a sequence, as well as the continuity between frames and sequences.

Third image The image created during slow dissolves, when the visual that is fading out is combined on-screen with the visual that is fading up, creating a third (transitory) image. This adds an artistic dimension to creative productions and is used selectively.

Chapter 5

Interviewing Techniques for Research and Sound Track Using Tape Recorder and Microphone

The art of interviewing is one of the least publicized skills in multi-image production. This skill is called upon in interviewing the client, in conducting extensive research, and in taping on-the-scene situations. Perhaps we take it for granted that anyone can ask questions and get answers. But what these questions are, how they are asked, and where and in what context they are used is not a simple undertaking. This chapter reviews techniques for preparing, conducting, transcribing, editing, and recording interviews for multi-image productions. It also covers selection and use of recording equipment, particularly microphones, in field applications.

Multi-image producers use the interview as a tool in several ways: (1) to interview the client and determine his or her needs; (2) to conduct preliminary subject matter research; (3) to enhance credibility in a production by using a first-person account or subject expert as a voice-over; (4) to create a sense of immediacy by on-the-spot commentary as events are taking place. Any way we choose to apply it, the interview is basic to the preparation of historical, informational, promotional, or social documentary multi-image presentations.

Multi-image (with one, two, or several projectors) is a natural vehicle for documentary, educational, and historical information. The still camera can be effective in copying historical images and relevant documents from newspapers, family albums, books, and archives. (See Chapter 3 on Fair Use.) Still photography also is the least expensive and most accessible tool, allowing us to document our travels, visually describe a culture, make a record of a historical event, or introduce a social program. With still camera and tape recorder we can remain mobile and flexible, able to cover both photographically and aurally events as they happen or re-create them as someone remembers them. Seeing these on a wide screen in sequential and progressive development, with integrated first-person commentary and music track, can only intensify an audience's appreciation of this material.

Through the documentary approach, the multi-image experience becomes more personal and credible to the viewer. The use of voice-over, particularly if the voice belongs to a person connected to the images we are seeing, lends an immediacy to the material. In this context, the interview takes on new significance.

PREPARING FOR THE INTERVIEW

As we have already stated, there are different kinds of interviews for different purposes. Interviewing a client (see the section on needs assessment in Chapter 2) is one kind of interview. Researching subject matter through interviews with individuals who are experts in their field is another use of the interviewing technique. Sometimes excerpts from these interviews can be included in the final production. Still another need is fulfilled in the direct live response to events as they are taking place. Once we have a clear idea of the types of interviews we will need, we can prepare the questions to be asked. The questions will always be tailored to the specific situation. But first we must make contact.

MAKING CONTACT

Contact by phone or letter is the most common way of introducing oneself to a potential interviewee, depending on the importance of the situation and the proximity and status of this person. If a mutual acquaintance acts as an intermediary, the responsibility for follow-through still rests with the interviewer. I would not call the mayor on the telephone, but I might call one of her aides to get an idea of her schedule and either make a preliminary appointment with her or write a brief letter outlining my proposal and requesting an appointment to discuss the matter.

But whether we reach our interviewee through phone or letter, we should always introduce ourselves, briefly tell the reason for our call, establish our credentials or credibility, and indicate our reason for selecting this particular interviewee. If it is relevant, we also might state why we think the project is important to the community, to the people involved, or to the history or art of the area. Obviously, we should be brief on the telephone, the purpose of the call being to set up an appointment to discuss the project more fully. Whether written or direct, the contact should be friendly and unpressured, and it should elicit support and even enthusiasm for the project.

With any interviewee whose time and energy are limited, it is important to let that person know, however subtly, that (1) he or she can be an important part of the process; (2) his or her contribution will greatly enhance the production; (3) the interview will take a specific amount of time and will be made at the subject's convenience; (4) the interviewee will not only be giving, but will be getting something out of the experience, whether in gratification, recognition, or remuneration.

INTERVIEWEE AS SUBJECT EXPERT

If we are interviewing only for background information that we need for the script, it is important to prepare a list of questions we think our expert can answer. Knowing something about the background of the interviewee can be helpful in designing the questions. Also, we should do some preliminary research and eliminate questions that can be answered elsewhere. Let's stick to our interviewee's area of expertise; otherwise it will be a waste of his or her valuable time and not conducive to continued goodwill. If the objective is to incorporate a part of this informational interview in the script, it would be helpful to indicate in the draft script where the commentary will be included and what the substance and duration of these anticipated remarks might be. This projection also can be helpful in focusing the questions we plan to ask in the interview.

In a recent script outline, I indicated three separate areas for including personal commentary. I soon realized that including three commentaries would make the script far too long. Instead, I decided to have most of the information related by a narrator and to limit the personal commentary to one person. The addition of a live participant breaks up (and wakes up) what might otherwise become a monotonous voice track. Using voice in a variety of ways can move a presentation along. Too many voices, however, can be disastrous. It should always be clear to the viewer—by voice, content, and imagery—who is doing the talking.

THE SPONTANEOUS INTERVIEW

The interviewer's questions will be removed from the final tape; therefore, the interview should be designed to elicit a complete response from the interviewee. Sometimes it is helpful to ask the interviewee to repeat part of the question as a statement in the response. When spontaneity is more important than the number of facts that can be incorporated in a limited space, the questions should be phrased in such a way as to allow the speaker to handle one idea at a time. We do not want our interviewee rambling on without getting to the point. The more prepared we are in eliciting the kind of responses that will add to the dynamic of the script, the more flexible we can become in allowing for deviation from the course, and the less work we will have later in editing the tapes. Following is a short example of one interviewing technique.

Question: *Can you tell us when you were born, and in what city?*
Answer: I was born January 3, 1904, in Ranger, Texas.
Question: *What was Ranger like in 1904?*
Answer: It was just a small farm town then. That was before oil was discovered.
Question: *Can you describe your town—before the oil discovery?*
Answer: It was flat as the eye could see. There was only one street, Main Street. My uncle's mercantile store was next door to the bank where my father worked. We lived at the south end of Main Street, about a mile out of town. The discovery of oil changed all that.

When we edit out the questions in the above excerpts, we will find continuity in the narration. If we feel more comfortable in allowing the interviewee to ramble without direction, we must plan to spend considerable time at the other end, creatively editing the tapes. I recently saw an effective multi-image production that used a number of short statements by noted public figures. These to-the-point remarks, set against a background of dramatic visuals, had been excerpted from six hours of taped speeches at a three-day conference. Many days of listening and notetaking had preceded the editing of these tapes, ultimately resulting in fifteen minutes of smoothly flowing slides and commentary. (See Figure 5–1 and the next section.)

• **The Re-recorded Interview**
Although short, spontaneous comments are a much-desired component in multi-image production—not everyone can respond succinctly on microphone. One way to handle a lengthy or free-flowing response is first to transcribe the tapes verbatim, then edit the typed material to fit the timing of the script. It is important to keep the essence and flow of the original, as well as its intent, but having the same person re-read the edited commentary has usually proven unsatisfactory in re-recording. A trained professional knows how to pace the material, where to add an inflection, when to pause or repeat a phrase in the event of error. Hopefully, the spontaneity and naturalness of the original voice can be recaptured. While this technique would not be my first choice, it does keep the commentary brief and to the point, and can save hours of cutting and splicing tape.

Always keep the unedited original master tapes and transcribed material on file for reference. Make duplicate tapes and photocopies for editing purposes. This is a good rule to follow whenever original material is being used because there may come a time when it will be needed.

SETTING UP TO RECORD THE INTERVIEW

If we are interviewing an individual and we do not have a sound studio available, the interviewee's home is quite adequate because our subject is more likely to be at ease in a familiar location. We can use the existing rugs and drapes as the soft area opposite a hard wall and ceiling to create a balanced acoustical environment (Figure 5–2). Also, rooms in a home tend to be of moderate size. If we were to record in a garage, with concrete floors and walls and plaster ceiling, the voice would bounce from one hard surface to another. If we were to record in a large, empty hall, the sound would reverberate, giving an echo effect. Ideally, we should have a soft surface (drapes, rugs) opposite a hard surface (ceiling, wall).

Since the objective of any interview is to create a comfortable, nonthreatening situation, the interviewer should be as unobtrusive as possible. This is another good reason for carrying lightweight, easy-to-assemble equipment. In a comfortable area, I usually arrange two straight-backed chairs at a 45-degree angle so that we will be able to maintain eye contact. Sitting on two sides of the corner of a table produces the same relationship. Sitting opposite each other with the table between us creates an immediate barrier. We want our contact open and conversational.

The mic is placed on a table in front of and toward the speaker, about six inches from his or her mouth. A soft rag or foam pad under the mic will soften the sound. If the interview is intended for informational purposes only, the accuracy of sound is not an issue. I find, however, that it is good practice to work toward quality recording no matter what the ultimate purpose.

INTERVIEW TRANSCRIBED VERBATIM FROM TAPE (Partial)

The police department just came out with some statistics, which we've refuted, because what they did was compared areas that we had organized with the rest of the city. You have to compare similar types of things. You have to compare one part of a neighborhood with another neighborhood that's similar, that's unorganized. You do it with like circumstances. Can't compare 34th Ave. with 18th Street. Every year we target a different district for concentrated organizing efforts. So for the Mayfair area which we targeted in 1981, the police department did an analysis, of crimes of burglary, before we came in and after we came in and we found out that burglary had been reduced almost 30 per cent in the areas which we had targeted. Police Department and Mayor's offices attributed this success in large part to these efforts. But when we pulled out from our concentrated efforts we found that burglary went up steadily, which also tells us something about organizing efforts and about people needing to continue those efforts. We have also seen, in some areas of the Colfax district which we targeted this year, that burglary has gone down.

EDITED VERSION FROM TRANSCRIPTION

Police department statistics in this case failed to compare neighborhoods in similar circumstances. They should have compared **like** neighborhoods; one organized, the other unorganized.

Every year we target a different district for concentrated organizing efforts. Before we went in to one targeted area, we asked the police department to give us a burglary analysis for that area. Then we went in and worked closely with the people there. During this period, crime dropped 30% in the neighborhood. The mayor's office attributed this success in large part to our efforts. But when we pulled out, we found that burglary went up steadily again. This tells us something about the need to extend our neighborhood organizing efforts over longer periods of time.

FIGURE 5–1
An interview transcribed verbatim from tape, before and after editing. In the transcribed interview, the writer keeps all the inflections and marks the gestures to stay true to the original meaning. If the intent is to keep the original tape, the transcript can be marked to indicate the sections to be cut out or transposed. If the intent is to edit for re-recording, the writer might make more extensive changes, keeping in mind the intent, rhythm, and feeling of the original.

FIGURE 5–2
In recording on location, drapes and carpets can act as soft walls opposite hard walls such as bare walls and ceilings. The mic should be close to the interviewee, and the interviewer should maintain eye contact. Equipment should be minimal and as unobtrusive as possible.

Many people are intimidated by a microphone, mostly because they believe they will sound foolish or because the tape becomes a permanent record of what they say. The less attention drawn to the equipment, the more spontaneous the repsonses will be. (See Figure 5–3.) Setting up quietly and efficiently is one way to minimize the impact of the technology. Maintaining eye contact and expressing interest during the interview also draws attention away from the mic.

The tape and recorder should be prepared in advance, with several seconds lead time (blank tape); then the subject's name, the date, and the location of the interview should be prerecorded. This information also should be written on the face of the cassette. After we set up the equipment in the interviewee's home, we should record an additional thirty seconds of blank tape to pick up the ambient sound in the room. This segment of tape can be used later if we need to patch in some additional tape during the editing stage; it makes a more faithful match.

Just prior to the interview, we should put the recorder in record mode and press the pause button to keep the record mode in a holding position. Now we set the tape counter to zero so that we can always return to this point. We then release the pause button and make a brief voice test of the interviewee to check sound level and make sure the equipment is functioning properly. This can be done while we are talking casually. Following any adjustments, such as increasing the volume level or moving the mic closer to the interviewee, we back up the tape to zero. We check to make sure the record and pause buttons are still depressed, and when we are ready to record, we simply release the pause button and turn our full attention to the interviewee. From this point forward, we will use the pause button to start and stop the record-

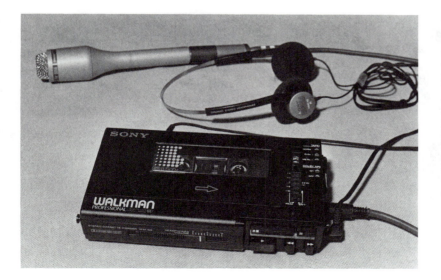

FIGURE 5–3
A tape recorder can be effective if it is small and of good quality. The microphone should be external to the recorder and of superior quality for best sound reproduction. Use the pause button rather than the stop button during recording to keep the record mode connected. (© Phiz Mezey)

ing. We should avoid using the stop button because it throws the machine out of record mode and makes a clicking sound on the tape each time it is disengaged.

Except for a quick visual check of the volume unit meter after the interview has begun, to assure ourselves that the voice is being recorded at an acceptable level, we should pay no more attention to the equipment until it is time to turn the tape over to side B. If there are any interruptions, such as someone coming into the room or a phone ringing, we can press the pause button and wait until the interviewee is ready to proceed. The recorder will remain in record mode.

INTERVIEWING IN THE FIELD

Ambience becomes a real problem when we are interviewing outdoors. To minimize outdoor ambient sound, we could use a lavalier mic or hold a directional (cardioid) mic with wind screen no more than six inches from the subject's mouth. It is advisable to try to get away from the wind or detach ourselves from a crowd, perhaps stand in a doorway or some sheltered spot. Specific sound effects that we want to include should be recorded separately on another tape and can be added (mixed) to the sound track at a later time.

USE A NEW TAPE FOR EACH SOUND UNIT

I find it most helpful to record each new speaker on a separate tape. A thirty-minute tape is preferable, but a sixty-minute tape is more available. We should label each tape carefully so that it can be easily identified when we get to the editing phase. We might end up with several voice tapes, a music tape, and a sound effects tape when we are done, so it helps to keep an index of what we have completed and the relative order in which it will be included in the final mix. We should keep the originals as master tapes, dubbing (copying) the best takes from each onto open-reel tape, which we can cut and splice without fear of destroying the original.

REVIEW OF STEPS IN INTERVIEWING

If we need information for our production, we should find an expert on the subject and interview him or her.

Some knowledge of the interviewee's background is helpful before undertaking an interview.

A letter or phone call should give the interviewee only the pertinent information about the project. Keep the call short, pleasant, and general. Indicate the importance of the interviewee to the success of the project.

Prepare a list of questions that will allow the interviewee an opportunity to deal with one idea at a time and maintain a smooth, logical flow.

Decide beforehand whether to record spontaneously on location or more formally under controlled conditions.

If the objective is to use the original tape, make a duplicate copy and edit the duplicate.

Indicate in the first draft of the script the substance and duration of the projected interview.

Transcribe (type) the interview as soon as possible, whether the plan is to edit directly on the tape or edit a transcript of the tape for later rerecording. Leave adequate space on your copy for editing marks.

Keep one copy intact (master); use photocopy for editing. Even if you are planning to edit directly on tape, you can indicate the desired cuts on the transcribed copy.

The edited, transcribed copy can be retyped in its final form and inserted into the script for final cueing.

Now that we are well prepared and have a good idea of where and how the interview technique can be used in a multi-image production, let's turn our attention to the equipment and techniques needed to record these interviews successfully.

RECORDING EQUIPMENT

For many years the only way to record in the field was to bring along a Uher or Nagra open-reel portable tape recorder. The equipment was state of the art, bulky, heavy, and prohibitively expensive. More recently small, lightweight, portable cassette recorders have replaced the earlier equipment, at a fraction of the cost. Sony has come out with a lightweight professional cassette tape deck used more and more by professionals in the field. This compact unit has much going for it, including a stereo component, VU (volume unit) meter, Dolby sound selector, pause button, a single-switch record component (instead of the more awkward two-switch record and play function), and many other features found only in more expensive units.

The major drawback to the cassette tape is its narrow width (⅛ inch) and slow speed (1⅞ inches per second, ips). It also is difficult to edit, so the sound track usually is transferred to an open-reel tape (two or four track, 7½ ips or 15 ips) for editing. For these reasons many professionals argue in favor of the open-reel recorder for field and studio use in all multi-image applications. My own experience in the field favors the lighter, smaller professional cassette deck, provided it has an excellent external microphone.

MICROPHONES

How does one choose the right microphone? First, we should identify our needs, in order of importance. If we are planning to conduct interviews in an indoor location under controlled conditions, as in a studio, we would select one kind of microphone. If, however, we plan to spend a good deal of time in the field, with lots of ambient sound in the background, we might choose differently. Recording live in a classroom or auditorium would require still another consideration in our selection.

Obviously, we are not going to be able to purchase a microphone for every need, so the best choice boils down to something of a compromise. As long as we keep in mind our primary uses and we find a microphone that is adaptable to those needs, we are on the right track. We also should keep in mind that the microphone must interface with the amplifier of the recorder we are planning to use. Impedance (a measure of resistance to current flow in an alternating current [AC] circuit, measured in ohms) and the type of connector we use are important considerations.

• Microphone Terminology

First, let's explore some common terminology relevant to microphones and their function. There are three main types of microphone: dynamic, ribbon, and condenser. The primary function of any microphone is to transform sound to an electrical signal. The *dynamic,* or moving coil, mic, by far the most popular because it is rugged and reliable in the field, has a vibrating coil attached to a thin plastic diaphragm. Sound vibrations cause the fine wire coil to move in the magnetic field that surrounds it, to produce electricity and generate a signal.

The *ribbon* mic is more delicate and is a variant of the dynamic principle, using a corrugated metal ribbon suspended between the poles of a magnet. Ribbon mics are not used much today.

Condenser mics have a lightweight membrane, an electrically resistant spacer, and a back plate. The small space between the diaphragm and the back plate is electrically charged and in effect becomes a condenser. The motion of the diaphragm in the charged field produces a small electrical signal. Capable of extremely wide-range response, most condenser mics require a battery or regular wall socket power to produce the charged field. One condenser microphone now on the market seals in a permanent static electrical charge on a coated plastic diaphragm. (See Figure 5–4.)

• Pickup Pattern

Microphones also are classified in terms of their response pattern. (See Figure 5–5.) *Omnidirectional* mics pick up sounds from all directions at once. A lavalier mic is omnidirectional, but because it is so close to the speaker, other sounds tend to be muted. *Bidirectional* mics have a figure-eight response pattern, rejecting sounds coming from the sides, and are useful in one-on-

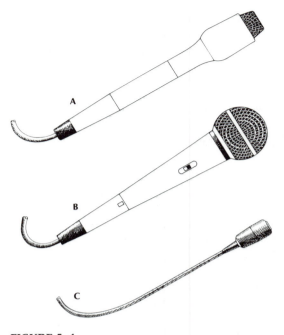

FIGURE 5–4
Three popular microphones used in multi-image production.

(A) The condenser microphone (also known as an electrostatic mic) requires its own power supply but is capable of extremely wide range response. The signal is generated by the variations in capacitance between two charged plates, one rigid and the other flexible, acting as a diaphragm in contact with the air. Depending on variations in the arrangement of the plates, this mic can be omnidirectional or cardioid in its response pattern. An inexpensive variation on this microphone is the electret mic used in consumer equipment.
(B) The dynamic microphone is most popular because it does not require its own power supply, has a high output, and is rugged and reliable. It uses a small coil moving in the field of a permanent magnet; the movement generates a current in the coil. This mic has a cardioid (heart-shaped) unidirectional response pattern, making it sensitive to sounds in an 80-degree frontal arc and less sensitive to sounds coming from the rear.
(C) The lavalier microphone is a personal microphone usually worn suspended around the neck or clipped to a shirt. It is omnidirectional, but because of its closeness to the person wearing it, external sounds are minimized. Unfortunately, the individual is attached to a power source, and excessive movement can cause problems.

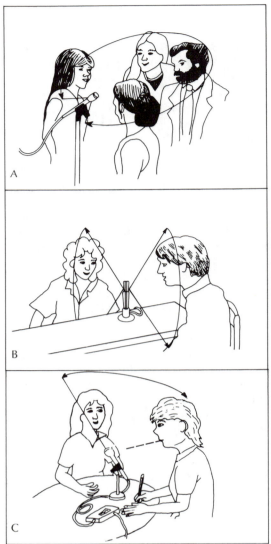

FIGURE 5–5
The pickup pattern of a microphone often will determine its application.

(A) In a group discussion, where the mic is centrally mounted, an omnidirectional mic is most appropriate because it accepts sounds from all directions. *(B)* Bidirectional mics reject sounds coming from the sides and are live on the front and back face—good for certain kinds of interviews. *(C)* Cardioid or unidirectional mics have a wide frontal acceptance of sound, but they reject sound coming from the rear and sides.

one interviews, unless the viewer places herself on the side of the mic that has no pickup at all. *Cardioid* microphones are *directional* mics that pick up sounds in an 80-degree arc in front of the microphone and reject sounds from the rear. They are the most practical microphones to use for interviews, sound effects, and other general purposes. They are called cardioid because of their heart shape, and look like a balloon with a finger poked in it.

Selecting a microphone is always a personal decision. I use a dynamic mic because it can stand up to rough treatment and is reliable in the field. It also has a high output. I frequently include interviews in my productions, as well as small, informal discussions. I also record interviews and sound effects outdoors. Although a cardioid mic would have been an acceptable choice, I selected an omnidirectional pattern because it gave me more latitude in my uses. I can minimize the ambient sound by controlling the environment and placing the speaker close to the mic. Finally, the mic I selected is shock mounted so that, when the occasion calls for it, it can be hand held without picking up any of the handling noise.

I could have chosen a lavalier mic—a small mic clipped to a shirt or suspended from the neck of the person speaking—eliminating the need for a shock-mounted mic. All lavalier mics are omnidirectional, but because of their closeness to the speaker, ambient sound tends to be minimized. One of the problems with using a lavalier mic is the cord, which needs to be attached to a transformer or recorder. This means that the speaker is *attached*. An inexperienced speaker moving about a great deal might create some problems. Then, too, it is limited to use by one subject. All things considered, I selected the most versatile mic for my purposes. Each person must make this decision for himself at the point of purchase.

• **Low Impedance/High Impedance**

I mentioned that it is important to match the microphone with the amplifier of the recorder we are using. This brings up another term that we should be familiar with: impedance. This is the biggest variable we will have to deal with in AV recording. Impedance means the amount of opposition to the flow of electricity. Microphone impedance refers to the AC (alternating current) resistance of the microphone. A mic with high impedance (10,000 ohms) has two signal wires, one already grounded. It is used most often with home equipment. A low-impedance mic (250 ohms) has two signal wires plus one ground. It is more often used in professional work when extended cables are involved. It travels well over long cable distances. We can change low impedance to high impedance by the addition of a transformer (adapter). I have a small transformer that converts my low-impedance professional mic to high impedance, to function with my Sony WD6 Walkman.

We also should become familiar with the plugs and jacks used with our equipment because we frequently have to patch one to another. XLRs (cannon plugs) are associated with low-impedance mics and amplifiers; RCA plugs are associated with high-impedance mics and amplifiers. (See Figure 5–6.)

GLOSSARY

AC Alternating current. An electrical current that reverses its direction regularly and continually.

Acoustics (1) The scientific study of sound, particularly its generation, propagation, perception, and interaction with materials. (2) The total effect of sound, especially as produced in an enclosed space.

Ambient sound Existing sounds in a room or location that are external to the subject being recorded.

Amplifier An electronic device or component that increases the magnitude of its input signal.

Bidirectional Having maximum response in two directions. A bidirectional microphone has two lobes of maximum sound response in what looks like a figure-eight pattern.

Cardioid Heart-shaped. A microphone with a unidirectional pickup pattern that can handle sound within an 80-degree radius.

Cassette tape A small self-encased tape that is ⅛ inch wide; developed by the Philips Co.

Condenser mic An electrostatic microphone in which the signal is generated by the variations in capacitance between two charged plates. It requires a power supply but is popular in the studio and field and can be as small as a lavaliere mic.

Context To weave together. (1) The whole situation, background, or environment in which an event occurs gives it its exact meaning. To select a part of it without reference to its relevant surrounding is to "take it out of context." (2) In multi-image this word is used to express the way in which sound and images are juxtaposed to enhance or distort a given meaning.

FIGURE 5–6
Plugs, jacks, and
adapters. *(A)* **Y**
adapter showing RCA
plugs and jacks; *(B)*
Cannon plug and jack
(also known as XLR);
(C) Mini phone plug
and jack; *(D)* RCA
plug and jack; *(E)*
phone plug and jack.

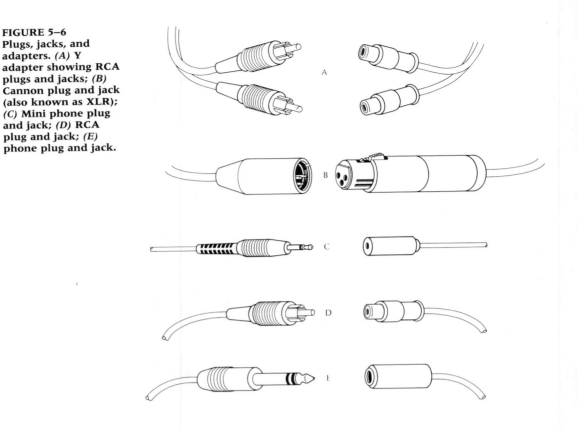

Directional Refers to a cardioid microphone, which has a unidirectional response
pattern. Cf Cardioid.

Four track (1) An audio recording system that lays down four separate sound
tracks and utilizes four separate channels.
Also known as quadraphonic. (2) Term
used to describe a stereophonic system in
which tracks 1 and 3 are used in one direction and tracks 2 and 4 are used in the
other direction. In this book I call this second system a *quarter-track* so as not to con-
fuse it with the four *separate* track system.

Interviewee The person who is being in-
terviewed.

Interviewer The person who conducts
the interview.

IPS Inches per second. The unit of measurement describing the speed at which the
tape travels past the tape head of the recorder. Recordings made at a certain ips
must be played back at the same ips.

Jack The receptacle for a plug connector.
The receptacle may be either an input jack
or output jack. Also called a *female connector.*

Mini phone A type of audio connector
noted for its small size. See Figure 5–6.

Omnidirectional A type of microphone
having a maximum response pattern in all
directions. See Figure 5–5.

Open reel Another name used to describe reel-to-reel tape recorders where the
tape is not enclosed in a cartridge.

Phone plug A common audio connector
used with headphones or microphones that
fits into a phone jack. Also called a telephone plug. See Figure 5–6.

RCA Connector A miniature audio connector developed by RCA. It is better than
the mini phone because it is more difficult
to accidentally disconnect. See Figure 5–6.

Ribbon mic A microphone whose signal
is generated by a magnetic field. This is an
older microphone with very delicate components. Ribbon mics are generally bidirectional. The *dynamic* mic also is generated
by a magnetic field but has much sturdier
components and is more popular today. Dynamic mics can have any response pattern.

Subject matter expert An individual
possessing expertise or experience in the
area being researched for a production.

Two track (1) An adjective describing a
recording system that lays down up to two

separate tracks of sound and uses two channels. (2) An adjective that sometimes describes a monaural system, which in this book is referred to as *half-track*.

XLR Connectors Also called *cannon connectors*. Heavy-duty, multipin connectors with interlocking outer shells—used in professional equipment.

Photographing for Multi-Image Production

In the past several years the introduction of leisure-time (memory) and computer programming to the multi-image field has enhanced the production of multiple-projector presentations. We can now include seamless panoramic vistas and a kaleidoscope of special effects. While much has been said about adding excitement to the multi-image screen through masks and special effects, too little attention has been paid to the image itself. Yet photography was the visual medium that started it all about thirty years ago.

While audio visual technology was reaching for the stars, the art and technique of *photographing* for multi-image was overlooked. Even the trade journals, filled with exotic ideas on computer graphics or seamless masks, virtually ignored the photographic component of multi-image. Little was said about this specialized field of photography in the 1970s, and although we are reaching technological peaks in multi-image today, limited attention is being paid to this special art in the eighties. This chapter addresses itself to this oversight.

Although this chapter is dedicated to the photographic image as it applies to multi-image production, we are not attempting to teach photographic exposure or principles of composition, how to select camera lenses, or related technical information. Rather we address the art of photographing sequentially and on multiple levels for multi-image.

In still photography, with its traditional emphasis on the single image, we look for the photograph that says it all, as in the phrase, "One picture is worth a thousand words." Most people today still think of photographic stills as single and separate images. Even if three frames of one scene are recorded on film, we expect only one of those frames to be usable, and we usually discard the others. For the past hundred years still photography has been based on this image-as-art, one-of-a-kind philosophy.

Photographing for multi-image projection breaks this mind-set and explores a whole new way of looking at 35mm still photographs. Traditionally, viewers look at a photographic print for as long as they are interested in the subject. But in multi-image there is no such luxury. A slide might be on the screen for two seconds or only a fraction of a second, and the viewer must receive and translate a great deal of information rapidly. The viewer also must be able to retain that information in preparation for the next slide, because multi-image is generally sequential, developmental, and multilayered. What comes before and after an image is as important as what emerges from a superimposition of images. In multi-image production not one image but a series of images, whether abstract or explicit, contributes to the development of an idea.

DEVELOPING A VISUAL CONCEPT

Each slide in multi-image can be thought of as a building block in a progression of images, like sentences that contribute to the development of a concept in a paragraph. Whether we are involved with story telling, documentation, instruction, or artistic abstraction, multi-image presentations rely on series or sequences of images that show a clear relationship between the frames. Every image must count. Each image must be relevant, interesting, and essential to the unfolding of the story or the realization of our objectives. And each image should project one idea or a step in the development of that idea. (This does not mean that there cannot be several levels of communication in one slide: color might be one level, juxtaposition of objects another, direction a third. But together they must communicate one idea.) Each slide should be clear in its intent and unique in its content. Clarity, simplicity, and internal movement are all part of the multi-image picture.

Continuity or flow are important whether we are preparing a one-projector, two-projector, or multi-projector presentation. With two or more projectors, the dissolves make image flow increasingly important because one image fades into another in a visual progression. If we concern ourselves with these relationships in the planning stage, the photographer is better equipped to think in terms of multi-image format techniques when taking his or her pictures.

If we photographed randomly without a plan, we could be missing important links in our sequences or including slides with no relation to the script. Planning does not restrict creativity but frees it to expand, elaborate, even change the original plan if the circumstances call for it. (See Figure 6–1.)

THINKING VISUALLY

The graphic artist usually creates the storyboard after the script has been completed. It is sometimes more effective to bring the writer, graphic artist, and photographer together at the beginning. This choice is usually the producer's, whose job it is to coordinate the different production components, keeping them fluid and interactive so that they will come together smoothly in final form. Since I usually write my own scripts and tend to think visually, I create the visual sequences in my mind's eye as I write. This does not mean that the images or frames are visualized in final form. I start with an idea of the sequences I hope to project and refine this as I go along. When writer and photographer are the same person, these two activities can evolve side by side. Generally, the writer, graphic artist, and photographer are three different persons, and it becomes the photographer's responsibility to familiarize himself or herself with the script and storyboard.

In preparing a script about crime prevention in neighborhoods, I could project in my mind's eye a number of scenes that might be included in the production. The opening scene could show aspects of the city, covering typical neighborhoods, people, and activities, and it might include a diversity of ethnic groups. All this could be covered in fewer than ten slides. Another sequence (scene) could show people meeting in a home. I would use an establishing shot, close-ups of people interacting, perhaps a role-playing series—all in fewer than ten slides. A third sequence would introduce a crime prevention specialist showing a resident how to secure her home. This previsualizing at the time of writing can be helpful in keeping the language of the script simple and to the point. During the production stage, as photographer, I must think sequentially and interactively. By that I mean that as I carry the visual line forward, I am also creating relationships between images through the effective use of dissolves. Line, color, dark and light areas, foreground and background, subject and symbol—all are key considerations in this process. (See Figure 6–2.)

Frequently we must work with existing slides, as in the case of the traveler who decides to make a slide presentation *after* the trip, or the client who already has a large slide file he wants to use. A good designer can make the most of this situation by selecting images that work together, using creative masking, and assigning a photographer to fill specific gaps. It is important here for the photographer to see the existing images and try to match them rather than overpowering them with his own style.

KEY IMAGE

I started out by saying that multi-image photography requires a special way of

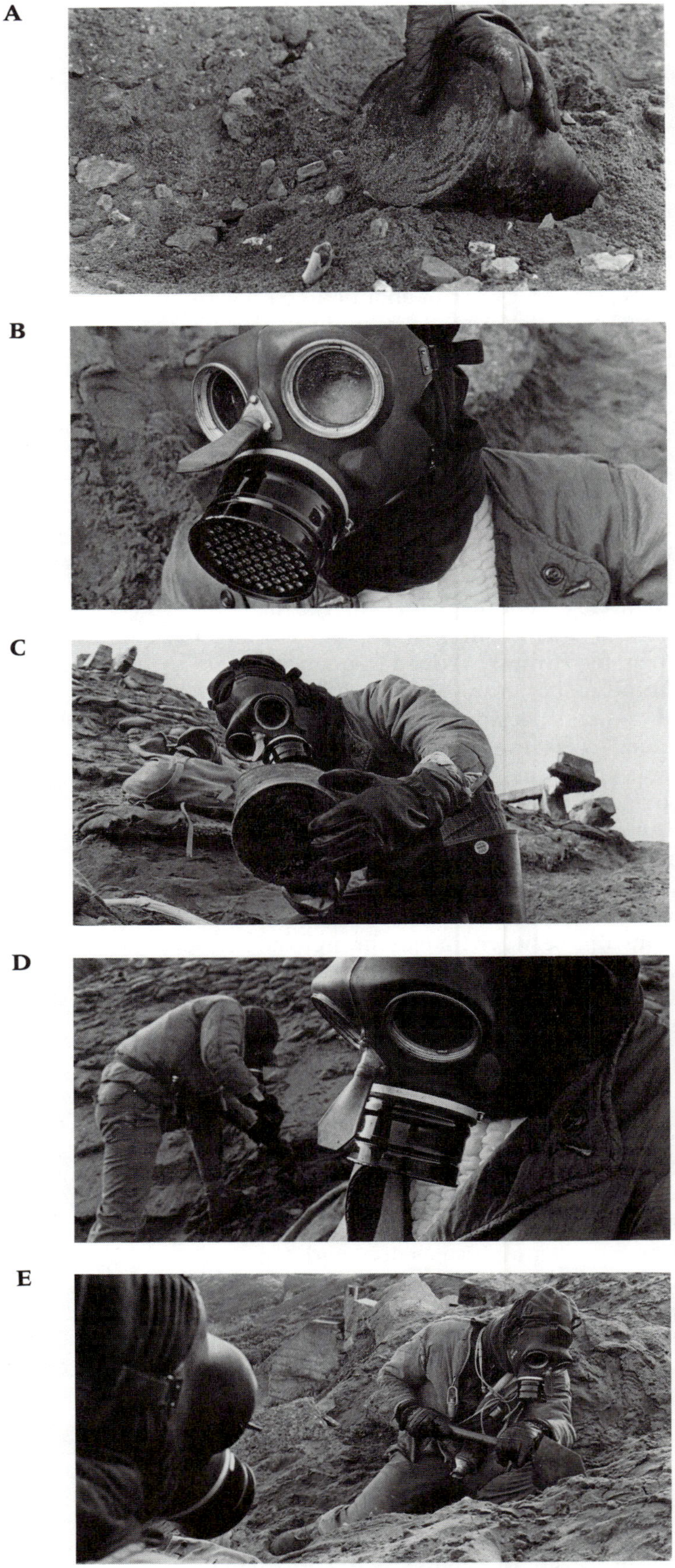

A

B

C

D

E

seeing and thinking, and that every image has to count. Yet in each sequence it helps to have a key image around which the others can build. In "Sunday in the Park," the skating production (page 52 and Figure 6–3), I wanted to introduce the idea that there is danger as well as pleasure in the sport. One of the skaters actually breaks a foot. The key image in this scene, which follows a lot of upbeat skating, is a waiting ambulance that prepares the viewer for a change of pace and mood. The waiting ambulance is preceded by a frame with two mounted policemen standing watch and followed by a frame showing members of the skate patrol also standing by. I have prepared the audience for the accident. Key images do not have to be the strongest images, but they should be pivotal and help focus the sequence.

I also stated that the viewer has to read, translate, and retain the information in each slide in a fraction of time. It is important, therefore, to keep unnecessary clutter out of the image. If a slide holds too much information, the viewer will be preoccupied with it when the next slide appears. As the viewer begins to lose a sense of visual continuity and clarity, frustration sets in, and he or she can become a visual casualty. *The photographer must put himself or herself in the place of the viewer, and record the scene with the viewer in mind.*

Clarity, simplicity, and compositional structure (visual organization within the slide) help the viewer grasp and integrate the material. And by showing a clear relationship between frames, we keep the story and the viewer moving along. Focus, line, camera angle, and direction in adjacent frames keep the visual line flowing. While a trained artist would have an easier time

FIGURE 6–1
This series is from a three-projector multi-image production titled "1994" and photographed in black and white by Doug Baird. All photographic images were shot with the viewfinder "masked" to produce a 2:1 ratio image. All final transparencies were mounted in Wess #6 glass mounts. The sequence introduces the initial characters and their environment. Music supports their desperate attempt at survival after a nuclear holocaust. Baird's storyboard reveals the following: *(A)* introduces the first human element of "1994"; *(B)* CU of main character; *(C)* MS of David holding a can; *(D)* MS of David looking down; reveals second survivor, Paulo; *(E)* MS of David looking at Paulo. (© 1984 Doug Baird)

managing this visual organization, all of us can master it in time. We must first become aware of "seeing" what we plan to photograph, then evaluating what we have shot. In time, through awareness and practice, we can organize the visual elements in-camera without conscious effort.

UNDERSTANDING THE MEDIUM

We said that photographing for multi-image is different from traditional still photography. Among other things, there is more implied movement in multi-image. But the designer or photographer should not try to emulate motion pictures. At twenty-four frames per second, the 16mm camera creates the illusion of continuous motion. The motion picture viewer follows the action. In multi-image the viewer anticipates the action. He or she is more likely to see twenty-four frames *per minute* rather than per second, forcing the viewer to fill in the gaps from his or her own experience. For instance, in a sequence of twelve frames, showing the accident in "Sunday in the Park," the viewer sees a waiting ambulance, mounted police, and the skate patrol, all of which add up to an idea of danger. Next, the viewer sees a skater on the ground grimacing in pain, with a woman and child bending over him. We make the quick assumption that he has been hurt, perhaps even broken a leg. The assumption is confirmed by the next photographs, which show one skate and sock removed from the injured man's foot, a growing crowd, and the arrival of an ambulance. It is the viewer who makes the connections from his or her own experiences and knowledge. (See Figure 6–3.)

The multi-image photographer must learn to selectively photograph for images that build a concept. If there are too many literal images, the viewer will lose interest. If the gaps are too wide, the viewer will fail to make the proper connections. Much of this tightening up of the sequences can take place in the editing phase, discussed in Chapter 10. Meanwhile, the photographer should follow through at the scene, mindful of the need for continuity, as well as the building and matching of images on the screen.

A good zoom lens can be the multi-image

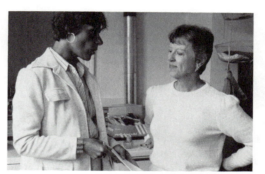

FIGURE 6–2
A house inspection sequence introduces a crime inspection specialist, with a voice-over, showing the resident how to secure her home. "SAFE in the City" was a two-projector, single-screen presentation. (© Mezey productions)

A

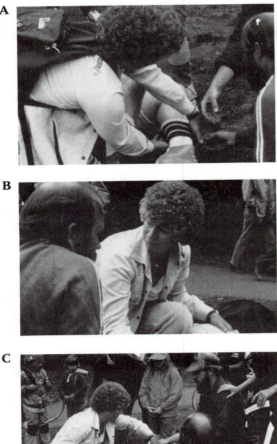

B

C

D

E

photographer's most valuable tool, permitting rapid changes in focal length (near and far) while keeping foreground and background objects (reference points) intact. The zoom can establish location in a long shot, then move to a more focused middle shot and finally a close-up. This is a versatile tool that can be used in many creative ways in multi-image photography.

MOVEMENT

What kind of movement do we want to create in slides? We are not talking about special effects, flashes, or movement suggested through narration, music, and other supportive techniques. We are still discussing the photographic image. Physical motion—such as walking, running, catching, bending, and stretching—is only one kind of movement. Movement in the sense that I am using it is psychological and cultural. This kind of movement is created by line, shape, form, direction, relative size, color, texture, contrast, balance, and placement of the subject in the frame. It also incorporates position (nearness, farness) of the subject and progression (development) of a story line through sequencing.

The camera must never allow a static moment, either within a frame or within a sequence. We can build our own awareness through viewing sequences that work and sequences that fail. We also can learn what to look for and what to avoid by photographing trial sequences and analyzing them. Following are a number of suggestions for creating movement in multi-image photography, all worth trying in preparation for a production. Although we might think of each of these elements separately, in actuality several elements can be combined in one frame or sequence.

FIGURE 6–3
"Sunday in the Park" is a production showing old and young, skating in the park. The ambulance scene required visual preparation through a few transition slides—police on horseback, an ambulance waiting, a volunteer skate patrol standing by. The key image was the waiting ambulance. The images shown here are the accident scene that follows this three-slide transition from a happier mode. (© Mezey Productions)

• 18 Ways to Create Movement

1. We use line, shape, texture, and form to create a dynamic within each frame and from frame to frame to carry our story forward. It is important to remember, when we are considering two- or three-projector dissolves, that proportion, line, shape, form, size, color, and so on must relate and should flow smoothly and creatively. (See Figure 6–4.)

2. Let's keep our direction consistent within the sequence. We cannot have the subject going in one direction and then have him come from the opposite direction in the next frame. Also, let's keep sequential images out of dead center, or the movement also will be stopped dead in midsequence. (See Figure 6–5.)

3. One way to develop a series, or sequence, with an eye toward visual continuity is to think of these images as building blocks in the unfolding of an idea or story. In addition to the intellectual progression, there must be visual progression, or the story will not go anywhere. Each image or group of images should move the story or concept forward toward its summation. It is important to develop one concept at a time; otherwise we might include too much. (See Figures 4–5, page 35, 6–1, 6–2.)

4. We never make just one exposure of a subject, especially if we are planning a

FIGURE 6–4
Line and shape can provide a sense of movement and continuity. (© Ken Burke)

FIGURE 6–5
Panning and catching movement a moment before it peaks extend the motion beyond the image frame. (© Phiz Mezey)

two-projector production. It is helpful to think of matching pairs when photographing; we can then change the second image in some way to indicate a progression. Examples: (a) Change the point of focus in frames one and two so that the audience is looking first at one subject, then at a second subject within the same location. For example, there are two students, one behind the other; first focus in sharply on one, then on the other. (b) If the opener is a sunrise, keep the next frame consistent in color, mood, and proportion. (c) Photograph a group or subject two times, but with a changed expression or physical stance, to indicate a progression. (d) Using a zoom lens, photograph one scene at 70mm, then at 100mm, and again at 200mm. (See Figure 6–6.)

5. It is important to familiarize our audience with the subject. One way we can do this is by exposing several frames of that subject, using different camera angles, changing lens-to-subject distance, or photographing around the subject. And we can focus in on relevant details. We also should pay attention to foreground and background and keep them simple. (See Figure 6–7.) The subject need not become an actor, but the photographer must be tuned in and move like a dancer.

6. One way to have an impact is to photograph the subject three times (front view). A zoom lens is helpful here. Take a medium shot (MS), a medium close-up (MCU), and a close-up (CU). Or, depending on the situation, we can start with a medium long shot (MLS) showing the whole person in his or her environment, then move in, getting closer with each frame. Be careful: Too many

frames will negate the effect. (See Figure 6–8.)

7. Desks and telephones make dull subject matter. In photographing inanimate objects, we can use different angles, photographing from above, from below, and at 45-degree angles to the straight line (the frame). This prevents the audience from being cut off from the image or from nodding off.

8. Bring human subjects close enough to the viewer to make contact. They can be shown facing the audience, or at least in a three-quarter view. Never lose this precious contact. (Side views shut out the audience.) Large images are effective, particularly with children, who need to identify with the subject matter.)

9. In multi-image photography we learn to think vertically in a horizontal framework. Unless we are planning to mask the images, photographing horizontally is the rule of thumb. With multi-projector presentations, slides should match visually and dissolve one to the other. Vertical slides are more difficult to incorporate in this visual flow; once the viewer has adjusted to the horizontal line, it is difficult to adjust to a vertical one. If we plan to include vertical formats, we also should plan to use a split frame or mask. With masking, verticals can be included in a horizontal format. (See Figure 6–3.) This is discussed in detail in Chapter 9. The images may be photographed vertically, then rephotographed to drop into a horizontal frame or format. (See Figure 6–9.)

10. Nowhere is the illusion of perspective more important than in multi-image photography. Creating depth through dark areas and converging lines is im-

FIGURE 6–6
Shifting focus from a foreground figure to a background figure through a dissolve also shifts the viewer's focus. (© Mezey Productions)

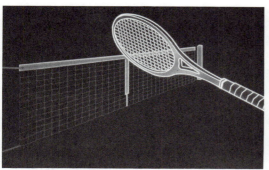

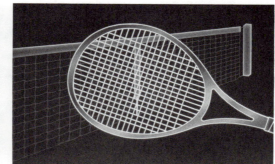

FIGURE 6–7
Creating movement through placement and size. This is shown through MS and CU, creating the illusion of movement on the screen. (© Bob Stolkin)

portant in bringing the viewer into our experience. Since we know that dark tones draw us into the image, we can use them selectively. But since bright colors jump forward—that is, the eye is attracted to the brightest colors first—we should be leery of bright, open skies and distracting reflections. I use a polarizing filter to minimize distracting reflective surfaces.

11. No one enjoys staring at a talking head. Once the camera has introduced the speaker, it can go about its business showing what the speaker is talking about; then, if it is relevant, we can return to the speaker again, shown with a dynamic expression or at a special angle so that the viewer will know that the same person is still speaking.

12. We should all become aware of body language. The body speaks eloquently. Photograph people in action, even if that action is a small gesture or a changing expression. Watch for expressions, gestures, and body extensions and contractions. (See Figure 6–10.)

13. Pay attention to facial expressions—surprise, conflict, anger, despair, humor. If the face is blank, use the subject's body language or change camera angle to create a sense of what is to be said. (See Figure 6–11.)

14. Show direction through pictorial line, subject placement, and, when people are the subject matter, through body extensions (for example, a runner, photographed from a three-quarter angle, with arm/leg extensions). Since we read from left to right, the runner should be moving from left to right so that the viewer will continue the action in his or her mind. Or we can photograph a hurdler, front view, in midleap

over a hurdle, coming directly toward the audience.

15. Yes, there is a decisive moment, just before the peak of action, to release the shutter. The tear is about to fall; the dancer has leaped but has not yet reached the top of the arc. This enables

FIGURE 6–8
Three slides of the same subject. A medium close-up and close-up work well with two-projector dissolves. In effect, the viewer moves closer and closer to the flower. (© Mezey Productions)

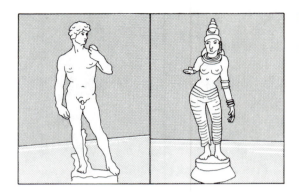

FIGURE 6–9
Verticals share a split frame where there is similarity of subject matter or relative comparison. Another technique with verticals (see Figure 6–3) is to duplicate the vertical in a horizontal format, allowing the sides to go to black.

the viewers to complete the action for themselves. (See Figure 6–5.)

16. Color can show a change in time. For example, changing colors might depict the four seasons or sepia tones might indicate a flashback. Color can imply continuity when it is carried through several frames. Use colors in their psychological context when a point needs visual support. Bright, cheerful colors jump forward and create a happy mood; cool blues and grays retreat and introduce a more thoughtful mood.

17. Show details, symbols, and signs with which the audience is familiar.

18. On occasion, use split frames to build a concept through progressive disclosure. Image one might be placed in the upper left quarter of frame *a*. Image two appears in frame *b* in the upper right corner. Image three appears in frame *c*, lower left. And all four images appear in *d*. To do this, four separate images can be photographed, then rephotographed with masks to fit one-quarter of the frame. (See Figure 6–12 and Chapter 9.)

CHOOSING THE RIGHT FILM

One of the most frequently asked questions in multi-image photography is "What film do I use?" The answer is at once simple and complex. We should use the transparency film that best suits the mood and purpose of our production. Now that I have said that, I must qualify my answer. We are, at this point, talking about trade names—Kodak, Agfa, Fuji, and so on—not the film speed (ASA). Each manufacturer has its own emulsion formula, and color rendition differs greatly. Some films are balanced for reds and warmer colors, while

FIGURE 6–10
Gesture works well in multi-image. Here an irate citizen shows her feeling with a gesture, which creates movement through an effective dissolve. (© Mezey Productions)

FIGURE 6–11
Facial expression is another way to create movement in slides. Here the viewer can respond to the sense of pain and anger referred to in the text. (© Mezey Productions)

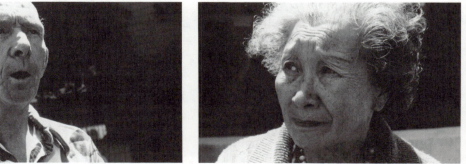

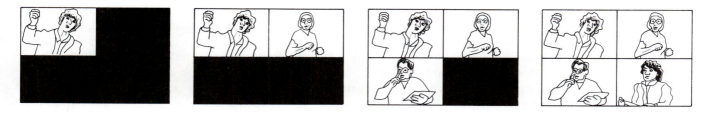

others favor blues and greens. Even the reds, blues, and greens are not the same within one product line. Kodachrome and Ecktachrome are not alike. For one of my multi-image productions on the Grand Canyon, I needed warmer tones to express my feelings about the Grand Canyon. But I learned that the processing plant of the manufacturer I had chosen was thousands of miles away, and that it would take weeks to get my processed film back. So I chose the product of another manufacturer, with a color balance that came close to what I had envisioned, and I added a skylight (warm-up) filter.

Ideally, for slide projection we might select a lower ASA, because the lower the ASA, the finer the grain, and hence the higher the color saturation. At ASA 25, we would have a richer color saturation and finer grain than at ASA 200. But choosing a particular ASA depends on other factors as well. First we must ask: What is the content and location of our multi-image production? Are we photographing people on the move? Are we photographing in low-light situations? Trying to work with ASA 25 under these conditions would force us to sacrifice depth of field and might even prove impossible without a flash.

We might then respond, "Well, I could use a faster emulsion (higher ASA) for the low-light and action scenes." But we must first make sure that the manufacturer has produced a film with a higher ASA in the same emulsion base. Let me give an example. Kodak produces Kodachrome in ASA 25, 40, and 64 and recently added ASA 100. Kodachrome is balanced to produce warmer reds and yellows and is usually selected for its rendition of rich flesh tones. Ektachrome, which has an ASA of 64, 100, 200, and 400, leans toward the cooler side and more natural colors. If we switched midstream in our production from Kodachrome to Ektachrome, it would be sharply apparent on our screen. Consistency in color balance is critical in multi-image presentations, and we should decide on one film and stay with it throughout the production. We would not want to mix warm hues and cool hues in a sequence, as it would distract from the continuity and flow. Similarly, we would not want to jump from an ASA 25 to an ASA 400, even if we stayed with one kind of film, because grain structure and color saturation would be vastly different between the slow and fast emulsions.

Let's assume, for the moment, that we would like to use Kodachrome 64 because of its tight grain and warm color qualities. We should plan to use a strobe light, or flash unit, for indoor and low-light situations. We also should take into consideration that only Kodak can process Kodachrome, as they keep their formula secret. And we can't effectively duplicate our show on Kodachrome because of its higher contrast. These are important considerations in choosing transparency film for multi-image production. Kodak recommends using Ektachrome Slide Duplicating Film 5071 because it is made specifically for this purpose and it seems reasonable that we can copy our Kodachrome slides on this film. Kodak S0 366 is excellent when duplicating with strobe light. I have also had good results in duplicating Ektachrome slides on Ektachrome Professional Tungsten (EPT 50) as long as I control the contrast. This is an individual choice.

Graininess increases with the speed of the film. An ASA of 64 or 100, a medium-fast emulsion with good resolution and color saturation, seems to be a good compromise. As already pointed out, this might force us to consider flash or special lighting in tight spots, unless we are willing to go to a faster film. If we started with Ektachrome 100, we could move up to Ektachrome 200, and the difference in grain and saturation would be minimal. But I would not recommend an ASA of 400 for multi-image projection. The grain will be obvious, and the color tends to shift consid-

FIGURE 6–12
Masking slides to create progressive disclosure can be effective if we are building on one idea. For example, a corporation might want to show four different workers, in different departments, all contributing to the growth of the firm. This four-way split might be an effective way of emphasizing their combined contribution.

erably. My own preference is to stay with one film emulsion throughout and use bounce flash when absolutely required.

When buying transparency film it is wiser to buy a quantity of rolls with the same emulsion batch number (printed on the box) to ensure that the color rendition will be identical from roll to roll. I store the unopened boxes in my refrigerator to increase longevity but take the film out of the refrigerator several hours before I plan to use it, to allow it to warm to room temperature. We also can buy 100-foot rolls of color transparency film, store it in a bulk loader, and spool it off into individual cassettes as needed.

A final note before leaving the subject of color transparency film. In response to the demands of professional photographers several years ago, Kodak developed a special category for its Ektachrome film, called Ektachrome Professional. In camera shops that cater to professional photographers, one can ask for Ektachrome Professional Daylight (EPN 100) or Ektachrome Professional Tungsten Film (EPT 160 or EPY 50). This simply means that after an emulsion batch has been processed at the Kodak plant, some film is earmarked for posttesting, and the *effective* emulsion speed is stamped in red on the information sheet inside each package. The effective ASA might be slightly higher, slightly lower, or identical to the emulsion speed marked on the carton. Thus, a film that is Ektachrome Daylight 100 might actually have an ASA rating of 80 in the retest. When a one-third–stop change is critical, it is wise to spend the few extra cents to buy the posttested professional film.

USING A FLASH FOR MULTI-IMAGE

I said that it is sometimes necessary to use supplementary light with multi-image photography. Ideally, if we could set up and control the scene, we might choose photoflood lights and reflector fills because we can replicate the soft, open quality of natural light photography. Sophisticated use of flash equipment can create the same effect. Since multi-image photography does not lend itself readily to studio setups, we often must improvise in the field. When strobe lighting is a necessity, it is important to try to keep that soft, open quality by using fill flash, diffused flash, or bounce flash rather than direct flash. This takes patience and some experience, but if we are serious about multi-image production, handling a strobe unit is an important part of the process.

It is not the purpose of this book to teach flash photography; there are many excellent books on this subject. Suffice to say that direct flash creates a harsh effect, usually with hot spots reflecting from heads that are in the foreground or from other reflective surfaces, making the resulting image on the screen distracting and unpleasant. By practicing how to bounce off a white surface, such as a ceiling or wall, we can diffuse the light and give the image an even, open look.

If there are no white surfaces to use, we can try to diffuse the light at its source (the flash head) with a handkerchief or tissue. Or we can purchase a small bounce attachment designed for the camera-mounted strobe unit. I find this attachment helpful when photographing one or two individuals at medium or close range. In a situation where the subject is backlighted, we can use our flash creatively as a fill, metering for the existing light while cutting down the flash power to fill in the shadows.

If direct flash is required to cover a large area, or if no other option is available, I would recommend trying a 1A (pale yellow) filter to diminish the cool blues and bring the image into balance with other slides that have been taken in natural light. We should always make several tests with our camera and flash unit before using them in a professional situation. This will help us familiarize ourselves with the problems we will face in the environment and work out any hitches that might arise with the equipment.

GLOSSARY

Aperture Opening. The diameter of the lens opening in a camera through which light passes.

ASA American Standards Association. Refers to the rating of film speed—that is, the light sensitivity of film emulsions.

Bounce light A light source that is bounced off a wall or other reflective object to illuminate the subject. This method tends to diffuse the light and open up the shadow areas.

Close-up The subject's head occupies the full screen.

Color saturation To soak up, imbue, or impregnate. In color technology, it means the vividness of hue; the degree of difference from a gray of the same brightness and lightness.

Depth of field The range of acceptable sharpness within which the subject (of focus) appears. Depth of field is determined by aperture, lens focal length, and the distance from subject to film plane.

Existing light The light that is there, whether it is daylight, reflected light, room light, or lamp light. As opposed to strobe light, photofloods, or any supplementary light added in the process of taking a photograph.

Exposure The amount of light hitting light-sensitive film during a given duration. This is determined by lens aperture and shutter speed based on an estimated or metered reading of the light on the subject.

Film emulsion The light-sensitive properties suspended in a gelatin base on the face of a film.

Filter Optical glass or gel of a specific color or property through which light rays are passed or absorbed for the purpose of intensifying or correcting the color balance of the exposed film.

Hot spot An undesirable concentration of light on one portion of the subject area.

Icon An image or representation where the relationship between the object and what it represents shows resemblance (for instance, a statue, photograph, or religious symbol).

Key image An image in a sequence that contains the pivotal reference around which all other images in the sequence revolve.

Light meter An instrument that measures the amount of direct light on a subject or the amount of light reflected by that subject, for the purpose of making an accurate photographic exposure.

Mask Usually a litho negative that changes the format of a slide by blocking out a portion of an image to create a special effect or change in image shape. There are also commercially available slide masks with special windows of various shapes and sizes.

Motion A meaningful or expressive change in the body or a part of the body; a gesture or physical action.

Movement In this book, it refers both to implied motion in still photography (for example, an outstretched leg or a subject shown first outside a doorway, then on the inside), and symbolic motion (for instance, red is warm, emotional; blue is cool, intellectual; a diagonal line is aggressive; a horizontal line is passive).

Polarizer A filter that splits up or divides a ray of light into two distinct refracted parts. Used in photography to reduce reflection from the sky or from surfaces in the image frame.

Sequence A group of related images, one following the other in an orderly manner to establish an aesthetic or dramatic unit. A visual paragraph.

Sign A conventional figure or device that stands for a word, phrase, or operation (for example, two fingers held up in a V shape stands for victory; a road sign showing a curved line signifies sharp curve ahead).

Split frame A type of visual effect where two or more distinct images appear in the same frame. This is generally created with the use of a mask.

Symbol Something that stands for or represents another thing; especially an object used to represent something abstract (for example, a dove represents peace). Language and numbers also are symbolic.

Zoom A lens with continuously variable focal lengths. A zoom effect on screen can be created by dissolving a series of slides of the same image photographed in various focal lengths.

Chapter 7

Creating the Music Track; Integrating Narration

At what point in production should the music track be put together? In filmmaking the music track usually is created after the film has been completed. Not so in multi-image, where the rhythm, emotional color, tempo, and instrumentation are tied to and integrated early on with the content of the show. Although the music track in multi-image is generally recorded after the narration has been taped, decisions about the music can be made as early as the scripting stage, and the music score can be prepared in rough at any time during production.

Although its function is to support the message of the presentation, not to call attention to itself, the music will play a key role in establishing the dramatic tone and pace of a production. As we have indicated, the content of the show will determine the choice of music. Audience is another factor to be considered. Although final decisions about the music might be put on the back burner while other media components are being organized, the multi-image producer has a good idea of the kind of music he or she wants overall. The producer also is aware of key (major, minor), mood, tempo, and instrumentation (orchestration), and he or she knows whether the music will be canned (library music) or original. Through all phases of production, the producer is listening to music and searching for the right sound.

LIBRARY MUSIC

Library music (stock music) is a popular choice for multi-image production because it is oriented toward the visual producer and can be dubbed for a minimal fee. It has been designed specifically for background sound, with little or no melody to distract the listener. Commercial music libraries abound in urban centers; some even produce catalogs from which records can be ordered by mail. For a fee, we can go to a music library and listen to hundreds of recordings with labels such as *urban upbeat, romantic, pastoral,* and *industrial.* When the choices have been narrowed down, the engineer often will make a tape of tentative selections for the producer or sound engineer to take back to the studio for further listening and consideration. Once the final selections have been made and incorporated in the sound track, a composer's fee, popularly known as a needle-drop fee, is charged for each of the music segments, which are now cleared for public presentation.

Of course, we can dub our own records and tapes at home for simple home and nonprofit use, but we are always at risk of copyright infringement if the production goes public—that is, if money is paid for the talent or fees are collected from an audience. (Refer to Chapter 3 for copyright information.) Using library music is one way to eliminate this uncertainty because the music is cleared when the needle-drop payment is made.

COMMISSIONING ORIGINAL MUSIC

Frequently original music is commissioned for a multi-image presentation. This is both the most costly and the most ideal choice because the composer is involved at the outset. The producer fills in the background of script and visuals for the composer, describing the intended audience and other information relevant to the production. The producer also gives the composer some idea of the kind of music desired. With a strong sense of the mood, pace, and instrumentation of the music, the composer can start to develop the theme. Typically, most of the multi-image music is composed in advance of the final mix, leaving natural breaks to allow for scene changes and narrative pauses. But not until the narration is taped and edited can the music score be completed.

Whether we use library music, live musicians, or an original composition, we should think of the narration as the lead instrument. The composer or editor works first from the script, then with the actual voice narration, working with the natural cadence of the voice and putting down the music on a separate track or tape in the order in which it will be played. The editor works one section at a time to edit the music to fit the voice, being careful never to overwhelm it. It is helpful to have some idea of the imagery as well. If we know that key images appear at certain points in the narrative design, a sound effect or a change of music key can be initiated.

TIMING THE NARRATION

It simplifies the work if each section of the voice master is timed out, so that we can cut a piece of music to fit exactly with each section of the narration. (It is assumed that the narration also has been timed out to allow for images to appear and dissolve on the screen.) We also can find the editing

FIGURE 7–1
A composer's sixteen-track automated recording studio. Here Chris Hedge is working at a sixteen-track computer-automated mixer. In front of this is another sixteen-track mixer. Just to his right is a tape deck autolocator, and beyond that is a sixteen-track tape recorder. To the right of his right shoulder is a digital synthesizer. Other equipment in the studio includes control room monitors (speakers), equalizers, amplifiers, and a turntable/cassette deck/digital audio recorder setup. (© Don Klein)

FIGURE 7–2
Home studio setups also can produce quality sound productions. They are easy to manage and cost-effective. Here we have a turntable, receiver, and cassette deck combination that forms the basic components of many home hi-fi systems. We have added an old Teac 124 cassette deck and a Numark 1550 mixer with mic input. Voila! An effective home sound studio. (© Phiz Mezey)

points where the music can be cut, faded out, or changed. Although it is helpful to know something about music composition, many of us who are neither musicians nor sound engineers respond intuitively to the rhythm and color of the sound. Intuition plays a very important role in this work. When library music has to be cut, a good point to keep in mind is to cut just before or just after the downbeat, never on it. For example, if we have a four-beat measure, we should cut on the second or fourth beat, not on the first or third. This makes the cuts less noticeable.

If there is no narrative track, the composer can work directly from the storyboard and slides to develop the music score, after consulting with the producer.

THE ROLE OF THE NARRATION

I said previously that the narration is the lead instrument in the audio track of a multi-image production. It also acts as the connective tissue between the aural and visual components. The tone and pace of the recorded voice will determine to a large extent the final number and cue time of the images. Of course, we have been working with script and images all along—selecting and ordering the images in a particular scene and reading the script aloud as we work with the images. We might have to add or cut out images on the light table, or indicate a pause, cut, or addition to the narration. But for many sound technicians, the script will be recorded before the music score can be completed. I have found that the final sound track is better if slides and narration have been fitted together before the final music edit, but that is a personal choice.

When the narration is ready to be recorded, we already will have selected the speaker based on the kind of voice we want. Selecting the narrator is a most important task, as it is the voice on which the other media will pivot. A professional generally knows what pace to set, when to pause, where to raise or lower the voice, and how to proceed when an error has been made. Although an amateur might be more spontaneous, the time consumed in directing the narration can be overwhelming, as is the time for editing out the bad takes.

Such time is better spent making the right choice of narrator. Until recently I was a proponent of the natural, unrehearsed voice. It also is true that until I decided on the professional voice, I spent several hours in rehearsal with an inexperienced narrator, and several more hours rough-editing the numerous takes, while my colleague, working with a professional, could record and make a final edit of the narration in one-quarter of the time.

SOME SUGGESTIONS FOR RECORDING AND EDITING THE NARRATION

If we do not have a sound studio available for recording the narration, we can duplicate many of the same acoustical conditions in our own home. If we do not want the sound to bounce like a ping-pong ball, one wall should be soft and the facing wall hard. Window drapery opposite a bare wall meets this condition. Similarly, a carpeted floor opposite a hard ceiling can keep the sound in healthier balance. A small or moderately sized room is better than a large, high-ceilinged one. A good microphone, appropriate for the situation and placed close to the sound source, also is important. (Refer to Chapter 5, the section on microphones.)

The experienced narrator knows just how close to the microphone to be. He or she also knows at what pace to read, when to raise and lower the voice, and when to allow for natural breaks in the rhythm. An experienced narrator usually can read the script in one reading, pausing momentarily after an error, then repeating the sentence correctly, without interrupting the flow of the narration.

When I work with an inexperienced narrator, I prefer to record the script in sections. I might record only a page or two at a time and will repeat each section until it records smoothly. There might be several takes for each reading, but one of them will be our choice in the final edit. The different takes can be identified on the tape with a voice identifier such as "Take 2, Part 1, Counter 125." The counter number refers to the counter window on the recorder, which operates during the record mode and on playback allows us to advance directly to a specific point in the tape.

If we have recorded on cassette tape, we will have to make a transfer to open-reel tape for editing purposes. When we have finished recording on cassette, we can listen to all the takes, transferring the best one in each segment to another tape (open reel) in chronological order. Now all the best segments are on a single master tape, ready to be edited. Of course, with this method, we have already lost a generation in the transfer of the original from cassette to open reel, but if the original recording is of high quality, the loss will be unnoticeable.

A more professional way to do this, especially when working with a speaker who can read through the script in one shot, is to work directly on open-reel tape. On playback we can mark the points of error on the tape with a low-frequency tone, adding a second tone at the beginning of the correction. When cutting, we just have to listen for the tones and cut out the sections between them to produce a first-generation smoothly narrated tape. This, of course, requires higher-quality equipment and know-how, but it does save many hours of listening, transferring, cutting, and splicing.

EDITING WITH THE THREE-REEL METHOD

One way to facilitate editing without losing track of all the cut-out strips of tape is to use the three-reel method (one for master tape, one for all the outtakes, and one for the final edit). (See Figure 7–3.) With the master tape on the supply reel, spin off the outtakes onto a second reel and the good takes on the third uptake reel. This might take a little more time, but it is a good way to keep track of all the pieces.

I have two additional suggestions for recording and editing voice narrations. For the best sound, voice should be recorded on a half-track open-reel recorder at 15 ips, with the Dolby and DBX switches in the off position. It can then be transferred to four-track open-reel tape for mixing. Since most of us work with less expensive recording equipment, including cassette decks, it is important to remember that the

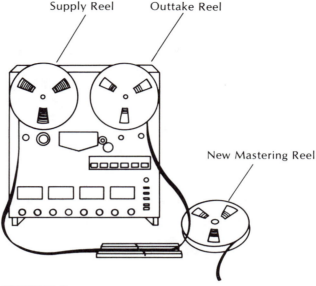

Supply Reel   Outtake Reel

New Mastering Reel

FIGURE 7–3
Three-reel method of editing. Splicing and keeping all the outtakes together on a separate reel ensures that the edited-out portions of the tape will be readily available and easy to locate should they be needed again. The alternative is to have countless disorganized strips of outtakes all over the counter or in the wastebasket.

voice cannot be better than the equipment on which it is recorded. The choice of microphone, tape, and tape recorder, as well as the acoustical environment for recording, is very important in the production process. If we are buying new equipment, we should do a thorough job of research to find the best equipment for the money we are spending (see Chapter 12).

GLOSSARY

Counter A device on the tape recorder that keeps numerical track of where a selection of audio is located on a tape. We can allow a counter to run consecutively from the beginning of the tape, or we can "zero" the tape—that is, set the counter at zero at any point in the tape to which we want to return later.

DBX A system of noise reduction (tape and electronic hiss) used in many professional sound systems.

Decibel (dB) A unit for measuring the volume of sound.

Dolby Named after its inventor, this is an audio tape recording and playback circuit used to improve the signal-to-noise ratio.

Dub   To make a copy of a prerecorded tape.

Hard wall   A smooth, hard, reflective surface that bounces the sound back to the room. A soft wall, such as drapery or rugs, absorbs sound. A good balance for recording purposes would be a hard surface opposite a soft surface—for example, a bare wall opposite drapes or a ceiling opposite a rug.

Intuition   The faculty of knowing something without the process of rational thought. A heightened sensitivity.

Library music   Recorded music that has been produced to satisfy a variety of possible needs in aural and visual production. Each track expresses a specific mood and rhythm but generally avoids melody, making it easier to mix and match with other music background. Sold by the needle drop, a fee that usually reverts to the composer.

Outtake   The edited-out portions of a recorded tape, or the slides not selected for a multi-image production.

Splice   In tape editing, the process by which two pieces of tape are butted together and held in place by a special tape.

Chapter 8

Some Basics in Mixing and Editing Sound

Some multi-imagists believe that the audio is fifty percent of the production. Although I disagree with that emphasis, I do believe that the sound track, which is the repository of all the audio we have created, is critical to the success of a multi-image production. If our narrative design has been executed well and our narration, music, and images are integrated effectively, we will have met most of the criteria for a successful presentation. A poor sound track could diminish the total effect.

Ideally, the final sound mix should be backed by engineering skill, experience, and quality equipment. That is why producers generally assign this function to a sound engineer who has a fully equipped studio. (See Figure 8–1.) Often the cost is prohibitive, however, and our only option is to do most or all of the audio preparation ourselves. That is why it is important to learn the basics about the mechanics and art of recording, editing, and mixing sound tracks for multi-image presentations.

OPEN-REEL TAPE RECORDERS

Open-reel (reel-to-reel) sound recording is considered the most professional way to record because of its accuracy in reproducing the original sound and the ease with which the tape can be edited. For the home user open-reel tape comes in a ¼-inch width and has a tape speed of 3¾ ips or 7½ ips (the number of inches of tape that passes the record head per second). Sound

engineers work with ¼-, ½-, and 1-inch widths. The wider the tape surface, the greater the sound accuracy. They use equipment that accommodates tape speeds of 7½ ips, 15 ips, and 30 ips. Faster tape speeds ensure better sound fidelity. Professional-quality open-reel tape recorders are therefore used by sound engineers and other professionals (1) in a studio environment; (2) in the preparation of master tapes; (3) for editing and mixing; and (4) for play-

FIGURE 8–1
Sound station (intermediate level), reading from left to right: four-track, two-channel Teac 225 sync recorder; amplifier (below); four-track, four-channel Tascam 22–4 open-reel tape deck; Teac mixer with eight inputs and four outputs and an eight-line-in to two-line-out submixer; Technics turntable; microphone. An editing splicer is taped to the table in front of the four-track Tascam recorder. (© Phiz Mezey)

back where sound fidelity is critical to the success of the production.

While tape width and tape speed are important factors in reproducing sound accurately, tape thickness also is a factor. A 1.0-mil tape, which comes in 1,800-foot lengths on the reel, might be too thin. There are only 1,200 feet per reel in 1.5-mil tape, but it is preferred for its strength and stability.

CASSETTE TAPE RECORDERS

Cassette tapes are closed-reel (encased) tapes. They are only ⅛ inch wide, and their standard speeds for general audio recording are 1⅞ ips and, for some professional units, 3¾ ips. It would seem that this would make a good argument against using cassette tapes in multi-image recording. But other factors balance the negative aspects of using cassette tapes in multi-image production. Their lighter weight, the convenience and ease with which they can be transported and set up for recording or playback, their moderate cost relative to open-reel units, and the tremendous improvements in the technology of cassette recording are some of the reasons cassette recorders and tapes are being used more and more in the field, particularly in recording the voice component of multi-image productions.

A carefully selected cassette recorder and superior-quality external microphone can go a long way toward starting us on the right track in recording the narration. Today cassette recorders are quite acceptable in the field for recording original voice and sound effects because of their lighter weight and convenience. The audio can later be transferred from a cassette to an open-reel recorder for editing purposes because it is not possible to cut and splice the narrow closed-reel cassette tapes, although electronic editing will be the next technological breakthrough in cassette recorder development.

We would generally leave our edited tape on open reel for playback, to take advantage of the better sound quality, particularly in a large auditorium. But if we did not have access to an open-reel deck for playback, the edited tape could be transferred back to the cassette format. There would be some loss of sound fidelity with each trans-

fer, but if the original was a quality recording, this disadvantage would be minimal and would be offset by the convenience of transporting and setting up the less bulky equipment.

TAPE FORMATS

It is a common misconception that the tapes we buy already have the tracks laid out on them. All tapes are essentially blank, with demagnetized iron oxide particles imbedded on the face. These particles are magnetized and rearranged to form a series of magnetic fields on the coated surface of the tape when sound waves, passing through a mic, are transferred to electrical impulses as the tape passes the record head.

The format of the tape (the number of tracks, the direction, the location of the sound, and the speed) is determined by the configuration of the record head and the type of recorder being used. Cassette tapes and open-reel tapes use the same three basic formats, but the order and direction of the tracks are significantly different. First, let's look at three basic formats we might find: monaural half track, stereophonic quarter track, and four track. The term *track* refers to the area or band of the tape that the sound signal occupies. Monaural recordings (from *mono aural,* one or more sound sources channeled into a single carrier) occupy one half of the tape for each "side" that is recorded. Monaural formats usually are referred to as half track. Stereophonic (stereo) formats are referred to as quarter track because they divide each half track into a right and left channel. Four-track tapes occupy the full width of the tape, and each track is independent and travels in the same direction. (We do not turn these over to play the "other side.")

Cassette tape at present has a narrower surface and a slower speed than open-reel tape. As we said above, the order and direction of the tracks are different on cassette tapes than on open-reel tapes. Developed by a man named Philips, all mono cassette recorders record on the bottom half of the tape width. When the tape is turned over, it again records on the bottom. (See Figure 8–2.)

Philips stereo cassette recorders also record on the bottom half of the tape, but this portion of the tape is again halved to accommodate a right and a left channel, both moving in the same direction. (*Channel* refers to the path that a signal follows.)

MONAURAL CASSETTE RECORDERS WITH A BUILT-IN SYNC SIGNAL

A synchronizer (sync) cassette recorder functions as a regular monaural cassette recorder but has the added function of being able to record a sync pulse on the tape when placed in the sync/record mode. We can first record our narration or music monaurally on the bottom half track of the tape. Now, with the machine placed in the sync/record mode, we can record an inaudible tone on the top half of the tape while listening to and without erasing the audio. In the sync mode both signals travel in the same direction. It is this 1,000-Hz sync pulse that will trigger the slide advance mechanism on the projector, causing a slide change during playback. It is important not to record any sound signal on the B side of the tape because that track is already occupied by the sync-pulse signal.

Synchronizer cassette recorders use the ANSI (American National Standards Institute) format, or separate track system, and are compatible with home stereo decks. We can do our original recording on cassette stereo (quarter-track stereo) at home, then transfer the audio to the monaural track on a cassette sync recorder, because both left and right audio signals occupy the same half track and are compatible. But we cannot put the sync pulse on the home stereo because it does not have the sync/record function (its side B travels in the direction *opposite* that of the audio on side A).

TRACK OR CHANNEL?

Two of the most confusing recording terms are *track* and *channel.* As I already pointed out, there are many different track arrangements, depending on the configuration of the record heads. *Track* refers to the area of the tape the recorded signal occupies, whether it is half of the tape or only a quarter of it. *Channel* refers to the path or line of amplification. For example, stereophonic

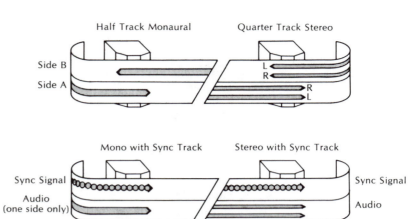

FIGURE 8–2
Cassette tape formats, showing the head configuration in half-track monaural and quarter-track stereo cassette tape recorders. The drawings at the top illustrate the typical consumer cassette recorder configuration. The tape can be turned over and played on the other side. The drawings on the bottom illustrate Philips ANSI format on cassette recorders with a sync-input and sync-track configuration. Audio is on one side of the tape only.

sound is laid down in two lines of amplification, a right and a left channel. Mono plus cue consists of a two-track, two-channel configuration.

OPEN-REEL HALF-TRACK, QUARTER-TRACK, AND TWO- AND FOUR-TRACK FORMATS

Although open-reel formats also allow for full-track, half-track, quarter-track, and two- and four-track configurations, they are formatted differently. Unlike cassette tape, half-track open-reel monaural tapes record from the top down. To record stereo sound on an open-reel quarter-track tape, the record head first records tracks 1 and 3, then records tracks 2 and 4 in the opposite direction. (Quarter track is sometimes called four track, but I make a distinction between quarter-track stereo home units and four-track professional modules in which each track is independent.)

A four-track, four-channel tape, whether open reel or cassette, will record all four tracks in the same direction. A two-track, two-channel tape will record both tracks in the same direction.

If we want to add a sync pulse to a four-track, four-channel tape, we can use two separate tracks for stereo sound, recording the music on one track and the narration on another, then skip one track (usually track 3, which remains blank) and record the sync pulse on track 4. (See Figure 8–3.)

RECORDING SOUND ON SOUND WITH HOME EQUIPMENT

If we have only a home hi-fi system to work with at the beginning of our multi-image experience, can we still mix narration and music? The answer is a qualified yes. Since the home recorder can take only one sound source at a time, we cannot mix the level of two sound sources internally. If we want to combine narration and music, they must be played back simultaneously onto a single track. Although the microphone can carry both the voice and the music in a crude, live mix, we should keep our sound tracks simple when our equipment is limited, settling for a music background only or a very simple combination of music and narration.

A sync pulse cannot be added on the second track of our home hi-fi equipment because this equipment does not have a sync-pulse function. (We cannot record both

halves of the tape in the same direction.) But once our music and sound are recorded on one track, we can add the sync pulse later, using an AV tape recorder (Philips ANSI), a programmer and tape recorder that has a sync input function, or a programmer with a four-track, four-channel deck.

HOW IT IS DONE

- **Solution 1: Recording Music and Narration on a Home System**

Let's assume we have a stereo receiver, turntable, and cassette tape deck of moderate quality. (See Figure 8–4.) On the rear panel our receiver has left and right tape-out jacks. From these jacks we are able to run a patch cord to our tape recorder or tape deck for the purpose of dubbing (copying) signals from our phonograph, radio, or other connected sound source. If we want to record a music background only, we can record through the system. But to mix music with narration, we must record them simultaneously in a live mix. Since we are limited to one external sound source at a time—either mic-in or line-in—we cannot control the levels of both the music and the narration. The only way to have the music background is to pick it up externally through the speakers, using the volume control knob on the receiver to fade up and fade out the music as we record live through the mic. The voice level can be adjusted internally through the level control (VU meters) on the cassette deck, while the music is adjusted manually with the volume control knob on the receiver. (Using the line-in instead of the mic-in function, the voice also can be dubbed from another tape, following the same process.) Since we are recording live, the narration must be free of mistakes, requiring a retake if anything goes wrong. This might not be a sophisticated solution, but it works. The sync signal must be added separately, on a recorder with a sync-input or sync/record mode.

- **Solution 2: Recording Two Tracks Independently, Then Mixing to One Track**

It would make more sense to record the music directly through the system by tak-

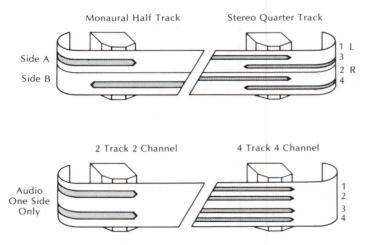

FIGURE 8–3
Open-reel tape formats, monaural and stereophonic, have a different head configuration from cassette formats and are not compatible with them. For editing purposes we would have to transfer cassette tapes, as well as open-reel tapes that have been recorded on both sides, to a two-track, two-channel—or four-track, four-channel—open-reel deck for editing. If you review Figures 8–2 and 8–3, you can see why.

ing the signal from the turntable or another tape recorder via a cable plugged into the input jack from the receiver. Today most radios and record players are fitted with input and output jacks. If we have access to an open-reel stereo tape recorder that will allow us to record the left and right tracks independently, we can mix a fresh program with an existing program, resulting in a single-track mixed signal, as follows (see Figure 8–5):

1. Record the narration on track 1 (left) of a quarter-track open-reel recorder. The recorder must have separate left and right record switches.
2. Disengage the track 1 (left) record switch before proceeding.
3. Edit the narration (cut and splice).
4. We now need two Y adapters. (One might have to be two male to one female, the other two female to one male.) Be sure that the left record switch has been disengaged before proceeding.
5. Connect the two Y adapters, one carrying the music from the receiver to the right input of the open-reel deck and the other carrying the narration from the left output to the right input of the tape deck.
6. Engage the right record switch (be sure the left is disengaged), and by adjusting the input and output level controls on the open-reel recorder, we will be able to get a high-quality mono sound on the right track.
7. If we wish, we may now use the left track for recording the projector sync signal.

• **Solution 3: Using a Cassette Tape Recorder as a Mixer**

It also is possible to use a separate tape recorder as a mixer to create a monaural recording, provided it has separate left and right level controls. We are going to combine (mix) the signals from different sources—turntable, another tape recorder, radio, or mic—into a blend of one (monophonic) signal. Let's call our recorder with its right and left level control knobs recorder 1. We can simplify the operation by completing it in two stages (see Figure 8–6):

1. We will simultaneously channel the music from our turntable, through a re-

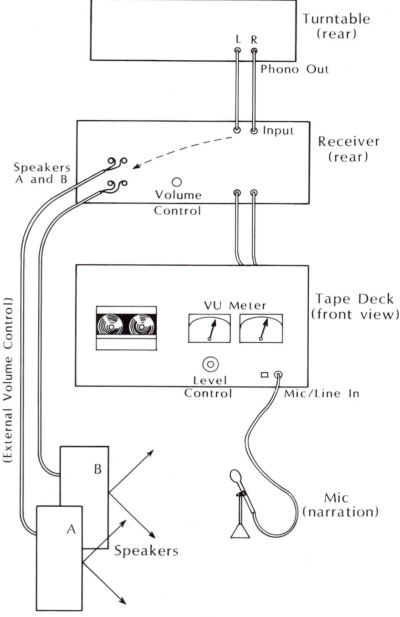

FIGURE 8–4
Solution 1: Home setup showing how music and narration can be mixed to one track, using a microphone and a mic-in jack for live narration and the speakers to play background music simultaneously. The recording level for the narration can be set with the level control (VU meter). The music background can be adjusted up or down by manually operating the volume control knob on the receiver during a live performance.

ceiver, into a left line-in on recorder 1, and the narration from a second source into the right line-in on this same recorder. This will establish two channels of information on one machine.

FIGURE 8–5
Solution 2: Recording two tracks independently.

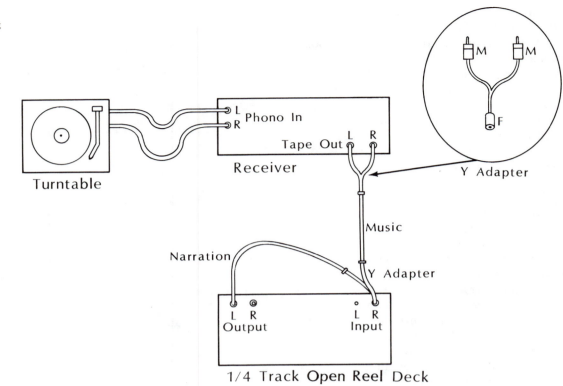

2. We should check to see that all noise-reduction systems on recorder 1 have been turned off, and when we are ready to record, we will put the machine in record/pause mode. Using earphones to monitor, we will practice manipulating the right and left level control knobs to establish the correct signal levels for each channel.

3. When we record, we will use the left and right level control knobs to fine-tune our blend, recording our sound on two separate channels.

4. Now we can mix these channels by patching them from recorder 1 to recorder 2. We use a patch cord from the left and right outputs of recorder 1 to the left only (or right only) input of recorder 2, using a Y adapter.

5. With recorder 1 in play mode and recorder 2 in record mode, we can now mix both channels down to a monaural track on recorder 2.

• **Solution 4: Recording with a Mixer and a Tape Recorder**

A mixer permits us to adjust the sound levels of several elements recorded sepa-

rately. With a mixer we can blend voice, more than one source of music, sound effects, and so on. We can fade up or fade down and in general create an integrated sound track. In effect, sound can be channeled through the mixer from different sources, mixed together, and fed to a single track or separate tracks on a recorder or tape deck. We can mix and edit as we go along.

A simple mixer will have either two or four inputs to accommodate audio from microphone, turntable, or tape recorder. With just two inputs we can still control the music level from one source by adjusting one of the "pots" (potentiometer, or sound level control knob) and the voice level with the other pot. With four inputs, we can crossfade two pieces of music—that is, fade out one piece of music while fading up the other, and at the same time control the level of the voice and sound effects through the two remaining pots. Most mixers have no built-in amplifier, although some will amplify the sound going through the system. The more expensive mixers will have VU meters (meters used to indicate the strength of the incoming or outgoing signal) and a

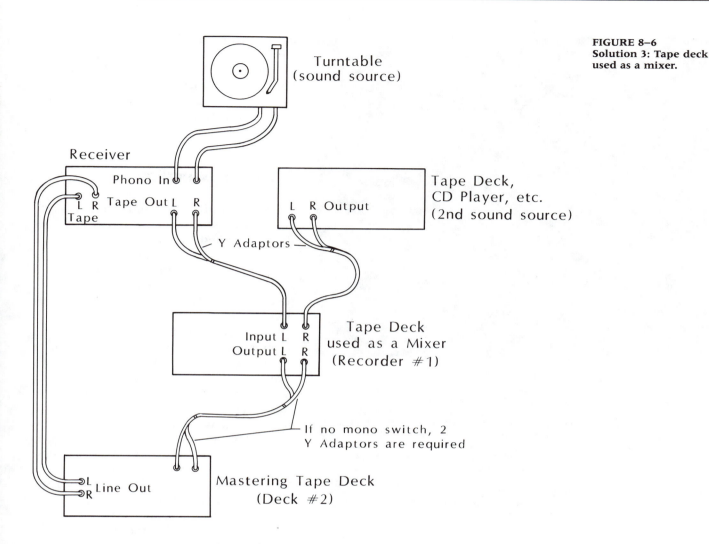

FIGURE 8–6
Solution 3: Tape deck
used as a mixer.

master level control so that all sources going through the mixer can be faded up or faded down together. (See Figure 7–2 in Chapter 7.)

EDITING OPEN-REEL TAPES

Editing open-reel tapes is relatively simple, as long as we remember that we cannot cut and splice ¼-inch open-reel stereo tape if the configuration has been recorded in both directions (on both sides). (Refer to Figure 8–3.) We will first have to transfer the ¼-inch stereo tape to an open-reel two-track or four-track deck with independent control of the tracks. (See Figure 8–7.)

Two-track and four-track open-reel tapes are easy to edit. (See Figure 8–8.) Since all tracks now travel in the same direction, we

will edit one track at a time, cutting out what we do not want or adding blank tape as required for spacing.

We assume that our open-reel tape recorder is designed to allow us to disengage the pinch roller while allowing us to manually rock the reels back and forth across the playback head to locate the beginning of the audio we want to cut. We can now mark with a grease pencil the exact point on the tape, over the playback head, where we want to begin our cut. Next, let's locate the end of the phrase or sentence we want to remove and mark the end of the desired cut area. Now we can back up and mark the beginning of the desired cut area.

Next, using a splicing block, with a groove to hold the tape and a 45-degree angled slot, we can lay the tape in the groove, face down (recorded side down),

FIGURE 8–7
Four-track, four-channel open-reel recorder/
reproducer. This deck is equipped with all the
functions needed for studio master multitrack
recording/reproducing: independent monitor
and record mode controls for each channel, mic/
line mixing, input and output level controls for
each channel, expanded scale VU meters, function and output select switches (which make
setting up record and sync channel assignments
easy), punch-in recording for rerecording of select sections of a track, and other capabilities.
(© Phiz Mezey)

and cut out the unwanted tape with a
straight-edge razor blade, using the slot for
a smooth angled cut. With the tape still
located in the groove of the splicing block,
we can join the tape ends smoothly and
bond them firmly in place with a piece of
splicing tape. Using the same technique,
we also can splice (add) blank tape or tape
from another part of the recording.

Here are two caveats: First, we should
always make a duplicate tape of the original
recording before we start to edit, just in
case we mangle a word or cut out too much.
Second, we should always save the edited-
out scraps in the event we want to piece
them back together later.

One handy way to simplify the editing
process is to use the three-reel method. Instead of cutting out the unwanted sections
of tape and leaving them jumbled on the
work surface, we can cut and splice them
onto an outtake reel, thereby keeping all
the outtakes together on one reel in the

event we might want to retrieve part of it
later. (See Figure 7–3 in Chapter 7.)

When we are satisfied with the results of
our editing of each of the narration, music,
and sound effects tapes, we can mix the
separate tracks down to one stereo or monaural format.

EDITING CASSETTE TAPES

As we already have indicated, cassette
tapes are enclosed in shells and are too frag-
ile to be edited by the above method. The
only way to edit a cassette tape is to transfer
the original tape from a source deck (deck
A) to a blank tape on a recording deck
(deck B), using the pause button on either
deck as the editor.

First, using a patch cord with the correct
terminals, we connect from the output of
our source (deck A) to the input of our
recorder (deck B). Deck A will be in playback mode, and deck B will be in record
mode. When we want to cut out a sentence
or segment, we first hit the pause button
on deck B, stopping the recording, while
allowing deck A to continue to play past
the unwanted section. We can release the
pause button on deck B and pick up the
sound again. To add silent space we reverse
the process, hitting the pause button to stop
deck A, while allowing the recording deck
to record a blank space. When we are ready
to pick up sound again, we release the
pause button on deck A. This is at best a
crude way to edit electronically, but it does
the trick when nothing else is available. I
use this method only for very simple or
preliminary rough cuts.

CONCLUSION

While most professional multi-image producers assign special tasks to experts in the
field—graphics to a graphic artist, sound to
a sound engineer, music to a composer—
the small producer usually handles most of
these jobs himself or herself. It is surprising
how much can be accomplished with limited resources if the producer is resourceful
enough to research the options. I usually
complete the rough edit of music and narration in my home studio, then rent commercial studio space for several hours to

a. Disengage the pinch roller (the rubber wheel that holds the tape tightly against the capstan, just to the right of the record heads). Now rock the reels back and forth across the playback head to locate the beginning of the audio to be edited out.

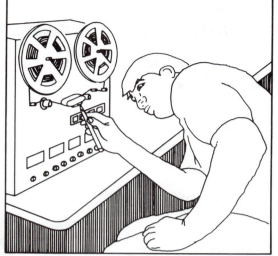

FIGURE 8–8
Editing open-reel tape.

b. Mark with a grease pencil the exact point on the tape, over the playback head, to begin the cut. Move to the end of the section to be removed and repeat this function, marking the end of the cut area.

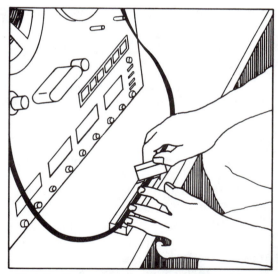

c. Put the first marked area in the splicer, over the diagonal groove, and cut with a straight-edge razor. Do not remove from the channel. Put the second marked tape in the channel area and make a second cut. Remove the unwanted tape.

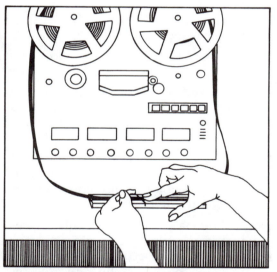

d. Both ends of the remaining tape will be butted together in the channel. Now rub splicing tape over the butt and remove from the channel. Rewind the tape. The edited portion can be spliced to the outtakes on a third reel or discarded after completion of the editing.

fine-tune the editing and complete the sound mix on state-of-the-art equipment. But back in the late sixties, I used all the techniques described as solutions 1, 2, 3, and 4.

Although multi-image production can be undertaken by one person as producer, writer, photographer, artist, sound engineer, editor, and programmer, it also lends itself to a team effort. We all have friends with special talents we can use in our production, and it is fun to solve problems with others. But whether we work alone or call on outside talent, multi-image production can be a gratifying experience that sharpens all our skills, fine-tunes our awareness, and produces a product that we can be proud to share.

GLOSSARY

Ampere Abbreviated, amp. A unit of electrical current equal to the flow of 1 volt across a resistance of 1 ohm.

Amplify To increase the volume or magnitude of an input signal by increasing the power or amperage in a circuit. A tape recorder has a built-in amplifier. A tape deck requires an external amplifier.

ANSI American National Standards Institute. An independent association for establishing standards used for AV equipment in the United States. (See Figure 8–2.)

Control knob Generally, a rheostat that adjusts the level of magnitude of a signal. Cf Level.

Deck Any audio or video tape recorder requiring external amplification.

Head The main component(s) of any recorder; its function is to record and play back the tape.

Hertz (Hz) Unit of frequency equivalent to 1 cycle per second.

Jack A socket or receptacle that accepts a plug. Cf Plug.

Level The degree of volume magnitude of the input source. To take a level refers to adjusting the volume unit meters to the highest magnitude without distortion.

Line-in/out An input or output terminal of a tape deck, preamplifier, and so on that provides a signal for amplification, recording, or monitoring.

Mic Abbreviation for microphone. A device that transforms voice, music, and other live sounds into an electrical current, which is usually fed into an amplifier, recorder, or other sound system.

Mix To combine electrically at varying levels two or more distinct signals.

Mixer A device that has two or more mic or line inputs that allows the operator to control and adjust each signal in the mix separately and to combine them linearly to produce an output signal. Cf Control knob, line-in/out, mic.

Monaural Mono aural. Sound heard from a single channel.

Ohm The basic unit of electrical resistance and reactance. Ohm's law: The dictum that states that the voltage (E) of a circuit is equal to the product of the current (I) and the resistance (R).

Patch cord A short cord with a plug or jack on each end to electronically connect two pieces of equipment.

Philips A standard of compatibility in head configurations for cassette recorders. Named after the man who pioneered the cassette recorder.

Pinch roller Also known as *capstan idler.* The mechanism in a tape recorder that comes in contact with the tape to drive it through the machine.

Plug A connector, usually male, that fits into a socket or jack.

Reel The spool on which the tape is wound.

Sound on sound The recording technique used in multitrack recording where audio material from different sources is recorded one track at a time and subsequently mixed with the other tracks.

Stereophonic The sound heard from two distinct channels or signal paths.

Synchronizer track The path on the tape that is used to record and play back the signal from a programmer or synchronizer.

Track

Full track A tape/head configuration in which the face of the entire ¼-inch tape is recorded in one direction only, creating one channel and using a single head that covers the width of the tape.

Half-track monaural The head configuration covers only half the tape in one direction. By turning the tape over, in effect recording in the opposite direction, a second pass can be made through the recorder.

Quarter-track stereo In this configuration each of the halves is divided to allow for a left and right channel of sound on each side of the tape. In cassette tape configuration tracks 1 and 2 are recorded in the same direction, and on the second pass tracks 3 and 4 are recorded in the opposite direction. Open-reel recorders take the stereo signal first on tracks 1 and 3, and on the second pass another stereo signal is created on tracks 2 and 4, in the opposite direction.

Two-track stereo Two heads are used to record and play back a stereophonic signal. In this configuration the tape is divided into two independent tracks, but it is recorded in one pass and one direction only. This is sometimes referred to as half-track stereo, but I find this usage confusing.

Four-track/four-channel The standard used in professional audiovisual productions. There are four tracks and four independent channels on the face of the tape, all traveling in the same direction. Each channel can be taped independently, then combined with the signal on any of the other channels. In multi-image production, we can combine music and sound from several different sources, using the channels independently in conjunction with a mixer.

Transistors Electronic switches that use semiconductor materials with an electrical conductivity.

Volume In this context it refers to the amplification of the sound on a tape recorder. When we turn the volume up or down, we are regulating the decibels through the speakers.

Volume units (VU) Volume units measure audio *level* power. By regulating the left and right channels, we can modulate the signal, keeping it in balance.

Y adaptor An audio patch cord in which two separate signals are combined before inputting into the recorder, receiver, and so on, or one signal is split into two when outputting.

Chapter 9

Graphics, Titles, and Special Effects Masks

Every production needs a title as well as credits to open and close the presentation. Many shows also include graphics and other illustrations in the body of the production. Graphics also are involved when we want to change the slide format (shape, size, position of images, and so on) through the use of special aperture mounts or slide masks. One does not have to be an artist to create effective layouts. Patience and attention to detail are the only prerequisites. For more complex special effects that require pin registration, we probably would hire a graphic artist, but preparing simple title and credit art and graphics is a relatively uncomplicated procedure.

How to prepare original title art and make slides from this artwork or copy is the subject of this chapter. We will cover planning the graphics, preparing title and credit art, and making the slides. We also will discuss copystand techniques, rephotography, screen formats, special effects masks, and the use of home computer graphics. This is a tall order for one chapter, so prepare to dig in.

One-projector shows or presentations using simple dissolves require artwork that is self-contained. To create a title over a visual, the two images can be sandwiched together in one slide or double-exposed in-camera to make a slide composite. More sophisticated dissolve systems make it possible to freeze (hold) a scenic slide on the screen while superimposing a title from a second projector. The principles and skills covered in this chapter are basic to all situations.

LAYOUT AND LETTERING TECHNIQUES

Every graphic starts with a rough layout—a previsualization of what the finished art should look like. The final art, of course, will be photographed on a copystand to make a 35mm slide transparency. The preliminary design can be hand-lettered but should be laid out in the slide format (a 2:3 ratio). Typeface and type size are important, as are the colors of the lettering and background. Before going ahead with the task, we should ask ourselves the following questions:

With which programmer and projection system will I be working?

Will I be designing a single slide composite to be executed in-camera in a single frame; a sandwich of two separate visual elements (two slide chips); or a programmed superimposition of title (projector B) over visual (projector A) on the screen?

What is the step-by-step procedure I should follow once I have selected one of the above?

What are the costs and availability of equipment and materials?

Are the format, design, and color of my artwork consistent with the content and tone of the production?

Is the type legible, large enough, and simple enough to read easily on-screen?

Is the title short enough for viewers to grasp quickly?

Will the title pique the viewer's interest?

Placement of the words, their size and weight, typeface, spacing, color, and choice of background are some of the important elements with which we must deal in the layout stage. Since our normal slide ratio is 2:3, our art layout should keep that ratio. Our original work can be laid out in a 6- by 9-inch or an 8- by 12-inch area, or a larger or smaller area, as long as we keep the 2:3 ratio. It is wise to leave extra space at the borders of the layout to permit extra "play" on the copystand. This is discussed further in the section on copystand techniques.

Dry transfer lettering is a popular choice for short titles because it has sharp, clean edges like commercial type; comes in a variety of typefaces, sizes, and colors; and can be purchased in sheets at most art or drafting supply stores. These rub-on letters transfer easily. A smooth, hard-surface matte white paper or illustration board is recommended. Illustration board handles well, and because of its weight, it will lie flat on the copystand, eliminating the need for a glass cover. A lighter weight translucent layout paper allows us to use an alignment grid underneath, while a peg bar and punched paper allows us to place one layout over another for more perfect alignment and registration. Although our alternatives are many, our choice will depend on the complexity of the graphic design we have selected.

WHAT WE WILL NEED

For our titling effort we will need the following (see Figures 9–1 and 9–2):

Smooth, white matte board (hot press) or translucent layout paper, punched paper, or punched acetate.

FIGURE 9–1
Preparing the artwork. Translucent layout paper over a layout grid, illustration board, or clear acetate over a layout grid are all effective materials for preparing art for multi-image slides. Dry transfer lettering, pictured here, or Kroy or Merlin Headliner lettering (Figure 9–5) can be used. Tools we will need include a drawing board, T square, burnisher, nonrepro blue pencil, ruler, masking tape, and X-acto knife.

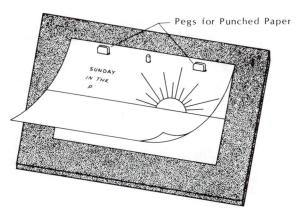

FIGURE 9–2
Peg board and punched paper or acetate are essential where several components in a slide must be in register. Using pegs and a layout grid allows us to make several overlays (for example, to create windows, drop titles over backgrounds, build a progressive, and so on), keeping each in alignment with the other.

A flat, clear surface, drawing board, or Acme-type peg board. We also might decide to use Tara, Format, or Proline lineup board (a pasteup board with a nonrepro blue grid).

Sheets of dry transfer letters, of the size and typeface we selected.

A burnisher to rub down the letters after transferring.

Masking tape to hold the board or paper in place and to remove transfer-letter errors.

A ruler and a T square.

A nonrepro blue pencil (if we plan to copy with photo lithography film), a soft-lead pencil and art eraser (if we are copying with color transparency film), or no marker if we plan to use a grid.

A rough layout of the artwork we are preparing.

Using the preliminary layout as a guide, follow these steps:

1. Carefully align the lettering on the paper so that the guidelines on the dry transfer sheet line up with the grid or hand-drawn guidelines.
2. Use the burnisher or a soft lead pencil, applied to the back of the dry transfer sheet, to transfer the letters to the art surface. Now place a clean sheet over the newly transferred letters and burnish again to ensure adherence.
3. Leave at least ¼ inch free space between the lettering and the edge of the frame. Never crowd the edge of the frame.
4. If a letter is crooked, it can be lifted carefully off the surface with a piece of mask-

ing tape and replaced with a new letter. Use the burnisher to rub the tape over the letter to be removed, then pull up gently.
5. Centering is not difficult. (a) First, measure the width of the layout area and mark the center point. (b) Count the number of letters and spaces in the title (let's say sixteen letters and spaces). (c) Divide this in half (eight letters and spaces). (d) Working from the center backward, transfer the first half of the title to the board, placing the eighth character first, at the center of the frame. (e) Then working forward toward the right border, lay down the second half of the title, starting from the ninth character, which is placed to the right of the center. (See Figure 9–3.)
6. Be sure to remove all guidelines and marks before photographing the artwork.

THINK "VOLUME"

One way to facilitate the process of even spacing between the dry transfer letters is to do it optically. Think of the spaces between letters as volume, rather than as linear measurement. Visualize these spaces as being filled with ink from an inkwell. Balance the spaces (volume) between letters visually. This might seem to be a slow and painstaking process, but with some practice the eye can learn to balance the spaces between letters. (See Figure 9–4.)

If the dry transfer technique seems too painstaking, we can use vinyl cut-out letters, which can be lifted off the sheet with an X-acto blade, then positioned and repositioned until they fit the area.

In some locations, local photocopy shops will rent for use on the premises a Kroy or similar lettering machine, at a fraction of the cost of typesetting. (See Figure 9–5.) After selecting a wheel or disk with the typeface and letter size desired, place the typewheel in the table-top machine and type or punch out the letters desired. They will appear on a continuous strip of clear film, with a paper backing. When the backing is peeled off, the strip can be mounted in place. This method saves us the trouble of aligning and spacing individual letters.

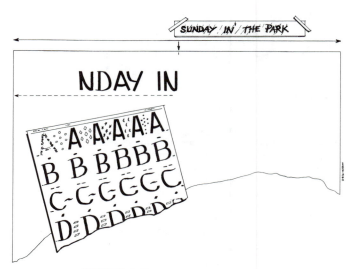

FIGURE 9–3
Centering: Find the center of the frame and the middle letter of the title, then affix the letter, working backward from the center to the left edge of the frame. (Courtesy of Angela Delaverson)

Although this technique works fine on white board, the clear acetate strips might show up on the slide if the lettering is applied directly to colored board. (See the section on copystand techniques.)

One choice, if the methods in this chapter seem too time-consuming, is to take the work to a commercial typesetter or hire a graphic artist who specializes in multi-image graphics and will handle the work from layout to finished slide. The cost is many times greater, since we are paying for someone else's time, equipment, and experience, but it is a choice to be considered.

SIMPLE TITLES

Because there are so many ways to go about making titles and other graphics for multi-image productions, I will limit this discussion to the basics and describe several of the more commonly used techniques. Original artwork can be photocopied on a copystand or outdoors under the open sky with 35mm daylight transparency film. Original art also can be generated on a computer screen and photographed directly. Copystand and camera techniques, as well as computer graphics, are covered in a special section later in this chapter.

For the moment, let's deal with three simple processes: black lettering on a colored background; black lettering on a textured background (see Figure 9–6); and black lettering on a scenic background.

• Black Lettering on a Colored Background

The surface should be smooth, hard, and nonreflective. Illustration board is a good choice for this purpose. "Hot press" board comes only in white and has a smooth, hard surface that holds ink and transfer letters well. "Cold press" board has more texture and comes in many nonsaturated colors, including white. Title backgrounds should be easy on the eye and nondistracting. I would recommend selecting one of the grays, blues, or beiges. These work well as backgrounds in multi-image production because cool colors tend to recede; warm colors move forward visually. If more saturated colors are desired, a special paper such as Pantone, Color Aids, or Chromarama can be purchased in most art stores.

FIGURE 9–4
Spacing dry transfer letters: Think volume and fill the wells between the letters, using the eyes rather than a ruler to balance the space. (Courtesy of Angela Delaverson)

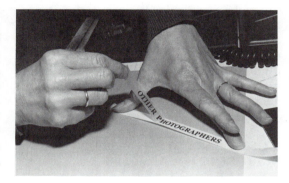

FIGURE 9–5
We can sometimes find a Kroy Lettering or Merlin Headliner machine at a shop where photocopies are made. This machine, which has different type wheels to choose from, will print letters on a clear acetate tape with a paper backing. We can peel off the backing and contact-mount the word strip on our layout board. (© Phiz Mezey)

FIGURE 9–6
Black lettering on a textured background.

These silk-screen papers, which are designed to match printer's inks, are used by graphic artists and come in a variety of richly saturated colors. For convenience and stability it is advisable to mount these papers on some firm backboard, such as bristol board or cardboard, before applying the letters or overlays. Another choice would be to use the paper as is, then place it under a sheet of plate glass to keep it flat on the copystand.

• Textured or Scenic Background

We also could mount our lettering on an imitation-texture wallpaper or contact-paper background. Some wrapping papers, and cut-out scenes from magazines, can make interesting backgrounds, too. An 8-×-10 color photocopy of a 35mm slide also can make an effective background. Remember to mount these photocopies in a 6-×-9 area on a cardboard surface. Be careful to mark your guidelines outside the area to be photographed, as color transparency film will reproduce everything in its field of view, including nonrepro blue.

MOST VERSATILE TITLES: BLACK LETTERING ON A WHITE SURFACE

The most versatile titles are created from simple black lettering on a white background. Through camera, copystand, and processing manipulations, one black-on-white title can spin off into a hundred different color and image combinations. By working with filters or with litho (high-contrast black-and-white) film, we can create any color background or title we desire. We can do any of the following: create a black title on a colored background by using a filter in front of the camera lens; use a litho positive film chip sandwiched with an existing transparency in a single slide; double-expose in-camera a color gel for background with a Kodalith title negative; create clear titles on colored backgrounds through reverse processing; or superimpose a title over a scenic on screen through the use of two or more projectors. These are only a few of the effects that can be achieved from original black-on-white art. It is highly recommended that the novice experiment with several of these techniques to become familiar with the process in order to evaluate the potential of each of these simple graphics in multi-image presentations.

• Adding Filters: Black Lettering on a Colored Background

Black art on a white surface can become a black title on a colored background with the application of a colored gel in front of the camera lens in the copying stage. Color transparency film "reads" red filters as red, blue as blue, and so on. Because we are working with two-dimensional art (on a flat surface), an optical gel is not required. Motion picture departments in camera stores sell sheets of saturated-color gels that can be cut to size and placed in a filter holder in front of the camera lens. Some theatrical gels also will work. Trial and error, along with careful notetaking, is the name of the game. Bracketing, which is covered in the section on copystand techniques, also is a good idea.

• Using an Acetate Overlay

Instead of applying letters directly to a solid background, we could put our title art on an acetate overlay. It is preferable to first mount the lettering on white layout paper and make a good photocopy of this. Next, using a Thermofax copier (many offices have them), we place an 8-by-10 sheet of 3M Thermofax transparency film, with the cut mark in the upper right corner, over the photocopied artwork and feed them through a Thermofax copier to create a clear acetate transparency. (The infrared energy of the Thermofax machine is sensitive to the carbon of the photocopy, transferring it as a clean, sharp-edged black title on the clear acetate film base.) This three-step process is extremely simple and avoids the possibility of error that can occur when applying the title lettering directly to the acetate. I also have found the indirect method more satisfactory because letters burnished directly onto acetate show a waxy edge that the camera can pick up.

Using the acetate as an overlay, we can now select any number of backgrounds for our title, including textured materials. Or we can overlay different titles and credits on the same background. Photographing these titles is discussed in the section on copystand techniques.

As our art becomes more complex, we should consider using a peg board and punched acetate or paper for more accurate registration when combining two or more elements in a title. I discuss registration on page 82.

• Using High-Contrast Film

Up to this point we have been preparing art under the assumption that we will copy it with color transparency film. But color transparency film cannot produce clean whites and tends to pick up colors reflected from other surfaces. This is particularly apparent in art where large areas of white are visible. If we want to project black letters on a clear background, or white letters on an opaque background, using high-contrast black-and-white (litho) film is the best answer. (See Figure 9–7.) There are several litho films on the market today, including Kodalith and Kodak Technical Pan film. While Kodalith, which has an ASA of 6, produces richer blacks, Kodak Technical Pan has an ASA of 125 and is somewhat easier for the novice to process. Kodalith can be developed in Kodak DK-50 or D-11 developer and requires some practice to arrive at the right exposure and development combination. Kodak Technical Pan film is developed in D-19 developer for four and one half minutes. Following the instructions carefully and conducting several tests is recommended. Both films, properly exposed, will produce a high-contrast negative (*clear letters on a black background*). This can become the basis for many variations in the final product.

To produce a *positive black image on a clear background,* we can make a positive through contact exposure with another strip of litho film or by copying the negative in-camera— that is, rephotographing it. An easier method might be to use Kodak LPD-4 film to photograph the original art. This gives a direct positive if black on a clear background is the desired result.

One way to get around the litho positive process is to use white transfer lettering on a black background in the original art. This will render, on the first pass, a litho negative showing black letters on a clear surface. If we plan to go this route, it is important to select an absorbent black background for the lettering rather than a reflective one;

FIGURE 9–7
Litho (high-contrast) negative and positive slides from original art (black lettering on a white background). See how the negative was used, in Figure 9–14. (© Mezey Productions)

otherwise, the black might not photograph as clear in the high-contrast litho negative.

• Colored Lettering on an Opaque Background

We have now produced a high-contrast black-and-white negative with clear lettering on an opaque surface. Projected, this will produce white letters on a dark screen. If we sandwich a colored acetate gel behind the letters of this negative, or color in these small areas with a special felt-tip pen (an acetate film marker), we can project colored letters on the screen. Inexpensive acetate gels can be purchased in sheets in the motion picture section of most camera shops. The felt-tip pens (for writing on acetate and film) can be found in an art supply store. Be careful not to apply them in large areas, as the colors will appear streaky.

• Clear Lettering on a Colored Background

White dry transfer lettering applied directly to a colored background is the most direct way to achieve this effect. It is important that the colored background offsets the white lettering and is "pure" enough to make a good projection transparency. Dark blues, dark greens, and deep reds are best for this purpose. Illustration board comes in these colors. Art supply stores also sell a special color-saturated paper called Pantone (there are several different manufacturers of similar papers, such as Color Aids). This is an excellent choice for multi-image projection and will reproduce as photographed. If we decide to use Pantone, we could mount it on cardboard for stability, then be very careful to avoid any errors in the transfer of the lettering. Alternatively, we could transfer the lettering to clear acetate and use it as an overlay, leaving the colored paper surface untouched.

• Double Exposure

A more efficient way of combining letters and background would be in-camera. Separately place the dark colored background on the copystand, being sure to fill the camera frame with color, and make an exposure. Then remove the original art on the copystand and replace it with the title art—white letters on a black background. Use the double-exposure function on a 35mm camera and reshoot, overexposing the title art for the white. It is helpful to use a peg board to keep the art in register.

Another way to accomplish this single-slide composite is to use a slide duplicator or optical printer. (See Figure 9–8.) In this

FIGURE 9–8
Beseler Slide Duplicator setup. Using a macro lens and bellows, the operator has the choice of flash or continuous lighting to make duplicate slides or create special effects. Kodak SO366 can be used with the flash, requiring little color correction. With Kodak 5071 and continuous light, images have a softer contrast, but the operator probably has to dial in some color correction. All copy work and special effects slides require extensive testing to find the right contrast and color balance. (© Phiz Mezey)

operation a color slide is used for the first exposure, but the film is not advanced, and a litho negative title slide becomes the second exposure, superimposed optically over the first slide. This title slide is overexposed and is appropriately called a "burn-in." We will have to experiment with exposures and take careful notes for reference. The end result should be a slide with sharp, clear lettering on a color-saturated background. A scenic background can be substituted for the solid color.

REGISTRATION

Before I go any further, I should say a few words about registration. While it is not required for simple overlays, it does become a factor as our composites become more sophisticated. Registration is the positioning of each graphic in alignment with the next. In flat art, cels (acetate) with holes punched at the top are laid over pegs on a peg board, keeping each new art component in register with the one before it. Translucent punched paper or acetate is usually used in this process.

Registration also is important for film, particularly when multiple exposures or other composites are in order. Special pin-registered slide mounts are available. The film chips (frames) are positioned on registration pins in the mount. Although perfect registration is not generally necessary when dropping in a title over a simple color or scenic background, registration becomes critical in the creation of more complex images, including drop-in windows and other special effects.

It cannot be assumed that all cameras keep film frames in register. Film-advance mechanisms wear out or might move the film erratically across the film plane. At some point it would be helpful to check the film and film transport mechanism of our camera. In 35mm film there are eight sprocket holes per frame. If our film-advance mechanism is not functioning properly and the film frames are not in register, we should try to correct the problem. One way to check this is to place an exposed strip of film on the light table and measure from a center line to the edges of the frame and from the center to the edges of the first and eighth sprockets. If both measurements are equidistant from the frame edge, the film is in register. If it is out of register, we can use variable slide mounts instead of pin-registered mounts for our slides. Or we can send our slides to a lab to be duplicated in register. (See Figure 9–9.)

PROGRESSIVE DISCLOSURE

Progressive disclosure is the presentation of one idea or sentence at a time, building progressively on the screen until all verbal elements appear on the final slide. (See Figure 9–10.) From the audience's viewpoint, it might appear that we are building one idea on another in a single slide, and that is the way we want it to appear. Actually, we are creating a series of slides, the first showing one sentence, the second two, the third three, and so on. This can be a very effective technique for making a point or clarifying an instruction, as long as it is kept within reason. Beyond four disclosures, the audience loses interest. This is a good time to use the peg board and punched paper to keep the artwork in position for each photographic exposure.

Assuming that we have put four ordered statements (black lettering on white paper) on one piece of flat art, we are ready to begin. With the camera and the peg board in position, we can begin by covering up all but the first statement; now advance the film to the next frame and photograph the first two statements; then three; then four. Or we can photograph in reverse order, first four, then three, then two, then one. It is important not to move the artwork, change

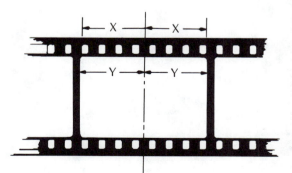

FIGURE 9–9
Checking frame registration: X–X and Y–Y are equidistant from the edges of the frame. If the edge sprockets were to the right or left of this center line, the frame would be out of register.

the focus, or bump the camera because once we move any of the elements, the slides are out of register. Using Acme-type punched paper and a peg registration board can minimize this problem.

When the four Kodaliths are ready to be mounted, one effective way to bring out each new statement is to highlight it with a bright color, while backing all preceding statements with a more neutral color. Color acetates taped behind the lettering are recommended.

CHANGING COLOR THROUGH PROCESSING

The high-contrast litho film method is not the only way to create clear lettering on a colored or dark scenic background. Another effective one-step method to create clear lettering on a colored background is to photograph the original black-and-white art with 35mm transparency film and a color gel that is the complement of the color result desired, mounted in front of the camera lens. If a green background is in order, we will photograph with a saturated magenta gel. We will not develop this film as a positive transparency (E-6 process), however, but as a *negative*. As a positive transparency it would produce black lettering on a magenta background. Since we want white lettering on a green background, we will ask a commercial processor to develop our transparency film in the C-41 line (negative film processing). This will produce a negative transparency in which the black lettering is reversed (clear) and the magenta background becomes its complement, green. Experiment with a roll of film, using different filters to produce the complementary colors you desire in the negative slide. Bracket and take careful notes for reference. This system also can be used effectively in progressive disclosure.

USING THE PROGRAMMER/ DISSOLVE

If the programmer/dissolve with which we are working has a freeze function, we can create a superimposition on-screen by designing or selecting separate slides for each effect. In a two-projector production, we

FIGURE 9–10
Progressive disclo-
sure: On-screen, one
statement is added
with each projector
advance. Viewers
think they see only
one slide, reading
each new statement
as it appears, yet
being aware of the
whole. This is an ef-
fective way of deliv-
ering a message. Pro-
gressive disclosure
also can be accom-
plished with images
or by adding new
components, one at a
time. (© Victoria
Schlintz) See also Fig-
ures 4–2 and 6–12.

can fade up projector A with a scenic and
freeze it on-screen as we fade up projector
B to superimpose a title over it or drop in
a series of different images on a special
format. Some programmers with independent access to each projector will then allow
both projectors to fade to black before ac-
cessing the next slide. Without this feature,
we have to fade out each projector separately, and the impact is lost. It is important
to check these functions before investing in
a programmer. A three-projector production allows us to bring up a new image on
the third projector while we fade out the
title superimposition on the other two.

COPYSTAND TECHNIQUES

In our discussion of artwork preparation
we have made several references to copy-

stand techniques. We cannot design the art
without an understanding of how it is
going to be reproduced. Let's take a closer
look at the copystand and how it can be
used most effectively in the production of
slides for multi-image production. (See
Figure 9–11.)

A macro (close-up) lens is essential for
this work because much of our artwork will
be less than 18 inches from the film plane.
Although a copystand with a camera
mounted on a rigid pole and attached arms
to hold the lamps can simplify copying, the
same results can be achieved under an open
sky with a 35mm camera, macro lens, and
tripod. We also can light the original art
with two photoflood lamps (3200 or 3400
degrees Kelvin) set on either side of the
camera and at a 45-degree angle to the art.
Our discussion of copystand techniques applies to other copying methods as well.

FIGURE 9–11
The copystand is
where most of the
original graphics
and illustrations will
be translated to
film. Adjust the
lamps to a 45-degree
angle to the copy
stage. Use a gray
card to establish a
base around which
to bracket future
exposures. Take
careful notes, and
eliminate glare and
extraneous light.
Develop a test roll
first, then make the
final slides based on
the notations. Since
hue and saturation
are particularly im-
portant in multi-im-
age transparencies,
developing good
habits at the copy-
stand can save time
and money by elimi-
nating unnecessary
reshooting. (© Phiz
Mezey)

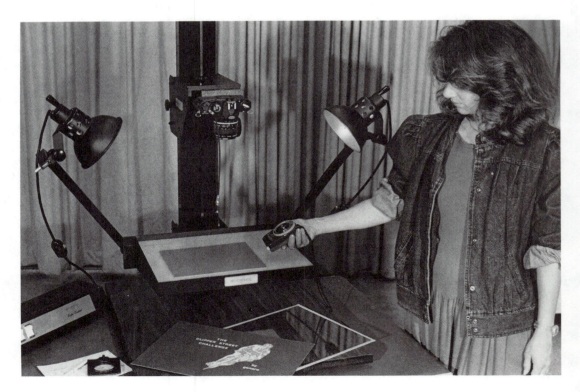

I like to work at a copystand with quartz halogen lights rated at 3200 degrees Kelvin. They have an average life of one thousand hours, and the lamp intensity remains constant throughout the life of the lamp. If I use color transparency film, I make sure the film emulsion is matched to the color temperature of the lamps, which in this case is 3200 degrees Kelvin. I generally use Ektachrome Professional *Tungsten* film with an ASA of 50 or 160 (EPY 50, EPT 160). There is a Kodachrome Tungsten film (KPA 40), which is balanced for 3400 degrees Kelvin, but I would have to change lamps to accommodate the color balance of this film. Ektachrome Daylight Film (EPD 25, 64, 100, 200, 400) is balanced for daylight but can be used in this situation only if I add a color correction filter (85A) in front of the camera lens.

• Gray Card Readings

With my camera loaded and my lights set at a 45-degree angle to the artwork, I take a gray card reading. Since artwork has both light and dark areas, I place a neutral gray card on the stage under the camera lens, rather than read the unevenly reflective art. Gray cards have an 18 percent reflectance and give an average reading—a zone V gray—which is a good place to begin in exposing the artwork. I might stop down the aperture when I come across artwork that is exceptionally high key—mostly bright reflective colors (yellow)—and might open up one-half stop for exceptionally dark art, but for the most part I recommend sticking to a gray card reading for average exposures. I usually set my shutter speed at one reading (for example, 1/30 second) and do not change it for the duration.

• Bracketing

I make three exposures of my gray card if I am working with new or unfamiliar equipment. The first is based on the neutral gray card exposure. For the second I close down one-half stop from the gray card reading. For the third I open up one-half stop over the gray card reading. This is called bracketing. (See Figure 9–12.) If my first exposure reads 1/30 at f/11, for my second exposure I will set my aperture between f/11 and f/16 and my third exposure between f/11 and f/8. Later, when I check back, the results will indicate whether the camera, light meter, and film emulsion are

functioning properly. The first exposure would duplicate the density and tone of the gray card, the second frame would be slightly underexposed and darker, and the third frame would be slightly overexposed and lighter than the original gray card.

I can now proceed with copying the artwork, bracketing each of my exposures as I go. This way I do not have to go back to the copystand again, as one of the three exposures will be right on. As I have indicated, exceptionally light or exceptionally dark artwork rates a beginning exposure that is either one-half stop higher or lower than the gray card exposure.

Since multi-image slides are projected on large screens, it is desirable to have more highly saturated colors. A slight (one-half stop) underexposure in the slide might give a richer saturation when projected. Until we have a show or two under our belts, however, it is best to stay within the guidelines stated above.

• Note Taking

It is helpful to have some ready-made forms on which to take exposure notes while working at the copystand. At the top, identify the film and effective film speed (listed in red on the directions that come with all professional film); also note the gray card reading, the subject matter, and the date the copying is completed. In the columns below this heading, list the number of the frame and the f-stops and shutter speed for each frame. Indicate whether a filter has been used and give a brief description of the image. Reviewing these slides with the note card in hand can show us where we have erred and give us the best exposure choice for future reference. This is invaluable information for the next copying session. (See Figure 9–13.)

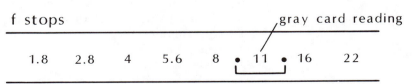

FIGURE 9–12
Bracketing: The gray card reading is f/11. After making this exposure, I adjust my aperture ring and take a second exposure between f/11 and f/8, and a third exposure between f/11 and f/16.

Film_____	Effective ASA_____	Emulsion #_____	Gray Card_____	Shutter Speed_____

#	Description	f stop	Filter	#	Description	f stop	Filter
1	_____	_____	_____	19	_____	_____	_____
2	_____	_____	_____	20	_____	_____	_____
3	_____	_____	_____	21	_____	_____	_____
4	_____	_____	_____	22	_____	_____	_____
5	_____	_____	_____	23	_____	_____	_____
6	_____	_____	_____	24	_____	_____	_____
7	_____	_____	_____	25	_____	_____	_____
8	_____	_____	_____	26	_____	_____	_____
9	_____	_____	_____	27	_____	_____	_____
10	_____	_____	_____	28	_____	_____	_____
11	_____	_____	_____	29	_____	_____	_____
12	_____	_____	_____	30	_____	_____	_____
13	_____	_____	_____	31	_____	_____	_____
14	_____	_____	_____	32	_____	_____	_____
15	_____	_____	_____	33	_____	_____	_____
16	_____	_____	_____	34	_____	_____	_____
17	_____	_____	_____	35	_____	_____	_____
18	_____	_____	_____	36	_____	_____	_____

NOTES:

FIGURE 9–13
Sample note card for keeping track of artwork and f-stop exposures on the preliminary test roll and final shoot.

• **Glare and Reflections**

When working indoors on a copystand or with photoflood lamps, be sure all other light sources are blocked off. The camera lens will pick up the color temperature of extraneous lamps and reflections from other surfaces. If the camera we are using for copy work has a chrome finish, the reflective surfaces should be blocked off by a sheet of black paper, with the center cut out for the camera lens. This can then be slid over the lens, eliminating all reflections from the camera body.

Some copystands come with sheets of polarizing material to cut out extraneous reflections. A polarizer in front of the camera lens also can be helpful. Since plate glass frequently is placed over artwork to keep the surface flat under the heat of the lamps, it is a good idea to check through the lens for any reflections from nearby objects and from imperfections in the glass. Some copystand technicians use nonglare glass, but I have found this unsatisfactory, as it seems to affect the image.

Acetate is another reflective surface. Earlier, I spoke of creating titles on acetate overlays for colored or subject matter backgrounds. If the colored background and acetate overlay are placed under glass, we might have another glare situation. Here is where a camera with double-exposure potential might be helpful. First, photograph the colored or subject matter background, being sure to underexpose slightly. Next, position the black acetate title on a translucent stage, with an even light source under the stage. Rewind the frame and take a second exposure of the title. Be sure to bracket several exposures and take notes. The process I have just described on the copystand can be carried out with a slide-duplicating system, double-exposing a 35mm color slide and negative Kodalith title slide.

REPHOTOGRAPHY: DUPLICATING SLIDES

Rephotography refers to the duplicating or copying of slides and masked images. This can be accomplished with a bellows and slide-copying attachment, a slide duplicator such as the Beseler Dual Mode Slide Duplicator, or an optical printer such as the Sickles or Marron Carrel. The difference between the duplicator and the optical printer is in function and price. The optical printer has a dedicated camera head (built-in) and a pin-registered film transport. It can be bulk loaded, has a roll-back feature, and has a reticle in place of the viewfinder. The reticle is a large viewing area with a focusing screen and grid etched into the ground glass. An optical printer can cost up to $60,000.

An economical bellows and slide-copying attachment or a duplicating projector can carry out most of these functions. For several years I worked with a 35mm camera, macro lens, bellows, copy adapter, and tripod. When using this copy attachment for straight duping, my light source was a strobe unit behind the image frame. We also could use a clear, open sky as our light source. But this method is not efficient if we must duplicate or mask slides frequently and in quantity. We probably will want to invest in a slide duplicator with a built-in light source and color filtration to save time and improve consistency.

THE BURN-IN TECHNIQUE

Photographing a title or other artwork over a scene or color background is known in the trade as "burning in." A burn usually means any discrete exposure of a graphic element that either removes all color from the emulsion (as in a white burn) or exposes into a solid-colored field or a previously masked area (as in color burns). It can be used almost synonymously with the word *exposure*, except that burns usually involve graphics, as distinguished from rephotography, which has to do with duplicating, making windows, masking, and so on.

Let's take the example of the black title overlay on a colored background described above. If, instead of the overlay, we used two slides—a Kodalith slide (black lettering on clear or white lettering on opaque) and a colored background slide (light-colored gel for black lettering, dark gel for clear lettering)—we could rephotograph (copy) the background slide first, rewind to the same frame, and reexpose (burn) the title over the background.

We also could burn a title over an existing subject slide, making sure that dark lettering appears in the light area of the slide and clear lettering appears in the dark area of the slide. (See Figure 9–14.)

FIGURE 9–14
A scene *(A)* with a negative graphic slide *(B)* burned in over it to create a title slide (© Mezey Productions). (See Figure 9–7)

CREATING A GLOW

To create a glow behind a title or logo, we need to expose through a combination of several elements: a pin-registered negative and positive of the logo; some form of diffusion material between them, such as tracing vellum; and, if we are using a negative carrier, a thin piece of glass. (If we are exposing through a registered mount, we do not use the glass.) In making an outside glow, the negative should be placed closest to the light source. Now add the glass and the diffusion material (or just the diffusion material), placing the positive on top. To make an inside glow, the positive must be closest to the light source in this sandwich.

Glows require long exposures, as much as five to eight stops above normal exposures. They can be combined with other elements to create a dramatic presentation on-screen. (See Figure 9–15.)

MASKING

Masking is covering one portion of a film or image frame with an opaque border or shape. The mask can be a film chip sandwiched in a glass slide mount along with the primary image. Its purpose is to modify the size, shape, or location of anything we have photographed or illustrated.

We can create our own masks with high-contrast litho film, making different formats possible within a frame, such as circles, squares, and split frames. We can position these shapes anywhere within the image frame. Masks also are used to change frame formats. We can create a 1:3 ratio, a 3:3 ratio, or even a square image with masking. The central shape can be transparent or opaque, depending on its function. Masks also can be hard edged or soft edged. This refers to the boundary line between the opaque portion and the clear portion of the mask. Hard-edged masks show a sharp separation between the opaque and clear area. In soft-edged masks, the black edge tapers off gradually, creating what we call a seamless border. The purpose of the soft-edged mask is to permit images to blend together. This is particularly useful when creating a panoramic effect.

We can purchase litho masks or film chips ready-made. If we do not want to create our own hard-edged masks, we can purchase special aperture mounts that produce the same effect. Into the clear section of the mount we would then strip in (tape in) the images we want or, using a full image, block out the portion of the image we do not want to project. (See Figures 9–16 through 9–20.)

To create a simple split image, we could use a split-frame slide mount and strip in two vertical images. A more efficient way would be to do this in-camera with registered split-frame mounts, exposing first the left mount and then the right mount onto one frame.

Another creative way to use a mask is to create a window mask (circle, square, or other clear shape) and project into that clear shape several different images on-screen. We also can create movement with masks. Placing each masked cut-out in a different position (on different chips, of course), we can move an image sequentially across the screen in a horizontal or diagonal movement. To be effective this is best accomplished with six or more projectors.

Masks add an exciting and creative dimension to multi-image. They open up possibilities for enlarging movement, creating a greater impact, and enhancing the design of a production. Unfortunately, these special effects can sometimes overwhelm a production. They should be used discreetly and never at the expense of content.

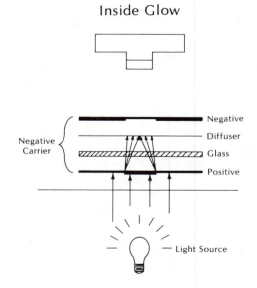

FIGURE 9–15
Inside glow requires both a registered negative and positive film chip, along with tracing vellum. To create an outside glow, reverse the procedure above. (Photo © Chuck Thursten)

CREATING AND PHOTOGRAPHING TITLES ON A HOME COMPUTER

Many of us have home computers, and there are numerous inexpensive software packages on the market that make it possible to build images with pixels to create color titles, credits, and other multi-image graphics on a color screen (although black-and-white also can be useful). Some programs that lend themselves to this are Digital Paintbrush by Computer Colorworks in Sausalito, California (Apple II, IBM PC, and PC compatibles); MacPaint (Macintosh); Thunderware by Thunderskin in Orinda, California; P. C. Paint; and Luminos, and many others. In addition, numerous software packages are devoted entirely to different typefaces, and many of these can be combined with existing graphics programs.

Once the graphics have been created and displayed with adequate resolution on the computer screen, they can be photographed with 35mm transparency film. Polaroid has created a sophisticated photographic system to be used with state-of-the-art graphics programs, most of which are prohibitively expensive. But anyone can use a 35mm camera to photograph on-screen graphics and titles. The results might not be as sharp or smooth as conventional artwork, but they are adequate.

To avoid the scan lines (diagonal stripes) on the monitor, set the shutter speed at ¼ second. The camera should be mounted on a tripod and all reflective surfaces draped in black to avoid reflections on the screen. Even the computer board light must be covered. To avoid placing our own reflection on the screen when making an exposure, it is helpful to stand to one side of the monitor, with a cable release in hand. The only light in the room should be coming from the monitor. We'll have to experiment with the lens aperture, depending on the speed of the film emulsion. At ¼ second, I would set the beginning test aperture at f/2.8 and close down one-half stop at a time. (See Figure 9–21 on p. 94.)

Remember, I am talking about home production here. There are state-of-the-art computers and rephotography systems on the market that create sophisticated graph-

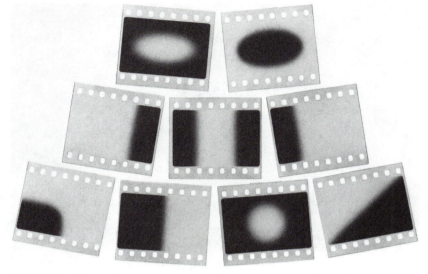

FIGURE 9–16
Masks are simply special film chips that are hard edged (as in windows and clearly defined separations) or soft edged, as shown here, to create undefined or soft edges for better blending of images. These usually are sandwiched with the image in the film mount (Courtesy Wess Mount)

ics and produce slides in a matter of minutes. But these systems cost thousands of dollars. There are also many graphics production houses that do this work efficiently and effectively for a fee. But the cost of having the artwork and slides produced on the Genographics or Dicomed systems probably is prohibitive for most of us.

In this chapter I have described the do-it-yourself method for producing inexpensive, effective graphics for multi-image productions involving one, two, or three projectors. Titles, credits, and other graphics can be created by anyone with the time and the patience to make them. The materials are readily available, there are numerous techniques from which to choose, and the cost is minimal. It is important, of course, to plan carefully by projecting the desired outcome, then working backward to select the materials and techniques required to achieve the result. Planning is the most important stage. After that, there is a step-by-step procedure, which, if followed, will have a most rewarding outcome.

Although not everyone can compose original music or mix sophisticated sound tracks, the availability of materials and formulas for creating effective multi-image graphics puts this art form within the reach of most of us who want to produce our own

FIGURE 9–17
An example of how masking can be used creatively. In this series, three slides have been created from a single layout *(A)*. Planned for a single-screen, three-projector show, each photographic image appears in a window on one half of the frame area opposite an identifying graphic. We can create the mask by exposing each title in the layout separately in register (covering up the other two), being sure to use rubylith for the windows. Then we can drop the color transparencies into the window area, either in-camera or by the cut-and-paste method on the light table. (© Doug Baird/ Phiz Mezey)

A

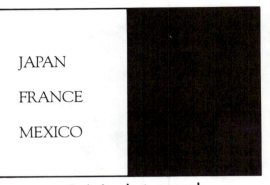

Original Artwork

multi-image shows. While there will always be some who will throw up their hands and say "this is not for me," many more will gain from the experience a sense of pleasure and accomplishment. If we think it through, keep it simple, and keep it in harmony with the rest of the production, it will be successful.

GLOSSARY

Acetate A transparent sheet or film base made of cellulose resin.

Acme registration A trade name for a three-hole punched-pin design that accurately aligns artwork overlays.

Align To arrange in a line; to line up. When superimposing slides, it is important that they are perfectly matched on-screen to ensure smooth dissolves. Alignment slides help ensure this registration. The peg bar keeps original art layout in alignment. The pin-registered mount keeps slide components in alignment.

Bracketing To ensure the best color saturation for multi-image projection, the photographer exposes a frame based on the light meter reading, then makes the next exposures of the same subject at one-half stop under and one-half stop over that reading. This makes it possible to select the best image for projection or reproduction purposes.

Burn In rephotography, when a litho title (clear letters on black) is superimposed over a darker background, whether scenic or solid color, the background is exposed first at normal exposure. Without advancing the film, we now slightly overexpose the title over the background, creating a burn-in.

Burnisher A tool with a smooth, curved head used to facilitate the transfer of dry transfer letters to a page by rubbing and smoothing the letters.

Cels Transparent sheets of clear acetate used to create overlays on the base art. Punched cels are available for the Acme and other punched-board formats used in registration.

Collage An artistic composition of different materials and objects pasted or glued to

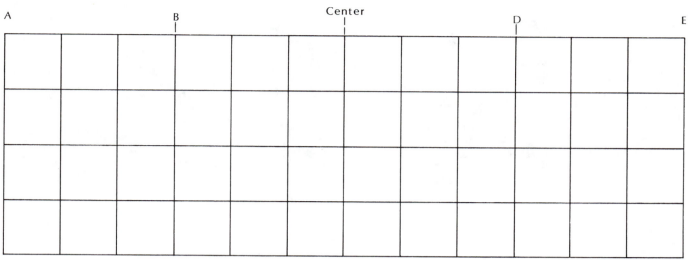

FIGURE 9–18
This grid can help us visualize how a multi-image designer working on a multiple-projector, wide-screen show can design layouts using different masks to change the formats to add another dimension to the art of multi-image presentations. On this screen we can project two full-frame images (AC, CE); three square images; or four verticals, one after the other, using split mounts to fill AB, BC, CD, and DE, in that order. (Grid design courtesy Chuck Thursten)

a surface, often with a unifying idea, colors, or lines.

Composite A slide or final image made up of different components blended together to create a single unified image.

Compound A special easel used with an optical printer that holds the artwork or slides in register with a set of registration pins. It can be moved in increments—still in register—left and right, up and down, and diagonally. Many compounds can light the artwork from below or above. If the compound is moved continuously during exposure, it creates the special effect known as a streak.

Contact print Sometimes called a proof print or contact sheet. A roll of film is cut into strips that are sandwiched directly in contact with a sheet of light-sensitive paper, creating a series of positive images the exact size of the negative. Used as a work sheet for selection in enlarging or reproduction.

Copystand Usually, a vertical column that holds a camera for the purpose of photographing flat art. It usually has extension arms with adjustable lights (placed at a 45-degree angle to the art) to ensure even lighting and an easel or base to hold the artwork.

Density To measure the degree of blackness of a tone on a processed negative, the quantity of light incident on the silver deposit being measured is compared with the quantity of light transmitted. Density,

therefore, is the degree of optical opacity of the medium or material being measured.

Double exposure In photography, making two separate exposures of the same film chip (or frame) before advancing the film to the next frame. Used to superimpose a title over a background or create a composite image.

Dry transfer A method of transferring letters or symbols to flat art. The letters, in alphabetical order, are arranged on a waxy sheet and can be easily transferred by rubbing the back of the transfer sheet. Letters are carbon based, with clean edges, and often are used in place of regular type.

Duping A term used to describe the process of duplicating transparencies in a 1:1 ratio.

Field guide Generally, a sheet of acetate that is used to position artwork in the area or field recorded by the camera. It has a grid system, which when placed on a light table, also makes it easy for the artist to align lettering and cut straight lines from masking material.

Filter A colored optical glass or gel that partially or completely absorbs certain light rays while letting others pass through to the film emulsion.

Flat art Any two-dimensional artwork.

Freeze A command term used by programmer equipment manufacturers to describe the technique of superimposition—projecting one image over another on-

L   C   R

screen, such as key words projected over a scenic. Also used to describe the technique of projecting several images on a single screen to create a montage effect. Projector lamps can be frozen at different percentage levels, giving each image a different intensity.

Gel From the word *gelatin,* used in the preparation of photographic film emulsions. Also a noun describing the color filters used in theatrical lighting and rephotography.

Glow An effect created by the addition of diffusion material behind an image, logo, or lettering to create a glow around the lettering. The first image is crisp, the second diffused. Together they can create an inside or outside glow, depending on how the materials are sandwiched.

Gray card A photographic board (usually 8-by-10) coated on one side with gray that has an 18 percent reflectance. This gray is the middle or neutral tone in the photographic scale. The gray card is used to get an average reading of the light source and is particularly useful as an exposure guide in copying flat art for color transparency slides.

Grid A framework of parallel or crisscrossed bars, used in photography to position the image.

Hot press White illustration board that has a smooth, hard surface; an excellent

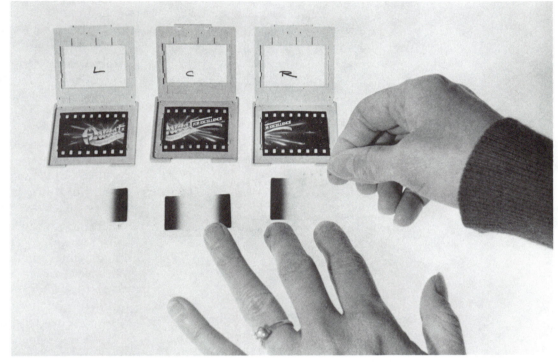

FIGURE 9–20
We can create a seamless panoramic across the entire screen area, using a slide that has been duplicated in register three times and is then sandwiched in registered glass mounts with special soft-edged masks. (Above, courtesy of Mind's Eye Productions; right, © Phiz Mezey)

surface for dry transfer lettering or pen-and-ink illustrations for reproduction. *Cold press* has a more textured surface.

Infrared Electromagnetic radiation having wavelengths greater than those of visible light and shorter than those of microwaves.

Kelvin (K) Unit of thermodynamic temperature used to designate the color temperature of a light source. Color transparency film emulsions are balanced to respond to various degrees Kelvin (K). Daylight film is balanced for 5600 degrees K, while tungsten film is balanced for 3200 degrees K or 3400 degrees K. An ordinary house lamp is about 2800 degrees K.

Kodalith Trade name for a high-contrast litho film used in creating titles and masks in multi-image photography.

Layout The positioning of graphics and artwork in a specific format showing what the final product will look like.

Litho film High-contrast film used by graphic artists in the preparation of artwork; also used in multi-image production for the creation of reversed titles with opaque backgrounds and in the preparation of masks for special effects.

Macro lens Used in close-up work in photography and in copying work where a 1:1 ratio is critical.

Negative An image in which the light areas of the film are rendered dark, and the dark areas are rendered light.

FIGURE 9–21
An Apple computer and graphics software can produce effective title slides and graphics. Though less sophisticated than those produced with professional graphics computers such as the Dicomed or Genographics, these affordable computers are being upgraded rapidly, and graphics software is abounding. The artwork is no more time-consuming to prepare than the flat art described earlier in this chapter, and it is easy to make slides from the computer screen. (Art courtesy of Charles Penalver)

Opaque Impenetrable by light, neither transparent nor translucent. In litho film light areas from a positive image appear as full black, and dark areas appear clear.

Optical printer Optical printers are essentially film duplicators. At the high end, they have a dedicated camera head, a superior viewing screen, a pin-registered film transport, a compound easel, and animation features, as well as the capability of bulk loading and rolling back areas of exposed film for the purpose of multiple exposure. At the low end, the camera body is separate, the camera may or may not be pin registered, animation functions and bulk loading are limited, but excellent dupes and composites are still possible.

Pixel Abbreviation for *picture element*. The smallest point that can be addressed on a display screen.

Process In this context, the system of operations in the production of a multi-image show; how and by what means it is put together.

Progressive disclosure The disclosing, in an ordered sequence, of an idea or statement, one step at a time; to the first phrase or image is added the second, then the third, and then the fourth, until the entire concept is shown in one all-inclusive slide.

Punched paper or acetate Special punched paper or acetate that will fit onto the pegs on a peg bar to provide alignment of all the graphic components in a layout.

Reflective art Original art has a reflective surface. In copying to slides, the light meter reads the amount of light that is reflected by this surface. Cf Gray card.

Registration The technique of precisely aligning artwork or slides with the use of a pin-registered camera, special viewing grid, field guide, peg bar and punched paper, and/or pin-registered mounts. Any, some, or all of these techniques might be employed in a single production.

Rephotography The art of duplicating original slides, making color corrections with special filters, or changing slide formats with the addition of special masks.

Rubylith A red "film" that photographs black and is used by graphic artists to create windows into which printers can drop halftones or rephotographers and programmers can drop images.

Sandwich Two slide chips placed together in a slide mount to project one composite image.

Saturation The intensity of hue based on the degree of difference from a gray of the same lightness and brightness.

Superimpose When one image (words, logo, and so on) is double exposed over a background in-camera or on the screen. By freezing the advance of one projector, it is being superimposed, or projected over another image.

Thermofax Trade name for a copy machine that uses infrared energy in duplicating printed or drawn material.

Chapter 10

Editing the Slides: Integrating Visuals with Audio and Cueing the Script

The first thing we must accept about the final selection and editing of slides, integrating the audio, and cueing the script is that it takes time—and patience. The editing phase—the pulling together of all the visual and aural components into a cohesive whole—is perhaps the most creative and demanding stage in production. The more prepared we are in conceptualizing and designing in the preproduction stage, and the more we shape and integrate visuals, voice, and sound as we go along, the less frustrating it will be to edit and program later on. But we are still talking about large, concentrated periods of time for the final edit, so be forewarned.

ORGANIZING A SLIDE FILE SYSTEM

The slide selection process, of course, is ongoing. If we are working from an existing slide file, preliminary selection can take place even before a script is completed. If we are designing all new material, previsualization takes place at the storyboard level. We should have a pretty good idea of some of the show's format, the graphics we will need, and how much of the production will be from file and what sequences will require new images. We stated in our cost analysis the amount of film we would need, depending on the ratio (number of frames shot to number of frames selected) we had decided on, and we reviewed storyboard and script with the photographer and

might even have prepared a shot list, grouping all the images that could be taken at each location. After each shoot, we reviewed the slides and discarded those that did not measure up, keeping only those that seemed to carry out the mood or concept we intended. We were rough-editing as we went along.

I feel that it is absolutely essential to establish a filing system at the beginning of production so that the slides do not become an incomprehensible jumble. After each photographic session I review and discard the technically unusable images, then identify by subject or sequence all the remaining slides. From these I select the slides that seem to work best with the script and music concepts and group them by sequence or category in twenty-frame plastic slide pages to keep them clean and visible. In these pages I include many more slides than probably will be used because I will be making choices later based on the final narrative and music score. But it is from these slide pages that I will build the show. Meanwhile, I box and label the discarded slides and keep them readily available for reference. Frequently I go back to this file to expand a sequence or replace a slide that makes a poor fit.

Each producer has his or her own way of setting up a file, depending on the space and help available. The important thing to remember is to develop a file and sort system at the beginning, then stick to it.

Many professionals will put their final selection in pin-registered glass mounts to protect them in handling, keep them from buckling in the projector, and keep them in register. This can be a costly and time-consuming process, but it pays off in the long run. I keep my original production slides in registered glass mounts but find that sometimes a client prefers a more economical plastic mount for the duplicates.

MARKING THE SLIDES FOR POSITION

One of the first things I do before storing the slides in plastic pages is to mark each with a dot in the lower left corner so that when I want to review a sequence, I can place them readily in the projector in the proper position (upside down, emulsion side facing the screen). This is a simple operation that can be carried out in minutes by looking at the slides on a light table so that they read correctly. When the slide is placed in the slot of the carousel, it should be rotated clockwise so that the dot appears in the upper right corner. In effect we have turned the image upside down, with the emulsion facing toward the screen—the proper way to load a carousel. (See Figure 10–1.)

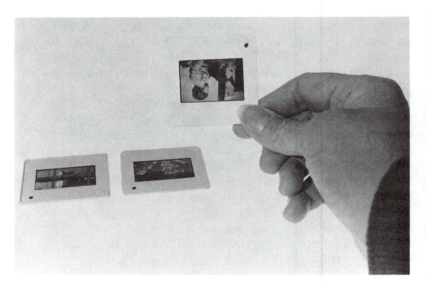

FIGURE 10–1
Marking the slides: Place a slide on the light table in reading position. Place a dot, or number, in the lower left corner. Rotate the slide so that the dot is in the upper right corner. This is the correct position for inserting it in the carousel slot. (© Phiz Mezey)

There might be occasions when we will have to flop the slide—that is, turn it over so that the subject faces the opposite direction—to conform with the flow of a sequence. In this case, do not forget to change the position dot to the lower left corner of the flopped (reversed) slide.

WORKING ON A LIGHT TABLE

Having a light table on which to lay out the show is a necessity in multi-image production. Light tables are expensive to buy but easy to make. A simple box painted white on the interior, with two parallel cool white fluorescent lamps evenly spaced near the bottom and a translucent Plexiglas cover, is all that is needed. I made my light box from plywood scraps, the biggest expense being the purchase of the two 4-foot fluorescent lamps. Now I can view seventy or more slides simultaneously. Since we tend to build a show sequence by sequence, this surface space seems more than adequate. Most photography stores sell plastic step-up light boxes that are reasonably priced. A couple of these, side by side, would make the sequencing much easier. (See Figures 10–2 and 10–3.)

When we are ready to work on the final edit, we will take the slides out of their plastic pages and arrange them in segments or by sequence on the light table, moving them around until they are integrated with the narrative design, music score, and voice narration in a smooth-flowing progression. We might have to add an image from the discarded slide file or remove images that do not fit. The giving up of a slide is frequently more difficult than filling in where script or music demand. I often have had to part with one of my favorite images because it did not fit the mood or tone of a sequence. We should keep these newly removed slides in separate, labeled slide pages, as we might want to use them elsewhere.

KEEPING ALL THE STRANDS IN MIND

As we view the slides on the light table, it is helpful to talk the script through to integrate the script and images more smoothly. Hearing and feeling the rhythm of the words can help us find the natural flow of the visuals. If I am working with library music, I usually work with the visuals and the music simultaneously, and frequently I will try to make a fit between narration, music, and the visuals while the slides are still on the light table. After the narration and music score have been mixed on a tape, I listen again as I view the slides on the table, searching for the right moment to project specific images.

Many producers, however, will have the music score mixed with the narration before the slide editing has been fine-tuned, especially if the music is an original composition. The visuals must then be fitted to the audio. But even the composer must be aware of the imagery when he or she creates the score, making the final design an interweaving of all the strands. Editing is the fine-tuning of this orchestration.

COMBINING SLIDES: GETTING THE BEST FROM THE MEDIUM

The content of the production will determine to a large extent the general organization of the slides. If we are following a story line, the slides must show some logical development or progression. The sequence does for multi-image what the paragraph does in written material: It introduces and develops a new idea. If we have photographed sequentially, our job now is to select the most effective slides for each sequence and place them in the appropriate order. But there are other considerations as well. We might want to change the visual format within the slide or on the screen to create verticals alongside horizontals or to make seamless panoramics. We must remember, however, that the more complex we become, the more projectors we might have to use to create these special effects. Whether our show is simple or complex, we should be cognizant that an upgraded technology makes it tantalizingly possible to stretch the potential of the medium.

The storyboard started the process of visual thinking for us; it helped us to see the relationships and visualize the continuity. Now, on the light table, we must be even more conscious of shape and density, size,

FIGURE 10–2
Light tables come flat or stepped. Here the designer studies slides that have been temporarily arranged by sequence in archival polyethylene pages. This is one method of organizing the material step by step while building the show. It also keeps the slides dust free. (© Phiz Mezey)

color, and direction, as well as the relationships made possible by multiple projection.

Here are some of the factors we should consider when editing our slides for a multi-image production:

With which format(s) will I be working?

Do the images implement the concept or theme?

Do they enhance the continuity of script, music, and imagery?

FIGURE 10–3
More expensive light tables might come with a flat as well as a vertical lighted box from which individual full-width frames with grooved edges can be hung, allowing the assembly of separate shows. Thus, when two or more shows are being produced in the same studio, one show can be removed intact in its frame, allowing work to proceed on the second show. This eliminates the problem of breaking down and setting up each time the material is worked on. (© Phiz Mezey)

How do they relate to other slides in the sequence in size, color, shape, mass, mood, tone, position, and direction?

In introducing a new idea, which slides will effectively create a visual transition between sequences?

How can I juxtapose visual ideas most effectively?

When is a superimposition called for?

Do the special effects add to the content and flow, or are they just clever distractions?

Are my visuals effectively integrated with the narration and music?

• Placement, Direction, and Size
Placement of the subject in the frame, direction of the subject, and size of the subject relative to the frame on either side should be consistent with the concept being projected. Whether it is a single- or multi-projector show, the frames must relate on several levels. When we look at our slides on the light table, we should consider all these levels.

• The Third Image
When planning slow or three-projector dissolves, we must keep in mind how the images will look as they overlap, one reaching a 50 percent fade-out, while another has faded up 50 percent. With independent control of the projectors, it also is possible to have one image fade out more slowly than the slide that is fading up. I call this the third image because it is, in effect, a projected sandwich. It is helpful to match these fading slides carefully for mood, subject, color, and balance. The dark areas of slide B should fade up in the light areas of slide A to create a balanced and intriguing third image. (See Figures 10–4 and 10–5.)

• Transition and Juxtaposition
Another consideration is the transition between sequences, which should prepare us for a change of pace or subject matter. This slide, or two or three slides, should contain elements of color or subject matter from the preceding slide(s) and elements of the new sequence to make the transition smooth. Going from outdoors to indoors or changing from a carefree moment to a cautious one requires subtlety in the selection of the transition slide(s). Too often we expect the music or the narration to make these transitions for us, but the visuals also should carry it through.

Juxtaposition of slides when a quick cut is needed is another light-table activity.

What kind of slides lend themselves to quick cuts, and which ones favor a slow fade? It is not just the script or music that determines this. Images of impending danger lend themselves to quick cuts, while warm family scenes work well with slower fades. Humor, irony, and all the other nuances in imagery have their own rhythm in the visual flow on the light table. (See Figure 10–6.)

As we lay our slides out in their nearly final order, we will become aware of the remaining gaps. Transitions might be jumpy, or an idea (slide) might be missing from the sequence. Our ending might be weak. It is here that we go through our "possibles" slide file again. Often I have found that a slide placed in a later sequence fits better in an earlier one. This juggling goes on until the pieces fit. At this late stage it is unusual for the photographer to go out and shoot specifically to fill the gap (this should have been done earlier), but it is not unheard of.

• **Arrangement on the Light Table**
Depending on whether we are preparing our slides for a one-, two-, or four-projector presentation, we might want to lay out our slides in a continuous flow. This is sometimes too much to encompass at one viewing. I usually begin with a continuous strand to establish the flow of sequence and story line. As the editing process becomes more complex, I work on individual sequences. Within each sequence I become aware of paired relationships (for a two-projector production) or grouped relationships (for a multi-projector production) so that both the story line and the relationship between slides are taken into account. Each editor has his or her own technique for grouping and regrouping slides. This is always a personal choice.

Each producer will decide the order of events individually, based on the specific production and his or her own artistic inclination. Regardless of these choices, the editing process cannot be fine-tuned until the music and narration have been recorded. Then the slides on the light table will be in their (almost) final arrangement. For me, nothing is final until I have projected the slides and experimented with the dissolves while listening to the audio master. In real-time programming this rehearsal time is essential. Even where the

FIGURE 10–4
When putting slides together, think of their relationship to each other, as well as to the content. For slow dissolves that build mood, dark areas should fade up through lighter areas. On the screen, an orange flower emerges behind the branches into a golden sky and then fades slowly behind emerging clouds. (© Chuck Thursten)

slides are programmed sequence by sequence on a computer screen, seeing a playback on the multi-image screen is important before finalizing the program. The beauty of using a memory or computer system is that the cues are not set and can be changed in seconds. Overall, memory programming is less time-consuming.

• **Numbering the Slides**
When all my slides are in the proper sequence, I usually number them in pencil just to the left of, or in place of, the position dot. (Note that when numbering the slides, we lay them out in projector position, with the dot appearing in the upper right corner.) The slides are numbered in the order in which they will appear in each projec-

FIGURE 10–5
Through creative dissolves, two images can be superimposed on the screen for a few seconds. This third image appears at the end of a sequence. Cueing directions: "Hold projectors B & C. Slow dissolve down projector B (CU of 'David') leaving CU of 'Luna' on screen." (© 1984 Doug Baird Productions)

CUEING THE SHOW

Cueing the show is always last, after the slides are all assembled on the light table and the audio track has been completed. Cueing is writing down, in shorthand form, all the commands we will give the programmer. We must decide when we want a projector to advance, in what order, and for how long it will fade up or out. We must indicate how many seconds we want to hold an image on the screen, whether to superimpose another image, and what kind of special effects we would like. Cueing the show can be simple or complex, depending on the production itself and the sophistication of the equipment.

Before we started the production, we chose the hardware we would be using. If we decided on a single-projector production, with a simple sync pulse, our graphics format was determined at the outset. Superimpositions, split screens, and progressive disclosures were planned for single slides, some in the form of sandwiches or in-camera composites. This makes cueing relatively straightforward and simple. But if we planned to use several projectors, superimpose images on-screen, alternate between projectors, and create pans or montages, we now have to plan the timing of the cues more carefully.

After the music and narration have been integrated and the slides arranged on the light table, some editors prepare a cue list directly on storyboard or script, working at the light table, sequence by sequence. Once the suggested cues have been noted, the slides are numbered and placed in the carousels, ready for programming.

For simple shows that use only a sync pulse or have only simple dissolves, I prefer to cue the slide changes at the light table, making my preliminary notations directly on the script page. This method gives me a quick overview of the show—narration, visuals, music track, and cues. It also is a replicable record from which I can work later while recording the cues on the programmer. I might start out with a dot just before the word I want to hear along with a particular image on the screen. Working with a simple programmer, I can later experiment with the timing, rehearsing in real time (live) until I get the pulses or simple dissolves just right.

tor—1A, 1B, 2A, 2B, and so on. If I am preparing a three-projector show, there will be a 1C, 2C, and so on as well. Or we might prefer to work out our own numbering method. The most popular system is to lay out the slides in the ABC sequence, designating projectors and following the number order stamped on the carousel slots. (See Figure 10–7.)

Some producers number their slides last, after the actual programming has been completed, but I feel safer when I can pencil in the numbers while the slides are on the light table, just in case of an unexpected upset. Later, when the programming is completed, I'll ink in the numbers. It is not critical when or how one numbers the slides, but it is very important that the numbering is accurate, consistent, and updated when there is any change in the slide order or designation.

It is a good idea to make a notation of which projector opens the production and whether we are planning to start on a blank slide or an image. It might be that A1 is a blank slide and B1 is the first image. Or we might dispense with the blank and designate A1 the first image. This is the more traditional choice. Indicate this in writing so that anyone setting up the production will know on which projector to begin. Also indicate whether the sound track precedes the visuals or starts with the visuals, to prevent unnecessary confusion on the part of the operator.

A separate cue sheet or program sheet is helpful in more complex productions. Unfortunately, I have not found too many professional producers who use them, most preferring to mark rough cues on the storyboard or script, or cueing directly on the memory programmer or computer.

• Cueing Slide to Narration

This question inevitably comes up: When should the visual appear? Before it is orally referenced? After? Or right at the moment? The answer is when the words and music say so. This is hardly a scientific answer. One generalization can be made here. If a specific image, voice reference, and musical beat reach the viewer simultaneously, the viewer will be forced to translate, in a fraction of time, three separate media codes (vocal, visual, and musical). It is inevitable that the impact of either the visual or the vocal will be diminished accordingly. I find that it is more effective to offset the visual and vocal just enough to allow the viewer time to decode one before the other. The visual might appear just before a key word or just after it, creating a sense of anticipation. This technique works particularly well in sequences where we are building concepts. Alternatively, when I reach a climax or dramatic conclusion, I might program all three media to hit the senses at the same moment.

• Cueing on the Script for Real Time

When I am working at the light table and making notations on my script, I might underline the key word just before which or just after which I want the image to reach full brightness. If I choose a two-second dissolve, then I know it will take two seconds for the image to fade up to full brightness at that key word, so I will have to start the dissolve x seconds before the underlined word. On the script, however, I usually enter the total wait time—that is, the dissolve time plus the on-screen time—and save the fine-tuning until later. If I write 5A–5, it means that slide 5 in projector A fades up for x seconds and remains on-screen for y seconds for a total of 5 seconds. Specific dissolve time and on-screen time can be decided when I rehearse the programming. I eventually might decide on a 2-second fade-up with 3 seconds on-

FIGURE 10–6
This sequence on self-protection has a series of short dissolves, then a cut on the fifth slide as the woman breaks the mugger's grip. (© Mezey Productions)

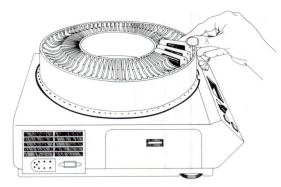

FIGURE 10–7
Using properly numbered slides in the carousel minimizes confusion if the slides get out of order.

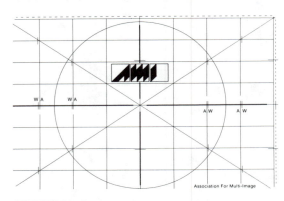

Association For Multi-Image

FIGURE 10–8
Alignment slides are invaluable in keeping the projections in register on-screen. Before each presentation, use these slides to align on-screen the images from different projectors. This effort will result in smooth dissolves and superimpositions and panoramics that are in perfect register. Alignment slides are available through the Association for Multi-Image (AMI), with national headquarters in Tampa, Florida. (Courtesy of the Association for Multi-Image)

screen, or a 1½-second fade-up with 3½ seconds on-screen. (See Figure 10–9.)

Some producers will time the cues on a stopwatch, but it is not necessary to be this anxious or detailed. Familiarity with the script, images, and music often puts the real-time programmer at ease with the material, and the timing comes naturally. Programming in real time cannot be as precise as programming in leisure time. One has to go with the flow, from one end of the program to the other, hopefully coming up with a good blend of dissolves that brings images, script, and music together in a successful orchestration.

I practice live with the programmer/dissolve, rehearsing with the slides, music, narration, and cue sheet until the slide

changes flow smoothly. At this time I make final cue changes on the script/cue sheet and remove or add slides as needed for a better fit. Each of us will develop his or her own system of cueing, particularly after we have learned it the hard way—through trial and error. Whatever choice we make, cueing on the script or preparing a preliminary programming sheet, we should strive for consistency, flow, and ease of replication.

• Cueing on the Computer

As our cueing options increase with more sophisticated programmers and multi-projector presentations, so will the complexity of our cueing process. Multi-projector cueing requires a carefully orchestrated program of cues that will help us visualize the sequence of commands required to achieve certain effects. This program of cues also will help us key audio cues with the appropriate commands and keep us abreast of projector status. There are many commercially available programming sheet formats, but ultimately we might prefer to design our own. Although programming sheets usually are not required for simple dissolve functions, by the time we are ready for multi-projector programming by computer, we would do well to consider buying or designing our own programming or cueing sheets, which we would prepare prior to actual programming by computer. This is discussed again in Chapter 11. (See Figure 10–10.)

SAVE THE MASTER

It is a good idea to dub a copy of the *uncued* master audio tape before programming the production, for backup purposes. Once the tape is cued, duplicate tapes should be made, and the cued master tape should be stored in a cool, dry, safe place. Similarly, when the production has been completed, a duplicate set of slides should be made, and the original slides should be stored in a cool, dry, safe place. Slides deteriorate with exposure to projector lights, heat, moisture, and handling. Tapes have been known to be lost, damaged, or erased accidentally by exposure to a magnetic field. With the stored master audio (synced) tape

Date _____	**Script Sheet**	Page __1__ of __5__
Title __SAFE In The City__	Writer __P. Mezey__	Draft No. 1·2 ③ Final

Visual Concepts

Titles, 6 slides

Script/Audio

(Music Up,

and Under ...) *A1 thru B6*

A7-5
NARRATOR: San Francisco is a beautiful city.
B7-4 A8-4
We pride ourselves in our friendliness,
B8-4 A9-4   B9-4, A10-4
our individuality, our outlook,
B10-5
and value the privacy of our homes.

So when this vision of ourselves and our community is
A11- Cut-2   B11-Cut-2
disrupted -- when a burglar breaks into our homes,
A12 cut-2
or a neighbor is mugged --
B12-5   A13-5
we react with pain and outrage.

Something should be done about it!
B13-4
Well, something is being done.
A14-4
All over the city people are organizing --
B14-4   A15-5
on their blocks, in their homes --
B15-Cut-2
to prevent breakins,
A-16-4
to keep violence off their streets.
B16-6
They are forming Neighborhood Alert groups.
A17-6
They are making their homes SAFE.

They are showing their concern for each other.
B17-5
More than twelve hundred Block Clubs in San Francisco

are now participating in a city-wide neighborhood
A18-4
alert program, and the program is working!

(Music change pace, and under)

Who are these people?

Why are they succeeding?

FIGURE 10–9
Cueing the script for real-time programming. No two programmers use the same method. Some cue on the storyboard, others on the script, and still others directly on the computer in leisure time. Ideally, one cues one sequence at a time, rather than all at once. (© Phiz Mezey)

FIGURE 10–10
Entering commands on a computer. In this example, a hypothetical show is being programmed on an Apple II using a Gemini programmer interface card and software. Shown are some practice fades, cuts, and flashes. *Fade* means a dissolve up or down; *time* refers to the length of the dissolve, in this case ten seconds; *proj* tells us which projectors are involved in the action; and *wait* time includes all the time that elapses between cues (a fade time of ten seconds, plus an on-screen time of five seconds). *Status* tells us where we are in the programming. (In this instance, we have just completed cue 21 with an elapsed time of 142.85 seconds.) See Chapter 11. (Courtesy of Robert Ferrer)

PROGRAMMING TEMPLATE
CUE #5-#21

CUE	COMMAND	TIME	PROJ	WAIT	STATUS 1	2
5	FADE	10	12	15.00		
6						
7	FADE!	10	12	15.00		
8	FADE!	CUT	12	.10		
9	FADE!	CUT	12	.10		
10	FADE!	CUT	12	.10		
11						
12	FLASH RATE=1		1	5.00		
13	FLASH RATE=2		1	5.00		
14	FLASH RATE=3		1	5.00		
15	FLASH RATE=0		1	5.00		
16	FADE	5	1	6.20		
17						
18	FLASH RATE=1		2	5.00		
19	FADE	10	2	10.10		
20	FADE	10	2	11.20		
21	FLASH RATE=0		2	.05	•	•
2 2						

ELAPSED TIME=142.85

PROJ 1   PROJ 2
%0   %0
04   03

and the original slides available, quality dupes can always be made.

Although by using duplicates we lose a generation in both slides and sound, the loss is minimal compared to the potential loss of the entire program. In addition, it is often difficult to tell a good duplicate from the original. Similarly, by making a duplicate set of slides we can correct for color balance, enlarge one section of a slide, mask images, or balance them for density. If we have our own duplicating equipment, we can do this work ourselves. Many commercial studios also specialize in this field, and they are listed in the phone book or are advertised in photography and AV journals.

GLOSSARY

Cue *(v.)* To *cue* a program is to write a set of instructions for the person synchronizing a multi-image production, indicating when to advance a projector, how long to make a dissolve, and how long to keep an image on-screen. *(n.)* A single command that is programmed and executed. It might take many cues to complete an action.

Cue sheet Also called a *programming sheet.* A series of commands or a list of cues written out in advance relative to timed dissolves, fades, and special effects, to be transferred to the programmer keyboard by the person programming a multi-image presentation.

Flop To invert an image, reversing its left/right orientation.

Juxtapose To put close together or side by side.

Light box Cf light table. Also see Figure 10–2, 10–3.

Lose a generation When one tape is duplicated, the new tape is said to have "lost a generation" in sound fidelity. If the duplicate tape is again dubbed, the new tape will have lost two generations of sound fidelity. When a slide is duplicated, it too has lost a generation in image quality.

Superimpose To place one image on top of another, either by projection, in a slide mount, or in-camera.

Chapter 11

Programming and Programmers

The integration of all the creative components—images, narration, and music—can be compared to the orchestration of a symphony, and the person who cues and programs the show is the conductor. It is the programmer's skill that will give our presentation its pace and vitality. It is the final, most critical step in production.

In this chapter I will discuss the different approaches to programming (putting the signals on tape), the various types of multi-image programmers on the market today, their advantages and disadvantages, and how they are operated. I will discuss real-time programming and leisure-time programming, and I have included a section on programming by computer. I also will cover the language of programming.

PROGRAMMING THE SHOW

Programming means entering commands on a programmer that instruct the projectors when to turn on and off and the rates at which they should do so. The cues, which have been written on a cue sheet, are entered into the programmer by an operator either in real time or in leisure time. When we interface a programmer with a computer, we enter our cues directly on the computer keyboard, reading them on a screen. Thus, two functions, cueing and programming, can be combined.

As I have indicated, there are two types of programmable dissolves—those that function in real time and those that are pro-

grammed in leisure time. Leisure-time units are more expensive than real-time units, since they have built-in extended memory capabilities. I will discuss this in greater detail later in the chapter.

Let's start with the simplest form of programming—recording a pulse tone using a synchronizer. This device is connected externally to a tape recorder or is built into a certain type of tape recorder, called a sync-recorder. It generates a 1,000-Hz signal on the tape. When the recorder is connected to a slide projector, the taped signal, on playback, tells the slides to advance. Syncing a show is a pretty straightforward procedure. Generally, it involves only one projector and a sync recorder. Most sync-recorders are monaural, with the audio track carrying the music and narration and the sync-track carrying the pulse tone. We can easily program such a show from cues we have written on a script page, and we will program in real time—that is, each time we tap the sync button as we listen to the sound track, we commit a signal on the tape. If we make an error, we probably will have to go back to the beginning of the tape and start syncing all over again. Since it takes approximately 1.2 seconds for the slide projector tray to advance, we must remember to wait 1.2 seconds after each advance before striking the next sync command.

Dissolves between two projectors create a better flow of imagery. A dissolve module controls the projectors' lamps in such a way that the images fade one to the other. As I pointed out in Chapter 1, early dissolve controls were connected externally with a synchronizer, but by the seventies, the synchronizer was built into the dissolve control module.

The next step up in the development of multi-image hardware is the programmer, which most often has the synchronizer and dissolver built-in. This device tells the dissolve control when and how to turn the projector lamps on and off; cycles the projector trays forward and reverse; and times the implementation of these functions. The operator has a number of choices in selecting dissolve rates and adding special effects, including commands such as "freeze" for superimpositions; "blink" or "flash" for animation between projectors; "reverse," "home," and "alt" (alternate between projectors without advancing the trays).

THE ANALOG SIGNAL

Early programmer/dissolves used an analog signal to control each function of the dissolve unit. With some two-projector programmers, a recorded analog signal alternately advances first one tray, then the other. At one frequency (1,000 Hz) the lamp on one projector will be on and the other off, and at the other pitch (150 Hz) the off lamp fades up and the on lamp fades down. Between these two signals, or frequencies, there will be a momentary blending or crossing of two images on the screen. This

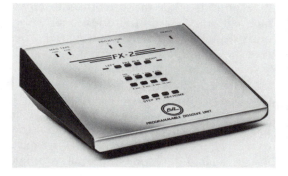

FIGURE 11–1
This AVL FX-2 two-projector real-time programmer features independent access to each projector. Posi-trak automatically locks the program to the audio track and will keep the show in sync if a tape error occurs. It also has seven button dissolves, seven alternate rates, up to sixteen seconds; blink dissolve, forward, reverse, step cue, home, and freeze. It can interface with an IBM-PC compatible through special software and an interface card designed for home use.

is accomplished by manipulating a knob or lever or by pressing a time button (¼ second, ½ second . . . 2 seconds) to encode the information on audio tape.

Analog programmers are limited in the number of commands they can execute and are much more susceptible to interference from electrical fluctuations in power lines, which can cause false cues. And since the tone is continuous, it cannot be edited easily. If we want to make a correction, chances are we will have to go back to the beginning and start recording the signals again. With the advent of multi-projector programs, a more functional signal system was needed to replace the analog tone.

THE DIGITAL SIGNAL

Our options increased with digital programming. Today most modern programmers have electronic microprocessors that create and store commands as digital information. The digital programmer allows for an unlimited number of commands and functions. It is also a more reliable signal than the analog tone since it is more resistant to extraneous interference and is easier to program.

Computer software allows digital data to be encoded on a cue track of an audio tape. Each activity of the projector and projector lamp is now assigned a binary code capable of telling the projectors what to do. At the moment a specific button is pressed, the programmer/dissolve unit puts the digital code on the cue track. With digital cueing, a more precise dissolve can be executed, and it becomes easier to control more than two projectors. Digital cueing also makes it somewhat easier to edit in real time because it is easier to locate a short digital cue on tape than it is to intercept a continuous analog tone.

Words such as *command* and *cue* have been used loosely, sometimes interchangeably, in the field. The programmer uses numerous command keys to cue a program. Time and function keys are command options. When we hit a command key, we tell the programmer what we want it to do. The cue, in this context, is the analog or digital prompt that starts the action. In microprocessor terminology a *cue* refers to the digital signal or short burst of numbers stored in memory to initiate an action. A sequence of cues, or a program of cues, is called a *cue list*.

REAL-TIME PROGRAMMING WITH TWO PROJECTORS

Most two-projector programmer/dissolves today are real-time units. The beauty of real-time programming is that it involves the operator physically and totally, as in a live performance. Once we are in sync/record mode, we are recording our cues as we listen to the sound track—in real time. One of the weaknesses of real-time programming is the possibility of human error, a missed cue, or a key pressed too soon, in spite of all the rehearsals. Whether our equipment has analog or digital cueing, once we start cueing in record mode, our cue is committed. Hopefully, several rehearsals and a good cue sheet will minimize the problem.

CUEING A DISSOLVE

A typical real-time programmer will have function and time keys. (See Figure 11–2.) The function keys tell the programmer what to do (dissolve, blink, freeze, and so on). The time keys tell the programmer for how long to do it (1 second, 3 seconds, 8 seconds). Every time a projector fades to

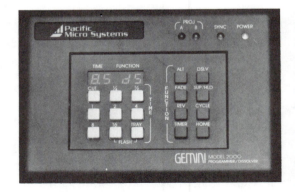

FIGURE 11–2
Compact and lightweight, this Gemini 2000 real-time programmer can be converted to leisure time through an interface card and software that works with the Apple II computer. In real time, however, it does not have independent projector control. It has a homing feature, reverses slides, and alternates and flashes. Time and function are always displayed in the LED readout.

dark, it will automatically cycle forward unless it has been cued otherwise. One non-programmable function in real time belongs to the operator. It is the time the operator allows the image to remain on the screen—by doing nothing. An image must remain on the screen until the operator initiates another dissolve cue. If one projector is at full brightness and the other is at full darkness, nothing happens on the screen until the operator gives another command. This cue-to-cue time is called wait time. Assuming that projector A is in the on position and projector B is in the off position, if we were to describe a command verbally, it would sound something like this:

(Cue 1) Begin cross-fade of projectors A and B for 4 seconds. When projector B image reaches 100 percent brightness, hold image on screen for 3 seconds.
(Cue 2) (Next command).

On the programmer keypad, it is as simple as this: press 4 seconds, press dissolve, and wait 3 more seconds before initiating the next command.

Function	Time
Dissolve	4 seconds

The wait time is the total time between two cues. Included in the wait time is the 1.2 seconds that it takes the projector in the off position to recycle. The wait time is the 4 seconds it takes the projectors to cross-fade (dissolve), plus the additional 3 seconds the image remains on the screen before the operator gives the next command.

It is important to include in our calculations the approximately 1.2 seconds it takes for a projector tray to cycle forward. If it takes an image 4 seconds to dissolve to black and another 1.2 seconds for that tray to recycle, the wait time between cues must be at least 5.2 seconds. In the example above, it was 7 seconds, so there was more than ample time for the off projector to recycle. But if we had kept the image on the screen only 1 second at full brightness, then initiated the next cue before the tray had a chance to complete its forward cycling, we would have thrown our program out of sync. It is a good idea to practice real-time programming before recording the signals on tape. When we program with multiple projectors, we can concern ourselves less with cycle-forward time because at least one projector will always be available for programming.

One real-time programmer/dissolve controlling two projectors can be linked with another programmer/dissolve and together they will control four projectors. By adding other compatible programmers, we can control up to sixteen projectors. Not only will the tray capacity and image flow be increased, but we can also program faster animation sequences. As the number of possible cues per second increases, however, so does our need for more sophisticated equipment to handle them.

INDEPENDENT ACCESS TO PROJECTORS

Another consideration is the need for independent access to each projector for better control. What if I wanted to give projector B two consecutive commands before cueing projector A? Heretofore, a 4-second fade-up of projector A meant an automatic 4-second fade-out of projector B, in ABAB rotation. Without independent access, if we executed a freeze on a scene in projector A, then superimposed a title from projector B, we would have no choice but to dissolve out the scenic from projector A first, then projector B, before being able to fade up a

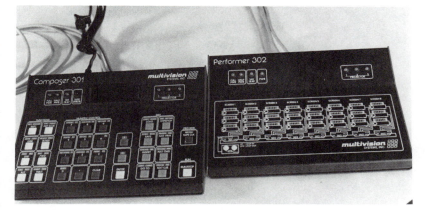

FIGURE 11–4
The Composer 301 links up with the Performer 302 to produce a six-projector show. Up to seven Performers can be connected to the Composer 301 via a communications loop, to program up to twenty-four projectors. (© Phiz Mezey)

new image in projector A. This would limit the effectiveness of our superimposition. With independent control of each projector, we can superimpose the title from projector B over the scenic, then fade out the title before fading out the scene.

Independent access allows the projectors to be activated in whatever order and for whatever length of time the cue specifies. With independent access we can hold an image on projector A and superimpose several different titles or credits over it from projector B, then fade out both projectors to black simultaneously. If we were working with a three-projector programmer, we would be able to fade up a new image from projector C while A and B were fading to black.

HOW MANY SCREENS?

Thus far we have been talking about programming on one screen. But another factor we must consider when determining the number of projectors and the type of programming equipment is the visual format. Will all the action take place on a single screen, or will there be two screens side by side, or an extended screen (two-screen center butt)? We must, of course, make these decisions in the planning stage of our production.

THE LANGUAGE OF PROGRAMMING

Although manufacturers have not yet standardized the vocabulary of multi-image, it is not too difficult to understand their meaning. Some manufacturers use the

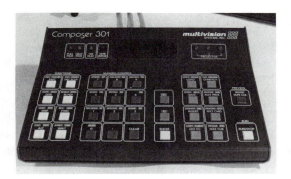

FIGURE 11–3
Each programmer has a different face (format) and might use a different name for some of its functions. But the basics are the same. This model is a three-projector memory programmer (leisure time). Presentations can be effectively programmed in segments, held in memory, and corrected before committing to tape. The Composer 301 also interfaces with the IBM-PC and IBM-PC compatibles through its OPUS/PC software. (© Phiz Mezey)

word *fade* to indicate a dissolve. But to be precise, *dissolve* generally implies a cross-fade between two projectors: One goes to dark while the other goes to bright. A *fade*, however, usually refers to the fading up or the fading out of one projector at a time. This does not become a significant distinction until we have independent access to projectors and leisure-time programming.

The terms *chop*, *hard cut*, and *fast cut* all say the same thing—cut to black or to bright fast. *Flash* and *blink* are not that far apart and mean that we can create an animated effect by blinking one or more projector lamps on and off. *Alt* also can mean to flash or blink, but it most often means a lamp change from one projector to another without advancing the trays. One programmer uses *Alt* as a function key in conjunction with *flash*, and this makes sense. *Loop* is used with leisure-time programmers and allows multiple commands to be grouped together so that the projectors can repeat a sequence. A loop can be created with any number of cues to repeat a segment many times. It is a way of saving time and memory space in leisure-time programmers. Other commands usually are explained clearly in the owner's manual, but let's look at some general terms in programming that need a little help. It is important to understand some of this programming language because we are using familiar words in a new context.

PROGRAMMING FORMS

We talked earlier about noting the cues in one- and two-projector productions directly on the original script or writing down the program instructions on a separate sheet, to be executed manually in real time. But as the number of possible commands increases, so does our need for a more formal cue information format, preferably one that resembles the programming system we are using. We can design our own program sheet template or buy one that is commercially available. It will have cue number, command, fade time, projector, and wait time information, and it also will have all the projector status information. For each cue we must anticipate which projectors to use. This requires that we know which projectors are on and off,

which are in the process of fading, what their tray positions are, and what each projector's percent level of lamp intensity is.

As the sophistication of cueing increases, so does the demand for equipment that can execute multiple cues in a short time. This is where leisure-time (memory) programmers can take over the work of real-time programming. With leisure-time programming, we are able to make multiple entries into the programmers, sequence by sequence, and have them held in memory until we have reviewed, changed, and fine-tuned them before committing them to tape.

LEISURE-TIME PROGRAMMING

I have made several references to leisure-time programming. With the appearance of the microcomputer came the development of a multi-image programmer with electronic memory. Many three- and four-projector programmers today are memory programmers with the capability of storing digital cues. Although memory capacity varies, we know that these machines can store the equivalent of more than a thousand entries, even though the average show will not use more than about three hundred entries.

This memory/storage capability gives us the leisure to cue and program our show *in segments*, changing and fine-tuning as we go along, before committing our program to tape. A leisure-time programmer has an alphanumeric keypad; the function and time keys are number and letter symbols. Using a keypad with numbers (for fade times) and letters (for other projector commands), we can store a linear sequence of cues in programmer memory. As we strike the key, our command appears in an LED (light-emitting diode) readout. When we have entered all our commands, we have completed our cue list—a program of all the action cues stored and ready to be executed. Now we can dump (transfer) our program to magnetic tape.

One of the drawbacks of memory programmers is that we can see only one cue at a time on the LED readout. It would be less frustrating to be able to see a sequence of cues on the screen. Perhaps that is why many programmer/dissolves and memory programmers are designed to interface with computers.

There are a number of keypad memory programmers on the market today, including the AVL Coyote, Clear Light Star Sentry 3, Electronic Saturn, Multivision Composer 301, and Arion 828. The Arion is really a four-projector programmer with a built-in keyboard, and it is capable of running three to sixteen projectors. All the above can program multi-projector shows by daisy-chaining additional external dissolvers that speak their programming language. Of course, we are talking about more money. While two-projector programmer/dissolves are in the $500 to $600 range, memory programmers start at around $1,650.

FIGURE 11–5
Clear Light's Memory Programmer 3 is another leisure-time programmer. It has eleven dissolve rates and sophisticated animation effects, including nested loops. Through its Program-Dependent Access, it eliminates time-consuming reprogramming when deleting or adding slides. It also is playback compatible with the Micro Diamond Star-3 and other modules in the Clear Light system.

COMPUTER INTERFACE

Some inexpensive two-projector real-time programmer/dissolves, such as the Arion Two Plus, the Gemini 2000, and the AVL FX-2, can convert to leisure-time programming through a special computer card and floppy disk software that make it possible to interface with either IBM-PC compatibles or Apple computers. A number of three- and four-projector memory programmers, such as the Composer 301, the Arion Four Plus, and the Entre 2004 Quad, also can interface with IBM-PC compatible computers. Multi-image programmer design seems to be pointed strongly in this direction. Industry standards today include the Clear Light Superstar software-driven system, which is a modified Apple or Standard Apple II fitted with a special interface card; the AVL Genesis, a self-contained multi-image computer programmer that can run other IBM-PC compatible programs; and the Electrosonic Apple/Sonic System.

Working with a computer keyboard, we no longer hit alphanumeric command keys but now type in the commands: fade, freeze, loop, and so on. We next type in the dissolve time and the wait time. All our commands and cues now appear on the screen. We can immediately access any cue or sequence of cues we want to change. Some computers also produce a printout, which can be very helpful in the editing process.

The following simple cue list is taken from a two-projector real-time programmer that can convert to a leisure-time programmer by interfacing with a personal computer through a board or card and floppy disk program. Again, there is no standardization, and computer formats and languages will vary in degree.

Let's look at a segment of a computer readout first, then describe what we have done in noncomputer language.

Cue	Command	Time	Projector	Wait
123	Fade	4	12	7.00
124	Fade	4	12	2.00
125	Freeze		1	2.15
126	Fade	2	2	0.05
127	Freeze		1	4.00
128	Fade	2.5	1	6.50

Explanation

Cue 123: Here we are requesting a 4-second fade on projectors 1 and 2 (one projector will fade up and the other fade down, in 4 seconds), and we have instructed projector 2 to hold the new image on-screen 3 seconds by listing a wait of 7 seconds before the next action command, cue 124.

Cue 124: As soon as we hit this cue 3 seconds after projector 2 reaches full brightness above, projector 2 will start to fade down and projector 1 will fade up for 4 seconds. Two seconds into the fade . . .

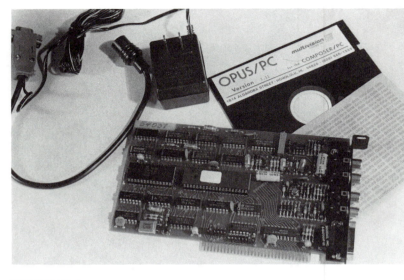

FIGURE 11–6 Multivision's (Composer 301) IBM-PC compatible interface card and software program. (© Phiz Mezey)

Cue 125: . . . or at 50 percent brightness, projector 1 is frozen. Meanwhile, projector 2 completes the fade-out and cycles forward.

Cue 126: Now projector 2 fades up in 2 seconds, superimposing over the image in projector 1. The 0.05 refers to the fraction of time it takes for a computer command to reach the dissolve module.

Cue 127: The second freeze command on this computer interface actually *unfreezes* projector 1, which is still at 50 percent brightness, and projectors 1 and 2 simultaneously fade to black.

Cue 128: Projector 1 fades up with a new image in 2.5 seconds, and after 4 seconds . . . the next action cue is ready to be struck.

KEEPING TRACK

Most programmers today have the capability of keeping the projectors in sync with the tape, even when the recorder is on fast forward or rewind, or when the projectors malfunction. Through the magic of digital systems, leisure-time programmers can keep track, between cues, of the tray position and the lamp status of the projectors. This digital tracking is referred to by many different names (Mate-Trac, PosiLock, Posi-trak), but they all do the same job: interleave projector status information with the cue data on the magnetic tape.

This is the way it works. During the pro-

gramming phase, digital information is being laid down between cues on the cue track in order to tell the programmer (on playback) where the projectors should be at that point on the tape to maintain exact synchronization. Thus, once the sync track has been recorded, we can move the tape to any point by fast-forwarding or rewinding it, and the projectors will follow it there. This is helpful during a presentation if we run into problems because we can go backward or forward on the tape in mid-presentation without losing our projector status (visual location). Projector status also is helpful during cueing, but once the cues are in the programmer, any cue change will change the projector status, and we will have to redo the cue track from that point on.

CLOCK TRACK

Clock track is another digital code that is put down on tape beside the audio track. It is simply a timing track (running clock) that establishes the relationship of all the cues in memory, one to another, in linear sequence. Remember how difficult it was, in real time, to get an image to come up on the screen at the precise moment we wanted it to appear? We either hit the time button too soon or too late and had to make several adjustments. With clock track, which appears on the computer screen in sync with the cues, each cue can be instantly accessed, and the cue time can be extended or shaved by a fraction of a second, bringing the image to the screen precisely when we want it to appear. Different systems use clock track in different ways, but it is generally found in very expensive equipment. The Composer 301, a three-projector memory programmer capable of using an IBM-PC computer interface, is the only one of the moderately priced leisure-time programmers that features clock track.

STATE OF THE ART? OR, WHAT WORKS BEST FOR EACH SITUATION?

For most of us, two-projector real-time programmers will continue to do a very adequate job. We always have the option of hooking up another compatible unit to

FIGURE 11–7
Programming a show on the AVL Genesis 16-bit leisure-time programming computer. It controls from two to thirty projectors and is expandable to 120 projectors. It uses Procall software, has clock track, and reads and generates SMPTE time code for video and slide sync. Dove X three-projector playback units will handle all Procall versions. (© Phiz Mezey)

make larger presentations. Or we can invest in a three-projector memory programmer, with the option of later interfacing with a home computer. Or we can add a two-projector programmer to our two-projector programmer and control four projectors. These decisions are individual and depend to a great extent on our goals, audience, and pocketbook.

We might ask, Can I get a dissolver/programmer/tape recorder in one package for a modest price? The answer is yes. There are several on the market today. Will it give me the dependability, quality, ease of operation, and results I want? The answer here must be qualified. Questions we must ask ourselves are, What are my expectations in a production? Will I be happy with a monaural system, or do I want stereo sound? Am I patient enough to work with an analog tone, or would I prefer digital signals? Am I willing to work with limited dissolve rates and a less-than-perfect sound system? Can I deal with the mishaps and frustrations that can occur in any production? Are compactness and simplicity important? Do I want to build a system, component by component?

Ultimately, what it boils down to is priorities and expectations. Is it important to carry a studio-in-a-suitcase for convenience and quick access to widespread audiences?

Or to mix and match separate specialized components for a more ambitious end product in a fixed location? We must again look at our objectives, our audience, and our funds. That is where it all starts, and that should be our point of reference when shopping for equipment. Of course, money is a major consideration. But it is possible to build a component system in stages, if that is what we want. It is possible to spend several hundred dollars and produce an exciting show. It also is possible to spend thousands and produce a poor show. Success does not depend only on the money or our system; it has a lot to do with what each of us is willing to put into the production. There is no question that the less sophisticated the equipment, the more time we will spend in production. But time seems a small cost if we achieve an equivalent amount of success in the final analysis.

Careful evaluation of our own needs, purposes, and motivations, plus a willingness to spend time in searching the market, are key factors in the purchasing of equipment for multi-image production. Twice now I have heard enthusiasts rave about a new product on the market, only to find out after I worked with the modules that there were several limitations. Fortunately, I had not yet made the purchase. It is important to ask questions, request demonstrations, talk to people who have worked with the product, read the spec sheets (though I find they give limited information), and consider and weigh all the pros and cons relative to what we need, want, and are willing to spend.

A small neighborhood outreach program can, with some outside help, produce a multi-image production that effectively informs and educates the community. But the equipment it rents or purchases, and the production it produces, will involve choices that differ from those made by an organization that has an industrial base, a permanent showroom, a large budget, and a sophisticated promotional goal. Each group should have the best product relative to its needs and funding. The equipment, materials, and production staff also should be selected relative to those factors. There is no point in insisting on six projectors if a well-conceived, well-executed two- or three-projector production can do the job creatively and effectively. Quality here is not dependent on quantity, but rather on careful planning and coordinating of all aspects of production—before actual production is undertaken. In Chapter 12 I list the various components of multi-image production, not by manufacturer, but by similarity in function and price.

When we have reviewed our needs, objectives, and budget, we should sit down and write a profile of the equipment for which we are looking. Then we should be able to go out and ask some intelligent questions before committing ourselves to a purchase. If it is possible to try out some of these components before investing, it is worth the extra rental cost to do so. Knowledge is money saved or at least money wisely spent.

Whether we are producing for our own pleasure or for a client, multi-image is an all-encompassing, richly satisfying experience. If we start simple and build wisely, we will not be disappointed.

GLOSSARY

Alternate   Turns off the lamp in one projector and turns on the lamp in the other, without advancing the tray, thereby allowing the operator to change the order of projection. It also is used as a command, ALT. Projector lamps can be programmed to turn on and off in split-second intervals without cycling trays forward.

Animation   Simulated motion by projecting progressively different images in rapid sequence. In multi-image a flashing sequence can give an animated effect on-screen, or a rapid and sequential showing of a number of related still images can give the appearance of movement. The number of projectors available and the sophistication of the equipment and materials determine the degree of complexity of the animation sequence.

Bump   The gradual increasing or decreasing of lamp intensity while the projectors flash on and off. This creates the effect of movement within a projected image. Images might appear to grow or shrink in size. Sometimes called a *fade flash*.

Chop   A dissolve at the fastest rate the equipment allows. A *fast cut;* also called a *hard cut*.

Cue link   This is the same as *wait*. The total time between one action cue and the next action cue.

Cut   A fast fade achieved by switching the lamp off or on in one projector.

Cycle forward   On command, the slide tray of a projector advances one slide at a time in approximately 1.2 seconds.

Dissolve   Generally, a cross-fade between two projectors. While one image fades up, the other fades down in a designated amount of time. The projector that fades down will cycle the tray forward when the lamp is completely off, thereby preparing it for the next dissolve cue. Cf Fade.

Fade   The fading out of an on-screen image until it reaches black, or the fading up of an image until it reaches the desired percent of brightness. Sometimes called a dissolve, but there is a difference in function. A dissolve implies a cross-fade, whereas with independent projectors images can fade up or fade out independently.

Field   A delineated area or background onto which is entered specific information or graphics. The area in any artwork that is to be photographed. A field guide helps to position that artwork correctly and in register.

Flash   In multi-image, the flashing on and off of one or more projector lamps, either in an alternating or independent pattern. Also called blinking.

Freeze   A command that stops and holds the dimming of one or all of the projector lamps at any given level. A background can be held on-screen, while a title is superimposed over it. Or an image might be frozen at a level less than 100 percent during a dissolve action. Also, a slide with a window might be frozen on-screen while different images are dropped into the window.

Hold   Some manufacturers use *hold* for *freeze*. It can also mean *standby*. (I sometimes use it to designate the time an image remains on-screen between dissolves.)

Home   The command used to return all trays to their original starting point.

Loop   A programmed cycle in which a series of commands is kept in memory and repeated. This is used in the creation of complex animation effects. It also saves the time and space of repetitive cueing.

Neon effect   A particular kind of glow.

Ripple   Sometimes called a *wipe*. An image or series of images are removed from the screen in a gradual sweep. Ripples are programmed by a series of continuous dissolves separated by a time interval. This is an advanced effect that requires multiple projectors and a two-screen butt center overlap to create a panoramic effect.

Toggle   Changes the direction of the lamps while the projectors are fading. A projector that is fading up will start to fade down, and vice versa.

Wait   Cue-to-cue time, which generally includes fade-up time plus the amount of time an image remains on-screen before the next cue. Wait time is a computer-generated term.

Chapter 12

Equipment Guide

What equipment will we need to begin our project? Once we have defined our needs, objectives, and budget potential, we can draw up a generalized list of required hardware and begin our search for the products that best match our purposes.

To begin we should consider not only the show on which we are currently working, but also the kinds of productions we think we will be involved with in the near future. Are we interested in producing two-projector or three-projector one-screen shows, or multi-screen, multi-projector presentations? Will we have a permanent installation in our home or studio, or is portability and easy setup an important factor in our presentations? If budget is a consideration, should we think of building a system over a period of time or get equipment now that meets our immediate requirements? Does it make sense to get equipment that is standard in the industry or to buy the product we personally prefer? What kinds of clients are we most likely to be working with?

Every multi-image producer must go through this question and answer process before making a final decision. Compiling a list of our present and projected needs is a first step in the long and complicated process of purchasing equipment. We will be spending a great deal of time and a lot of bucks on this system. We can save time and money if we invest in the research first.

SYNCHRONIZERS, DISSOLVERS, AND PROGRAMMERS

We could begin with a one-projector format and a simple synchronizer or dissolver. We could program live in real time with a manually controlled music tape. Our investment for either device would be under $200, assuming that we owned a slide projector. Then, if we enjoyed putting a show together, we could look around for a more sophisticated multi-image system that would fit our needs.

For approximately $500 to $900 we can purchase a high-quality tape recorder with a built-in dissolve device. In the trade these are called PDTRs (programmer/dissolve/tape recorders) and combine several functions in one piece of equipment that will record, dissolve, program, and play back. It is portable and easy to handle, but it might be limited somewhat in sound fidelity and the number of dissolve rates and special effects it can offer. Some will handle only one projector internally (Recordex) but feature a sync-in/out jack that accepts an external programmer to create two-projector shows. Other AV tape recorders have built-in dissolve devices (Arion Producer TD) or feature stereo formats that accept a sync signal on the fourth track (Sharp 688AV). Since most of these units come with external jacks that accept almost all programmers, we can at any time add an external programmer component for more sophisticated effects. PDTRs are an effective solution for the multi-imagist who is involved with smaller productions and desires compactness, easy portability, and convenient setup and playback features.

We also can begin to build a system of separate modules that interface and are interchangeable and expandable. The initial cost might be $500 for a programmer/dissolve that can handle two projectors, or up to $1,650 for a three-projector memory programmer/dissolve that can operate as a separate unit or interface with a home computer. The tape recorder or deck (and amplifier) would be separate but necessary components. Thus, the costs are higher for a system made up of separate modules, but the applications are unlimited.

In this chapter I will list and describe numerous programming modules and components, from the simplest to the most sophisticated. They are grouped by function and price. I include specifications for Audiotronics, Califone, Sharp, Arion, Tiffen, and Tascam units, which are among the many AV cassette recorders available. I also cover Clear Light (Cornerstone), AVL, and Electrosonic as well as other manufacturers. Although I could not list them all, I have included many cassette and open-reel tape recorders and tape decks that lend themselves, however differently, to recording multi-image programming cues on a separate track. I realize that new models are continually coming on the market, but this list can give the reader a basis for understanding the functions and attributes of the various systems.

COMPATIBILITY

It is important to recognize that modules manufactured by different companies usually are not compatible. Some manufacturers, however, have made components for outside companies. Arion produced a programmer for Kodak, which still interfaces with some Arion components. The Califone 275-Ten tape recorder has a built-in Entre dissolve unit. When researching the purchase of multi-image components, it is helpful to keep in mind (or in a notebook) some of these relationships.

Some AV manufacturers, such as Cornerstone, AVL, and Arion, produce only multi-image equipment and are system-oriented. Most of their modules will interface. Once we decide on a particular system, we can build our own multi-image production system, module by module—from a simple two-projector dissolve to a six-, nine-, or sixteen-projector production, and from real-time to leisure-time to computer-programmed presentations.

In the past few years several companies have developed computer software and interface cards to enable the multi-imagist to cue and edit presentations on a home computer. These companies include AVL, Arion, Cornerstone (Clear Light), Multivision, and Gemini Electronics. We list these special products in the specifications that follow.

PROJECTORS

Since most multi-imagists quickly graduate to multi-projector productions or might want to transfer productions to videotape, it would be wise to buy two projectors at the outset. It is possible, however, to start with one projector, as long as the second projector we buy matches the first. If we start with an Ektagraphic II, our second projector should also be an Ektagraphic II, since the Ektagraphic III lamp system is different. The Elmo Omnigraphic 300 slide projector is comparable to the Ektagraphic II (no longer manufactured), has a better optical system, and is well worth checking out.

PROJECTOR STANDS AND PROJECTOR TABLES

A projector stand is nice to have. I worked from an ordinary table for years until I got tired of stacking books under the projectors to limit keystoning. But nothing can replace a good projector stand, called a stack stand, and I now wonder how I ever did without it. We can buy a one-tier, two-tier expandable, or three-tier stack stand. I purchased a two-tier stand, with the option of adding the third tier later on. Sleeker, less-cumbersome projector stands and tables are coming on the market each year. If we are planning to go to three-projector production and have the funds, it is wise to purchase a three-tier stand at the outset.

SCREEN

A screen is another necessary piece of equipment. A 6- by 9-foot screen that is in the same 2:3 proportion as the slides is ideal, but for home use a 4- by 4-foot silver lenticular screen will do nicely. Although a screen might not be a priority while we are building a production base, it will greatly enhance the presentation and eventually becomes a must, along with projector stands and tables. A smooth white matte wall will do nicely as a temporary projection surface.

MIXER

A mixer can be a simple disc module listed at under $100 at Radio Shack or at music stores, or it can be an elaborate board of buttons and sliders priced at more than $1,000. Some modules, such as the Tascam Ministudio and the 246 Tascam Portastudio, have incorporated a cassette tape deck. (Some cassette tape recorders, such as the Tascam 225 or 234, might have a limited mixing function and can serve this purpose if necessary.) Most mixers require external amplifiers and speakers, yet some of the inexpensive models have preamplifier features and can be played through existing home hi-fi systems. If we do not plan to have the sound mixed professionally, a mixer, however simple, is an important piece of equipment to include on our multi-image list.

EQUIPMENT SPECIFICATIONS

The following listings begin with simple one- and two-projector manual dissolvers and synchronizers priced under $100, followed by specifications for several AV tape recorders with built-in sync and/or dissolve functions in the $400 to $900 range. I then describe two-projector programmer/dis-

solves with add-on capabilities in the $600 to $1,500 range; three-projector and leisure-time programmer/dissolves from $600 to $1,650; computer interface programmer/dissolves in the same range; and one or two computer programmers costing considerably more. Listed separately, but limited in number, are specifications for inexpensive audio mixers. Projectors, screens, light tables, and microphones are not reviewed in this chapter.

It is impossible to list all the devices and components on the market today or to keep up with the new models and price changes that occur daily. The intention of the following listing is to acquaint multi-imagists with products and product capabilities, to get us started in the research process, and to help us select the best group of components for our particular needs. A complete and updated listing can be found in the 15237/frmtDirectory of Audio-Visual, Computer, & Video Products, an annual equipment catalog (about $25).

SIMPLE SYNCHRONIZERS AND DISSOLVE UNITS

Manufacturer	Impact Communications, Inc.
Model	Pacer II
Price	$129.50
Type	One-projector synchronizer; works with any standard cassette or open-reel stereo tape recorder; will record/playback high-quality audio tapes.
Tones	One frequency, 1,000 Hz (generates narrowband tone, rejecting false signals; minimizes crosstalk problems on standard stereo recorders).
Functions	One-function controlled.
Weight	14 oz. Dimensions: 2½ × 1½ × 4¾ inches.
Power	120 V, 60 Hz. Unit available with international (220 V) power pack ($139.50).
Notes	Kodak projector cord included. Relay activated output; can be used to program all types of equipment.
Other models	2- and 3-channel models available on special order.

Manufacturer	Kimchuk, Inc., AV Division
Model	Auto-Fade GO-1
Price	Under $100
Type	Single-projector dissolve control.

Projectors	One-projector controlled: Kodak Carousel or Ektagraphic including B-2AR International model; 300 watts maximum.
Dissolve Control method	2½ seconds, fixed dissolve rate. Standard Kodak hand-held remote; 1,000 Hz synchronized sound/slide tape recorders; automatic timer.
Power	Derives power from projector, no AC outlet needed; 50/60 Hz.
Weight	7 oz. Dimensions: 1¼ × 4¼ × 3¼ inches.
Notes	Plugs into remote socket of most Kodak slide projectors; no additional cables needed.
Other models	GO-2: has built-in variable automatic timer for continuous or unattended showings; kit for Kodak AudioViewer or Telex/Singer Caramate slide/sound projectors available. DuoFade DU-2 or DU-4, single and dual projector dissolve controls work with AV recorders that have contact closure capability; built-in variable timer for continuous showings.

FIGURE 12–1
Pacer II, from Impact Communications, Inc.
(Impact Communications, Inc.)

Manufacturer	Image Two, Inc.
Model	Slide Dissolve SD-102
Price	$159
Type	Manual dissolver for two projectors.
Projectors	Two; 300-watt limitation.
Control method	Manual at dissolve control; not programmable; independent access to each projector, making superimpositions possible.
Weight	Approx. 1½ pounds.
Notes	Order direct through Image Two, 1124 La Paloma Drive, Cupertino, CA 95104. (RMF 2225 is another manual dissolve control that operates by moving a slider back and forth. The RMF 2225 requires live input; will not record and play back).

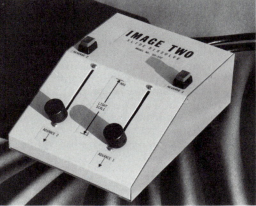

FIGURE 12–2
Auto-Fade GO-1, from Kimchuk, Inc.

Manufacturer	Entré Electronics Corp.
Model	Entre 7605
Price	Under $199
Type	Self-contained programmer/dissolve, programmable in real time; quite small.
Projectors	One or two; 500 watts maximum; compatible with Kodak, Singer, Leitz, and others using Kodak plug format.
Control functions	Infinitely variable dissolve rates from 0.3-second cut; pause, sway, superimpose, flash; audible signal track.
Signal output	(Run/record) approx. 1.3 V P-P AC coupled, 100 ohms source impedance, tone from approx.

FIGURE 12–3
Slide Dissolve SD-102 from Image Two, Inc.

	1,050 Hz to 1,450 Hz. Recommended record level 0 to 5 VU. Signal level and frequency compatible with AV sync and stereo hi-fi (home) recorders.
Signal input	(Tape/play) Autogain 0.05 V P-P minimum, 3 V P-P maximum, −10 VU or higher. Input compatible with AV sync and stereo hi-fi recorders.
Power	90 to 130 AC, 50/60 Hz.
Weight	1¾ lbs. Dimensions: 2¼ × 4½ × 4 inches.

Tape recorder Interface with any tape recorder that has separate channel access for signal or hi-fi stereo.

Other models Entre 7610 PD has rotary or optional slider for easy programming; will function directly with 1,000-Hz sync recorders; has delayed power sequence that delays lamp and advances system 3 seconds to allow power buildup. Entre 7620 has automatic mode, built-in timer, Kodak remote socket for use with live presentations.

Manufacturer RMF Products, Inc.
Model 2325 Image Blender
Price $235
Type Two-projector synchronizer/dissolve; will record and play back.
Dissolve Continuously variable duration, ½ to 10 seconds; push button initiates dissolve and generates cue for tape, separate track.
Control method Manual, at dissolve control or remote connection for optional synchronizer, projector remote control, or other control device.
Special effects Superimpositions at full lamp brightness.
Power 120 V, 60 Hz.
Weight 4 lbs. Dimensions: 3¼ × 6¾ × 8½ inches.
Accessories Automatic timer.
Special features Tape recorder input/output connections.
Other models 2225 Image Blender, $130; this is a manual dissolve unit. 500 Imatronic Image Blender, $545; programmer built-in; also will function directly with 1,000-Hz sync recorders. 2600 Image Blender, $450; combines a digital programmer and a dissolve control into one package. Designed as a companion for the RMF Tri-Cassette Recorder.

FIGURE 12–4
RMF Image Blender.

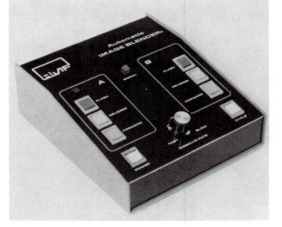

Manufacturer Audiotronics Corporation
Model Dissolve Control D-101B (see p. 121)
Price $199
Type Two-projector controlled; generates an analog signal; operates with any American-made slide projector, including Ektagraphic III, that has a seven-contact remote control socket; 500 watts maximum projector. To function, it must be connected to an Audiotronics sync cassette unit.
Dissolve Rotating knob manually selects dissolve rates of continuously variable duration, ½ to 10 seconds.
Control method Manual; remote control.
Power Derives power from projector, no AC outlet needed.
Weight 2½ lbs. Dimensions: 7 × 5½ × 3¼ inches.
Special features Projector cables permanently attached to dissolve unit; socket for Kodak remote control.
Other models Listed in following section.

AUDIO CASSETTE TAPE RECORDERS WITH BUILT-IN SYNCHRONIZER; PROGRAMMER/ DISSOLVE TAPE RECORDERS (PDTR): $300 to $600

The multi-imagist interested in getting started is often confused by the wide variety and dissimilarity of components in multi-image. Some manufacturers combine components in one module, while others make separate but compatible modules. Even so, there is little similarity or compatibility of equipment between manufacturers. In reviewing the following AV cassette tape recorders (with sync capability), it is important that we pay attention to the specifications of each product. Does it have a built-in synchronizer? How many projectors does it control? Does it have a built-in dissolve control? What is the tape format? Does it have a sync-input jack for external programmers? What are its limitations? The answers to these questions will influence our choice in selecting the hardware that best fits our needs.

Manufacturer Audiotronics Corporation
Model 154 S2 Sync Recorder
Price $330
Type A sync cassette tape recorder (built-in synchronizer); a D-101B dissolve unit can be added externally, $199.
Projectors One or two.
Control functions 1,000-Hz visual advance; 150-Hz program stop; separate track for live audio input; controls two functions; external dissolve unit

permits two-projector production.

Tape function
Record/playback; monaural. Tape speed: 1⅞ ips. Wow and flutter: 0.2%.

Audio section
Frequency response: 40 to 10,000 Hz +3 dB.

Power
120 V, 60 Hz; UL and CSA listed. Speaker 6 × 4 inch dual cone.

Inputs
Mic in, auxiliary in/out, sync in/out.

Outputs
Speaker, standard ¼ inch.

Weight
5¾ lbs. Dimensions: 4½ × 11⅜ × 9¾ inches.

Special features
Five-position LED level array; LED function indicators; jacks for access to control track for separate programmer and duplication of audio and sync track; bidirectional sound; full-function low-flutter tape deck; cables for Kodak projectors included; PA function.

Other models
162S-2 with D-101B dissolve permits three-projector shows; 162-SD has built-in dissolve.

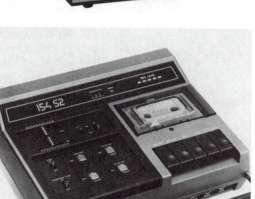

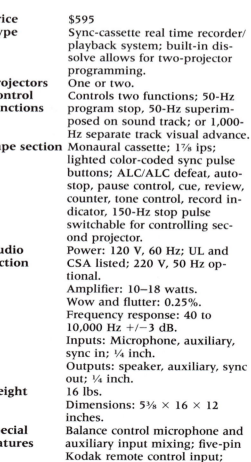

Manufacturer Recordex

Model
2870 AV (formerly Wollensak-3M)

Price
$605

Type
Sync cassette recorder (meets ANSI standards) for single slide projector or two slide projectors, using external dissolver. Standard monaural half-track format, with cue signals on upper track. 150-Hz program stop.

Projectors
One; a second projector can be added with external dissolver.

Control functions
1,000-Hz visual advance cue in sync mode; 150-Hz program stop; compatible with external dissolver.

Tape section Monaural cassette plus cue track (Philips ANSI). Tape speed: 1⅞ ips. Signal-to-noise ratio: 54 dB minimum. Wow and flutter: less than 0.2%.

Audio section
Amplifier: 10 watts RMS. Frequency response: 50 to 11,000 Hz; ±3 dB. Speakers: 3¼ × 7⅝ inch elliptical.

Inputs
Mic in, line in, sync in.

Outputs
Line out, sync out, external speaker out.

Weight
16½ lbs.

Other models
2851 AV; 2820 AV.

Manufacturer Califone International, Inc.

Model
5275 Califone tape recorder with built-in Entre 7610 dissolve. Same as Entre 275-Ten.

Price
$595

Type
Sync-cassette real time recorder/playback system; built-in dissolve allows for two-projector programming.

Projectors
One or two.

Control functions
Controls two functions; 50-Hz program stop, 50-Hz superimposed on sound track; or 1,000-Hz separate track visual advance.

Tape section Monaural cassette; 1⅞ ips; lighted color-coded sync pulse buttons; ALC/ALC defeat, auto-stop, pause control, cue, review, counter, tone control, record indicator, 150-Hz stop pulse switchable for controlling second projector.

Audio section
Power: 120 V, 60 Hz; UL and CSA listed; 220 V, 50 Hz optional. Amplifier: 10–18 watts. Wow and flutter: 0.25%. Frequency response: 40 to 10,000 Hz +/−3 dB. Inputs: Microphone, auxiliary, sync in; ¼ inch. Outputs: speaker, auxiliary, sync out; ¼ inch.

Weight
16 lbs. Dimensions: 5⅜ × 16 × 12 inches.

Special features
Balance control microphone and auxiliary input mixing; five-pin Kodak remote control input; four-pin Cinch-Jones projector

Other models	output; PA/monitor switch. 3675 for $479.95.
Manufacturer	Audiotronics Corporation
Model	162 SD Electro Sync Mate-Trac
Price	$1,096
Type	Monaural cassette sync recorder with built-in dissolve; digital, microprocessor based; Philips cassette EIA RS-399 standard; twelve-position keypad; interchangeable with Kodak and Arion two-projector programmers.
Projectors	Two.
Control functions	1-, 2-, 4-, and 8-second dissolve rates; flash, reverse, freeze, superimpose, tape stop/start, home, cut, etc.
Tape section	Half-track monaural cassette plus cue; record/playback. Signal-to-noise ratio: −45 dB unweighted. Wow and flutter: less than 0.20%. Tape speed: 1⅞ ips.
Audio section	Power: 10–18 watts. Frequency response: 40 to 10,000 Hz +/−3 dB. Speakers: 10-inch oval. Inputs: mic, auxiliary, sync in. Outputs: speaker, headphone, external amplifier, sync out. Power: 120 V, 50/60 Hz, 16 watts AC. three-wire cord.
Weight	14½ lbs. Dimensions: 6½ × 14 × 10 inches.
Special features	ALC/ALC defeat, pause and tone controls, review, autostop, cue, counter; built-in Mate-trac (slides will always be in perfect sync with program).
Notes	Bidirectional sound, full autostop, "live-in-play" LED level array, LED function indicators; PA capability, monitor.
Manufacturer	Sharp Electronics Corporation
Model	RD-685AV
Price	$350
Type	10-watt heavy-duty slide/sync and dissolve tape recorder; produces and plays back; built-in electret condenser microphone.
Projectors	One or two.
Control functions	1,000-Hz cues recorded on tape produce the first rate, and 150-Hz cues produce the second; first rate can be quick cut to 8 seconds; separate sync jack allows for external programmer; program stop for live input.
Power	120 V, 50/60 Hz, or external 12 volts DC source (for audio function only).
Inputs	External mic/line (auxiliary) in.

Outputs	Line out; plus speaker/headphone out.
Tape section	1⅞ ips monaural; Philips ANSI format; second track for cue; will accept any cassette.
Audio section	Speaker system: 6 × 4 inch woofer plus separate piezoelectric horn-type tweeter. Frequency response: 100 to 6,000 Hz. Wow and flutter: 0.2% WRMS. Signal-to-noise ratio: 44 dB.
Weight	16.1 lbs. Dimensions: 14³⁄₁₆ × 6½ × 11 inches.
Special features	PA system, record monitor, and switchable ALC (automatic record level control) all built-in; VU meter for monitoring audio level in record mode; input jack for external microphone.
Other models	See Sharp 688AV model, described on p. 125.
Manufacturer	RMF Products, Inc.
Model	Tri-Cassette Three Channel Recorder. (See Figure 12–8.)
Price	$545 (System: with Model 760 Speakers, $80; Model 765 Carrying Case, $75; and Model 2600 Image Blender, $450.00).
Type	Three-channel stereo cassette standard format recorder with built-in synchronizer; real time programmable with synchronizer or external dissolve control (2600 Image Blender or other module).
Projectors	One or two.
Control functions	With button or any external programmer. A 1,000-Hz cue signal permits control of single projector or simple dissolve system. Access to third channel available for use with more sophisticated programming equipment. Records and plays 500-Hz to 10,000-Hz external pulses; one-function controlled.
Tape section	Quarter-track stereo format; three channels. Speed: 1⅞ ips. Signal-to-noise ratio: Dolby off, 50 dB, Dolby on, 60 dB. Wow and flutter: 0.12%.
Audio section	Frequency response: 35 to 17,000 Hz +/−1.5 dB. Amplifier: 7.5 watts RMS. Speaker: 4 inch. Power: 120 V, 60 Hz, 15 watts. Amplifier: 7.5 watts.
Inputs	Mic/line in, sync in is six-pin DIN.
Outputs	Line, speaker, headphone, sync out is six-pin DIN.
Weight	7 lbs. Dimensions: 11⅝ × 3½ × 8¼ inches.

Special features	Three-channel recorders permit stereo sound in addition to a sync track; Dolby circuitry; cue and review; tape equalization, dual VU meters, and stereo headphone jack. External speakers available.

Manufacturer	Tiffen
Model	Pro-Dissolve recorder and dissolver. (See Figure 12–9.)
Price	$499
Type	Digital and analog real time programmable dissolver/cassette tape recorder.
Projectors	Two (or one).
Control functions	Analog: 1,000 Hz initiates first projector advance; 150 Hz advances second projector or stops tape deck to allow live input. Digital: dissolve rates: cut to 10-second dissolves; title, alt, flash.
Special effects	Variable dissolve, alternate, and flash rates to create limited animation effects.
Tape section	Monaural plus cue. Tape speed: 1⅞ ips. Tape track configuration: Two-track/two-channel system. Wow and flutter: 0.3%.
Audio section	Amplifier: 10 watts RMS. Frequency response: 63 to 10,000 Hz. Speakers: 4-inch round.
Inputs/ outputs	Mic and speaker/headphone ¼-inch jacks; auxiliary in/out; external sync in/out.
Weight	6 lbs. 5 oz. Dimensions: 13¾ × 10 × 3⁵⁄₁₆ inches.
Special features	PA switch allows use of Pro-Dissolve's amplifier and speaker with the hand-held microphone; tone control; variable sync volume control; LED readout.
Other models	Pro-Corder cassette tape, 5 watts RMS, $249. See also Tiffen Memorizer, Digital Leisure Time Programmer, $499.

Manufacturer	Arion Corporation
Model	Mate-Trac Producer, Model TD. (See Figure 12–10.)
Price	$1,395
Type	Cassette tape recorder with built-in two-projector digital dissolver; built-in 15-watt speaker; computer compatible; built-in microprocessor. Will record or play back shows using any program signal (AVL, Clear Light, Electrosonics, etc.).
Projectors	Two; may be linked to external Arion Omni Loc or Omni Mate equipment for multi-projector shows.
Control method	Synchronization/dissolve functions built-in. Trays stay in sync

with the tape regardless of tape direction or speed. Will sync one projector or dissolve between two projectors. Will accept external programmable dissolves.

Tape section Half-track monaural cassette with cue and review; Philips ANSI format; 1⅞ ips. Signal-to-noise ratio: >55 dB. Wow and flutter: 0.06%.

Audio section Amplifier power: 15 watts. Frequency response: 19,000 Hz. Built-in speaker; built-in PA; mixing function; separate controlled mic and line in.

Inputs/ outputs Sync in/out; separate mic in, line in; external speaker output.

Weight 13 lbs. Dimensions: 4½ × 15 × 10½ inches.

Special features Time display on front panel reads tape time in minutes and seconds rather than conventional tape counter numbers; separate treble, bass, and volume controls; Tray-Loc automatically synchronizes slide trays to tape; all key operations available on accessory remote control panel; auto replay and remote operation functions.

Other models Mate-Trac Producer available in three models: TS is basic single-projector sync signal operation plus external sync in/out, $795; TR has same as TS but includes capability of complete remote operation and auto present features, $995; TD is the top model, described above. Mate-Trac Two Plus and Keyboard, $695; Mate-Trac Four Plus (see Programmer Dissolves); 828 Omni-Mate Memory Programmer (see Leisure-Time Programmers); Mate-Trac Express Four (see Playback-Only Modules).

TAPE DECKS WITH CUE INPUT/ OUTPUT (EXTERNAL SYNC)

Manufacturer Sharp Electronics Corporation

Model RD-688AV

Price $550

Type Cassette stereo plus cue; sync control separate track; compatible with external programmer/ dissolve modules; double cassette for dubbing, editing; portable.

Record/ playback Double-cassette tape recorder: tape 1, playback only, four track/ three channel; tape 2, record/ playback, four track/three channel; two built-in condenser microphones.

Tape section Monaural/stereo cassette; compatible with all grades of cassette tapes—normal, chrome, metal. Speed: 1⅞ ips. Wow and flutter: 0.07%.

Audio section Built-in amplifier: 5 watts RMS per channel (26 watts total peak power). Speakers: Two 6½-inch woofer and 2-inch tweeter built-in speakers. Frequency response: 30 to 17,000 Hz.

Inputs Mic in, sync in, external amp.

Outputs Speaker, headphone, external amp, sync out, monitor headphone.

Weight 19.8 lbs. Dimensions: 12⅝ × 20⅞ × 5⅞ inches.

Special features Double cassette allows instant dubbing, tape editing, sound-on-sound voice-overs; also, ALC/ALC defeat (automatic level control equalizes the sound input); pause, tone control; cue and review; VU and sync signal meter selector; treble/bass control.

Auxiliaries Model RCC-688 carrying case, #110; model MC-78DV microphone with desk stand, $40.

Manufacturer Tascam/TEAC

Model 133B

Price approx. $1,250

Type Four-track/three-channel cassette tape deck; stereo plus cue; requires external programmer/dissolve; standard line level output is compatible with any amplifier configuration.

Tape 3¾ and 1⅞ ips; dual tape speed provides professsional-quality (3¾) or standard (1⅞) recording (or playback); meter on cue track. Standard tapes made on 133 will play back on most recorders. (ANSI format, half-track configuration, can be replayed on the 133 with some limitations.)

Configuration Two heads/two motors; three tracks, each individually recordable; complete three-channel simul-sync operation.

Audio Wow and flutter: 0.06% at 1⅞ ips. Frequency response: 30 to 8,000 Hz (1⅞ ips). Signal-to-noise ratio: Built-in Dolby noise reduction improves signal-to-noise by +10 dB.

Inputs/ outputs Input/output impedance: balanced; mic and line inputs; cue input/output; line output; headphone output.

Features	Simul-sync (listen to one track, record second track for sound-on-sound synchronization); punch-in recording; built-in 25-Hz tone generator allows you to program stop and wait for live talk; endless loop logic for continuous unattended presentations; programmable home command.
Other models	Tascam 234 is four-track/four-channel, 3¾ ips (only) cassette tape deck; Model 234L has 1⅞ ips speed; see also Porta One Ministudio, approx. $550, and 246 Portastudio, under Mixers.
Note	The Tascam 133 and 234 are compatible with most programmers.

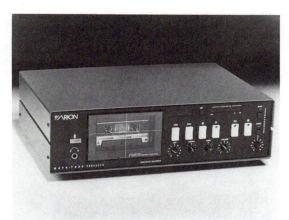

FIGURE 12–10
Arion Mate-Trac Producer.

PROGRAMMER/DISSOLVES: $400 TO $1,000

Manufacturer	Cornerstone Associates
Model	Micro Diamond Dissolve
Price	$399
Type	Self-contained digital record/playback programmer/dissolve unit; Time Division Multiplex Signal (series of pulses that contain synchronous information and data and control the time between the pulses); nine functions controlled; will interface with any tape recorder that has a separate cue track.
Projectors	Two.
Dissolves	Selectable durations: cut, 1-, 2-, 4-, and 8-second.
Special effects	Hold, animation, superimposition, ripple, and reverse dissolves.
Weight	3 lbs. Dimensions: 2½ × 6 × 8½ inches.
Special features	Will interface with Micro Diamond Memory Programmer to make up to six-projector shows.
Other models	Micro Diamond Memory Programmer; Star Sentry Series Memory Programmer 3, Performer 2, etc.

Manufacturer	AVL (Audio Visual Laboratories)
Model	FX-2
Price	$595
Type	Real-time programmer; simple keyboard.
Projectors	Two; 300 watts maximum.
Control method	Seven button dissolves, seven alternate rates, up to sixteen-second variable; blink dissolve, forward, reverse, step cue, home, freeze, independent access to projectors.

FIGURE 12–11
Sharp RD-688AV.

FIGURE 12–12
Tascam 133 tape recorder.

FIGURE 12–13
AVL FX-2.

Power	AC 115/220 V, 50/60 Hz. Power Consumption: 30 watts (not including projectors).
Weight	10 lbs. Dimensions: 8.3 × 8.85 × 3.25 inches.
Special features	Posi-trak locks program to audio track and will automatically synchronize show if tape error occurs.
Other models	Coyote, see p. 128

Manufacturer	Entré Electronics Corp.
Model	Entre 7620
Price	$450
Type	Real-time analog programmer/ dissolve; compatible with any model projector; 500 watts maximum per projector.
Control functions	Knob control for continuously variable duration, 0.2 seconds to infinity; selectable durations, cut to 10 sec/1-second increments; external rotary or slider and internal set-a-rate control, plus built-in timer control and Kodak remote control socket system for live presentations.
Projectors	Two.
Special effects	Titling, pause, sway, and animation programmable.
Power	90 to 130 V, 50/60 Hz.
Inputs/ outputs	Tape recorder in/out.
Weight	2½ lbs. Dimensions: 2 × 3⅛ × 6 inches.
Tape recorder	Can interface with any tape recorder in which a separate channel can be accessed for the dissolve signal (i.e., all AV recorders with external sync channel access or "true" stereo systems and decks).
Accessories	Included: 5-foot extension cord; S-100 stacker, $40; C-200 remote slider, $25.
Other models	Entre 275-10 (Califone 5275 AV recorder with built-in Entre 7610 programmer/dissolve) $210; also 7903, three-projector programmer/dissolve, $575; 7906 six-projector programmer/ dissolve, $825; 2004 4-projector digital dissolve, $995; export models available.

Manufacturer	Eastman Kodak Company
Model	Kodak Ektagraphic Programmable Dissolve Control
Price	$557
Type	Real-time digital programmable dissolve; preprogrammed button controls; may be linked to other

	dissolve controls for larger presentations.
Projectors	Two, four, six, or eight.
Dissolve	Selective duration: cut, 1-, 2-, 4-, and 8-second.
Control method	Manual at dissolve control or remote; programmer built-in; also can accommodate external programmer.
Special effects	Freeze, superimpose, reverse, flash, animate.
Power	110 to 130, or 220 to 225 V, 50/ 60 Hz, 15 watts maximum; voltage switch on rear panel.
Weight	4.2 lbs. Dimensions: 2.4 × 7.9 × 8.8 inches.
Special features	Audio track will automatically move trays to proper position if error occurs in playback. Arion compatible.
Accessories	Kodak remote controls EC-1, EC-2, EC-3, EC-4.

Manufacturer	Gemini Electronics
Model	Gemini 2000
Price	$549
Type	Digital real-time programmer; push-button manual operation; no independent access to projectors unless converted to leisure time through computer card and program disk.
Projectors	Two; other Geminis can be linked to produce multiprojector productions.
Control functions	Twenty-eight programmable dissolves, from hard cut to 30 seconds in 1/10-second increments; alt, fade, hold (freeze), reverse, cycle off, projector forward or reverse, home, flash.
Special effects	Continuously variable animation, superimpose, loop effects for alt, dissolve, reverse dissolve, fade, super, freeze.
Power	AC 115/220 V, 50/60 Hz. Power consumption: 30 watts.
Weight	6 lbs. Dimensions: 3.25 × 12.625 × 8.25 inches.
Notes	Sync-Lock; LED display of all cues; programmable self-timer works with all effects and times; expandable to leisure-time programming with PC interface card and disk; compatible with Apple II computers.

Manufacturer	Arion Corporation
Model	Mate-Trac Two Plus Dissolve; with remote keyboard
Price	Mate-Trac Two Plus, $575; keyboard, $175; both, $695.

Type	Digital real-time dissolve/programmer. Several Two Plus dissolve units will link up to be controlled by single keyboard for programming; no keyboard required for playback.
Projectors	Two projectors controlled; any Ektagraphic or Carousel, 500 watts maximum; link up to four Two Plus Dissolves to make eight-projector presentations.
Control functions	Seven dissolve rates plus cut, freeze, reverse, flash, home, program stop, projectors on/off, etc.
Special effects	Superimposition, loop, build, wipe, blink.
Power	120 V, 60 Hz.
Inputs/ outputs	¼-inch phone in/out jacks; compatible with most recorders.
Weight	4.2 lbs. Dimensions: 2.4 × 7.9 × 8.8 inches.
Tape recorder	Will function with most AV tape recorders.
Special features	Mate-Trac keeps projectors in sync.
Other models	See Leisure-Time Programmers.

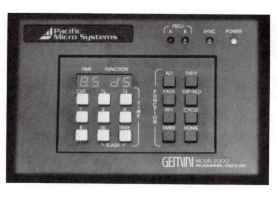

FIGURE 12–14
Gemini 2000 real-time programmer and interface card.

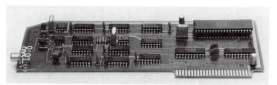

LEISURE-TIME (MEMORY) PROGRAMMERS: $600 TO $3,000

Manufacturer	Cornerstone Associates
Model	Clear Light Micro Diamond Memory Programmer
Price	$599
Type	Real-time digital programmer with memory assist for the more complicated sequences; Time Division Multiplex Signal; independent projector control; built-in programmer/playback for two projectors; can program and play back three to six projectors *with addition of Micro Diamond Dissolve units*. Compatible only with other Clear Light modules.
Memory	Simple memory-assisted real-time hybrid programmer; memory storage capacity 127 cues; keyboard built-in.
Projectors	Two or three; up to six projectors may be programmed by linking additional dissolve units.
Control functions	Controls twenty-eight functions with basic model.
Dissolve module	Five dissolve rates: cut, 1-, 2-, 4-, and 8-second; freeze/hold, standby/home, auxiliary, loop.
Power	120/220 V, 50/60 Hz; switchable.
Weight	4½ lbs. Dimensions: 2½ × 8½ × 10 inches.

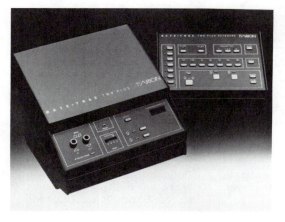

FIGURE 12–15
Arion Mate-Trac Two Plus.

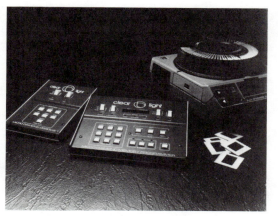

FIGURE 12–16
Clear Light Memory Programmer/ Dissolve.

**FIGURE 12–17
AVL Coyote.**

**FIGURE 12–18
Multivision's Composer 301 and Performer 302.**

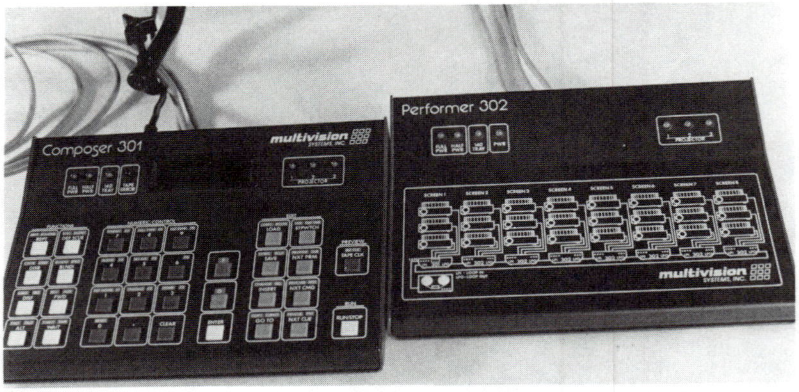

Special features	Programs up to three screen areas; has built-in dissolve for screen 2, uses Micro Diamond Dissolve for screens 1 and 3. Cycle Sentry automatically resyncs projectors in event of power failure or tray jam.
Other models	Optional companion module, Micro Diamond Dissolve, $399. For more sophisticated programming, Star Sentry Series Performer 2 with remote keyboard, $795; Star Sentry Memory Programmer 3, $1,295; Superstar AMPL Programming Software.
Manufacturer	AVL (Audio Visual Laboratories)
Model	Coyote
Price	$995
Type	Memory programmer plus three-projector dissolver; built-in keyboard features tactile response points instead of keys; alphanumeric display window shows cues and commands being entered.

Memory	Up to nine hundred cues; ten to twenty cues per second.
Projectors	Three or two projectors controlled; 500 watts maximum; building block for larger systems.
Control functions	Dissolve rates: 1 to 37 seconds; cut, freeze, smooth, blink, add, delete, reverse. Repeat X enables series of cues to be repeated unlimited times; wait X, automatic insertion of the proper timing between action commands for precise synchronization with audio.
Special effects	Superimpose, ripple, animate, control intensity of dissolves.
Sequencing	In sequence 3 mode, all three projectors are accessed in ABC order; in sequence 2 mode, only left and right (A, C) are accessed. Projector B can be assigned independently with a command and projector B designation.
Power	AC 115/220 V, 50/60 Hz. Use 115/230 V switch.
Inputs/ outputs	RCA play-in jack for all ingoing data; record-out jack for all outgoing data; remote-out jack to advance and reverse Coyote from a remote location.
Weight	5 lbs. Dimensions: 3.25 × 12.625 × 8.25 inches.
Tape recorder	Will function with tape recorders that have separate cue track.
Special features	Posi-trak locks program to audio track and will automatically resync show if tape error occurs.
Other models	AVL Genesis, a computer programmer.

Manufacturer	Multivision Systems, Inc.
Model	Composer 301
Price	$1,595
Type	Leisure-time digital programmer/dissolve; keyboard with alphanumeric display; Composer system is modular and designed to fit a wide range of system sizes; can program up to twenty-four projectors.
Projectors	Three; programmer/dissolve/playback; 500 watts maximum.
Memory	Holds four thousand cues.
Control functions	Two hundred fifty dissolve rates, hard cut to 25 seconds soft cut, freeze, unfreeze, alt, reverse, repeat X, home, blend in/out, wait X, etc.
Special effects	Superimpose, animate, etc.
Inputs/ outputs	Record and playback jacks; daisy-chain and communications loop.

Weight	5 lbs. Dimensions: $3 \times 10 \times 13$ inches.
Tape recorder	Will function with any tape recorder that has sync or line in.
Special features	PosiLock timing for faultless synchronization; CycleGuard projector sensing for absolute tray positioning; SuperCue allows up to nine separate cue lists to run simultaneously; Clock Track: This is the only programmer in this price range that features clock track.
Accessories	IBM-PC compatible interface and program disk permits PC computer programming through Composer 301.
Other models	Conductor 303. Up to seven conductors can be connected to Composer 301 via communications loop, to program up to twenty-four projectors.
Notes	Special Composer PC interface card and program disk allow interface with IBM-PC compatibles.

FIGURE 12–19
Arion Mate-Trac 828 and the CAMI interface card and software.

Manufacturer	Arion Corporation
Model	Mate-Trac 828
Price	$2,795
Type	Digital leisure-time projector programmer and playback; with built-in four-projector dissolve, and 8k memory
Projectors	Operates one, two, three, or four projectors, expandable to sixteen with additional Arion, Kodak, or 3M dissolve controls; 500 watts maximum per projector.
Control functions	Sixty-four dissolve rates from hard cut to 99 seconds; cut, freeze, tray forward and reverse, flash, loop, repeat, wait, etc.
Special effects	Unlimited.
Power	110/220 V switchable, 60/60 Hz; autosensing.
Weight	Dimensions: $2.9 \times 13.9 \times 1.8$ inches.
Tape recorder	Interfaces with any tape recorder in which one track is available for cue signal.
Playback	Play back through 828 or take along a lightweight Two Plus or Four Plus for playback on the road.
Special features	Mate-Trac keeps projectors in sync with tape; built-in battery backup to protect memory in event of power interruption; built-in projector outlets; editing

capabilities with change, add, delete, and help keys to guide operator through each program entry.

Note	IBM-PC compatible with CAMI circuit board and disk.

PLAYBACK-ONLY MODULES

Manufacturer	AVL (Audio Visual Laboratories)
Model	Dove X2
Price	$1,645
Type	Computerized dissolve playback module. For three-projector presentations programmed on AVL equipment; incorporates AVL Posi-trak and Cycle-trak to ensure constant synchronization; plays back Procall language X-1 and all other Procall language versions including Show Pro.

FIGURE 12–20
AVL Traveler.

Manufacturer	AVL (Audio Visual Laboratories)
Model	Pro-Traveler X2
Price	$2,695
Type	Digital dissolve/tape playback unit for shows programmed on AVL equipment. Controls two to three projectors; a compact, portable system with speakers; logic-controlled front-load cassette mechanism; LED power meters; slide control for bass to treble; 30 watts RMS per channel.
Compatibility	Philips format, stereo, Teac 133 compatible.
Special features	Posi-trak, built-in PA system; auto selectable function for either beginning of tape or counter zero; stereo/mono switch; shipping/carrying case.

Manufacturer	Arion Corporation
Model	Mate-Trac Express Four
Price	$2,195
Type	Four-projector presentation system with integrated stereo sound. Built-in dissolve control; one touch activates projectors and stereo; expandable to sixteen-projector presentations with additional Four Plus, Two Plus, 3M, or Kodak dissolve controls.

FIGURE 12–21
Arion Mate-Trac Express Four.

PROGRAMMABLE COMPUTERS

Manufacturer	Cornerstone Associates
Model	Clear Light Superstar AMPL/M Programming Software and Interface Card
Price	$1,395
Type	Runs on any Apple II, II+, or II/e computer or equivalent (needed to create programming system). Integrates with other Cornerstone Clear Light components (see "Accessories") to complete a system capable of controlling from 2 to 30 projectors.
Control functions	Includes AMPL/M Applesoft BASIC, DOS 3.3. AMPL/M allows up to one hundred cues/second from memory; type-in script to appear alongside cues; up to four separate programs (time lines or tasks) running independently and concurrently to simplify multi-image programming; comments anywhere in the program; run-time variables; conditional program branching; clock track synchronization during programming; extensive disk and file backup function; word-processing type interactive editing.
Accessories	System components allow simple or more complex systems to be built. Components include: Star-3 Dissolve ($995), Star Sentry Dissolve 3 ($1,395), Star Sentry Memory Programmer 3 ($1,295), Star Sentry Series Controller ($495), Star Universal Interface Card ($1,495).
Other Models	Superstar AMPL/15 programming software and interface card ($995), interfaces with components to run 2 to 15 projectors; Superstar AMPL/X software and interface card ($1,995).

Manufacturer	AVL (Audio Visual Laboratories)
Model	Genesis
Price	$4,095
Type	Sixteen-bit multi-image leisure-time programming computer for up to thirty projectors. Flexibility and ease of operation reduce programming time. Compatible with existing AVL programs.
Projectors	Two to thirty projectors controlled; expandable to 120 projectors.

Control functions	Keyboard contains eighty-four keys, including ten function keys and complete numeric key-pad; five thousand cues; MS-DOS operating system; 640K Dynamic RAM; Dual 5¼-inch floppy disk drives; Procall GX language allows flexible formatting.
Notes	Posi-trak allows show to start at any point. AVL Clock-trak allows time syncing of cues to audio track; reads and generates SMPTE time code (NTSC SMPTE) for video and slide sync; Dove X2 three-projector playback units playback Procall X and all previous Procall versions including Show Pro.
Other models	AVL Genesis portable, $4,395.

FIGURE 12–22
Clear Light Superstar Computer.

FIGURE 12–23
AVL Genesis Computer System.

INEXPENSIVE MIXERS

Manufacturer	Radio Shack
Model	Realistic Stereo Mixer 32-1100A. (See Figure 12–25.)
Price	$69.95
Type	Stereo audio mixer.
Application	For home studio, semiprofessional applications. Cue function permits individual monitoring of each source via headphones.
Input channels	Stereo mic; two-stereo phono for turntable or changer; high-level input for tape deck or other source.
Outputs	Mono/stereo mode switch permits mono to both output channels; tape recorder output connections.
Equalization	Not required (according to literature received).
Power	Four 1.5 V AC cells (6 V DC) or AC adapter.
Metering	Dual VU meters to monitor output levels.
Weight	1.8Kg

FIGURE 12–24
Radio Shack Realistic Mixer 32-1100A.

Manufacturer	Radio Shack
Model	Realistic Stereo Mixer 32-1200B
Price	$119.95
Type	Home studio or semi-professional; mobile; portable.
Input channels	Three mic in; two phono in; one tape in.
Metering	Dual VU meters.
Power	AC 120 V, 60 Hz for US and Canada.

Manufacturer	Numark Electronics Corporation
Model	Numark DM500
Price	$124.95

Type   Stereo audio or audio/video mixer.

Input channels   Two phono, two line, one mic; for magnetic cartridges, with stereo input level slide controls.

Input levels   Phono: 2.5 mV; line: 150 mV; mic: 0.5 mV.

Equalization   RIAA for phone inputs.

Outputs   Multitrack outputs: stereo master outputs (L & R); tape outputs (L & R).

Connectors   RCA phono jacks; mic ¼-inch phono jack.

Power   120 V AC, 5 watts. Weight: 6 lbs.

Manufacturer   Numark Electronics Corporation

Model   Numark DM1550

Price $299.95

Type   Stereo audio studio mixer, with six-channel stereo equalizer.

Application   Audio or audio/video.

Input channels   Two phono, three line, one mic.

Input levels   Phono: 1.20 mV; line: 70 mV; mic: 0.5 mV.

Equalization   Built-in six-band stereo with +/−15 dB; 40 Hz, 125 Hz, 400 Hz, 1,250 Hz, 4 kHz, 125 kHz. Equalizer can be deleted from the mixer by switching the equalizer defeat switch to defeat position.

Outputs   Multi-track; two master, two line.

Metering   Two VU meters.

Connectors   RCA phono jacks; mic ¼-inch phono jack.

Power   120 V AC, 8 watts.

Other models   Numark DM1900 mixer/preamp/equalizer.

FIGURE 12–25
Numark DM1550.

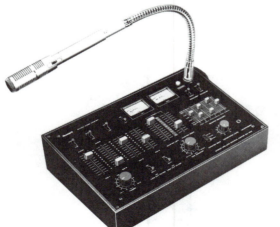

Manufacturer   Fostex Corporation of America

Model   X-30 Multitracker

Price $499

Type   Four-track cassette tape deck with built-in mixer; operates on AC; use a regular tape deck to record in stereo; overdub, ping-pong tracks, mix down to stereo or mono; monomix section has gain and pan controls for each track so that you can hear what you are doing; Dolby C.

Inputs/outputs   Stereo line in, mic in; line out, tape out, headphones out.

Equalization   Independent bass and treble tone controls for each main channel.

Record track   Four tracks, one direction.

Recording tape   Compact cassette, C-60 or C-90 IEC Type II for use at high bias level and 70-microsecond EQ.

Metering   Two linear slide faders for the main level controls with LED bar graph indicators.

Weight   6.4 lbs. with battery pack.

Manufacturer   Tascam/Teac

Model   Ministudio

Price $595

Type   Four-channel multi-track compact cassette recorder for field or studio; battery operated with optional AC adapter; built-in mixer; for use with standard format (1⅞ ips) cassettes; tracks can be "bounced" (combined), allowing for up to ten different parts without rerecording any one part more than once.

Inputs/outputs   Four input channels can be assigned to any track; four independent tape-out jacks, including stereo headphone to hear exactly what you are doing during recording and overdubbing.

Input levels   Mic/line input: −60/−10 dB V; switchable dbx noise reduction; input channel mute (off) switch lets you bring channels into mix without having to change any control settings.

Equalization   Each channel has two-band EQ with center defeat detents.

Metering   Four VU meters provide visual monitoring of any input, tape, or program bus signals.

Power   Runs on batteries: SUM-2, C size, R14 or equiv.; PS-PI AC/DC adapter available.

Audio   Frequency response: 40 Hz to 12.5 kHz.
Signal-to-noise ratio: 85 dB (weighted with dbx).

	Wow and flutter: 0.05%, NAB weighted.		
Weight	7.7 lbs. with batteries. Dimen-	Other models	sions: 13 × 9³⁄₁₆ × 2¾ inches. 246 Portastudio has two tape speeds, approx. $1,300.

Appendix A: Sample Needs Assessment Questionnaire

The purpose of the attached Questionnaire is to help us better understand the scope of your project. Please answer as completely as you can at this point in your planning. It will help us to work together for a product that is accurate, valid, effective, and appropriate to your needs and the needs of your audience.

1. What is the subject of your project?
   _____
   _____

2. What is the primary function of the materials?
   _____ to train personnel on specific procedures
   _____ to promote a product
   _____ to present information to a conference or seminar
   _____ to document a particular case, procedure or finding
   _____ to provide support of a lecture/demonstration
   _____ to replace a lecture/demonstration as the primary source of information
   _____ to educate patients
   _____ Other (specify) _____

3. Who is the primary audience for this material?
   _____ Sales personnel (specify) _____
   _____ Staff employees (specify) _____
   _____ General public
   _____ Organization members
   _____ Health professionals
   _____ Conference delegates
   _____ Other (specify) _____

4. In what setting will the material be used?
   _____ by a small group in an informal setting
   _____ by a speaker in an auditorium
   _____ large group presentations (no speaker)
   _____ permanent installation (i.e., museum)
   _____ by individuals at a trade show
   _____ Other (specify) _____

5. Which of these are major goals of the materials?
   _____ to promote a product
   _____ to provide learners with information
   _____ to teach techniques or skills
   _____ to motivate or stimulate
   _____ Other (specify) _____

6. Does the intended audience have any special characteristics: i.e., unfamiliarity with this material, inadequate background in this area, language differences, etc.?
   _____
   _____

7. Has similar material been produced elsewhere? Yes_____ No_____
   In what form _____

Appendix A   Needs Assessment Questionnaire, continued

Needs assessment (cont.)

8. State briefly the content of the material that you intend to produce.
   _____
   _____
   _____

9. How will this material fit in with your organization's overall goals?
   _____
   _____

10. What resources (or equipment) are available for this project?
    _____
    _____

11. How much money do you expect to commit for the development of the material?
    $_____.   Do you see this as total funding, or (?)_____
    _____

12. What personnel support do you expect to provide (time per week and type of
    personnel). _____
    _____

13. What (if any is needed) support materials do you expect to provide?
    (Space, specialized equipment, etc.)
    _____
    _____

14. Do you have a particular medium? Yes____ No____   IF YES, which:
    ____ Videotape   Running time _____
    ____ Slide/Sound   ____ projectors   Run. time ____
    ____ Videotape from Slide/Sound production
    ____ Other (specify)_____

15. Briefly explain why you have chosen this medium.
    _____
    _____

16. How do you plan to measure the effectiveness of this material?
    _____
    _____

17. When would you like to begin producing the material? _____

18. By what date would you like the project completed? _____

Signature _____   Date _____

Title _____   Company _____

Appendix B: Sample Proposal Form

```
                  PROJECT PROPOSAL (First Draft)

Name_____ Class_____ Date_____
STATEMENT OF PURPOSE:_____
_____
_____
_____

RATIONALE:_____
_____
_____

AUDIENCE (Specific Characteristics):_____
_____

OBJECTIVES (Desired Outcomes):_____
_____
_____
_____

PROJECT OUTLINE:_____
_____
_____
_____
_____

PRODUCTION DESIGN:_____
_____
_____
_____
_____

EVALUATION (Basis for Measurement):_____
_____
_____
_____

RESEARCH SOURCES, RESOURCES:_____
_____
_____
_____

MATERIALS & COSTS:_____
_____
_____
_____

PRODUCTION SCHEDULE:_____
_____
_____
_____
            (Use Back of Paper for Additional Information)
```

Designed by Phiz Mezey

Appendix C: Standard Production Agreement: AMI

THE ASSOCIATION FOR MULTI-IMAGE
STANDARD PRODUCTION AGREEMENT

TO: [CLIENT'S NAME]

               [CLIENT'S ADDRESS]

FOR: Audiovisual Production Software/Hardware As Below —

DATE: [DAY/MONTH/YEAR]

REF: [IF ANY]

JOB NO: [IF ANY]

COPIES: [IF ANY]

The following will constitute the overall terms by which **[NAME OF SHOW]** will be produced for **[CLIENT'S NAME]** by **[PRODUCER'S NAME]**.

1.) TITLE & SUBJECT:

    A.)   **[NAME OF SHOW]**: _____

    B.)   **[DESCRIPTION OF SHOW & SUBJECTS COVERED]**: _____

_____

(NOTE: IF YOU INTEND A LENGTHY DESCRIPTION OF THE SHOW(S) AND/OR PRODUCTION SERVICE(S) TO BE RENDERED, THESE SHOULD BE WRITTEN IN THE FORM OF A PROPOSAL, IN WHICH CASE DESCRIPTION OF SHOW CAN READ "PER ATTACHED PROPOSAL.")

2.) FORMAT:

    A.)   **[LENGTH OF SHOW]**: _____

    B.)   **[NUMBER OF SCREENS]**: _____

    C.)   **[SCREEN ARRANGEMENT/LAYOUT]**: _____

    D.)   **[NUMBER/TYPE OF PROJECTORS]**: _____

    E.)   **[AUDIO CONFIGURATION]**: _____

    F.)   **[THEATRICAL/SPECIAL STAGING EFFECTS]**: _____

_____

    G.)   **[SPECIAL OR "LIVE" TALENT]**: _____

    H.)   **[OTHER]**: _____

3.) ACCESS TO INFORMATION/VISUALS:

    A.) You will supply or cause to be supplied to us all the information, research materials, advisory personnel, visual materials of an historical nature, access to appropriate people, locations **[LIST ANY OTHERS]** within the framework of this project at no cost to us and with no copyright risk to us.

    B.) As currently contemplated we will require you to supply to us the following:

[LIST ALL MATERIALS REQUIRED ALONG WITH DATES MATERIALS ARE NEEDED FOR PRODUCTION.]

©Association for Multi-Image

Appendix C   Standard Production Agreement: AMI, continued

4.) COPYRIGHTS:

[AMI DOES NOT SANCTION THE USE OF COPYRIGHTED MATERIALS WITHOUT OBTAINING A LICENSE FROM THE OWNER OF THE COPYRIGHT. HOWEVER, IN CASES WHERE THE CLIENT INSISTS UPON USING SUCH MATERIALS, THE FOLLOWING CLAUSE (A) MAY LIMIT PRODUCER LIABILITY.]

A.) Should the use of other materials, such as art work, photographs, music, or others be required, and if such are protected by copyright, trademark, or otherwise protected, it is our understanding that we are not responsible in any way as a result of such use, and that you hereby agree to indemnify and save us harmless in the event any claims or suits are made on such account, including reasonable attorney's fees.

B.) **[WE]** own the copyright to the finished presentation, and grant **[YOU]** the license to use this show intact for screening to **[ANY]** audiences, **[EXCEPT:** _____] for a period of **[NUMBER]** years from signing of this Agreement.

C.) At no time can any components of this show be reproduced or utilized in any manner without prior written consent of **[PRODUCER'S NAME]**, and it is understood that all rights to any and all materials so produced belong to **[PRODUCER'S NAME]**.

D.) No rights are granted until final payment is made.

E.) If **[CLIENT'S NAME]** contemplates the use of any artwork or photographs produced by **[PRODUCER'S NAME]** in print promotion or advertising (including annual reports), additional use fees will be paid to **[PRODUCER'S NAME]** per the following schedule:

- Advertising (per picture, per ad):
Full page:	$[AMOUNT]
1/2 page:	$[AMOUNT]
1/3 page or less:	$[AMOUNT]

- Brochures/Posters (per picture, per use):
Cover:	$[AMOUNT]
Full page (poster):	$[AMOUNT]
1/2 page (poster):	$[AMOUNT]
1/3 page (poster) or less:	$[AMOUNT]

- Annual Report (per picture, per use):
Cover:	$[AMOUNT]
Full page:	$[AMOUNT]
1/2 page:	$[AMOUNT]
1/3 page or less:	$[AMOUNT]

- **[OTHERS]**:
[LIST]	$[AMOUNT]

F.) If additional use of elements of this show (including audio, graphics, photography, or **[OTHER]**) produced by **[PRODUCER'S NAME]** in other audiovisual, motion picture, television, or **[OTHER]** productions is contemplated, it is understood that such use requires the written approval of **[PRODUCER'S NAME]** and additional fees which will be separately negotiated.

5.) BUDGET:

A.) There are three parts to this presentation:
- Software (slides, audio tape and program cues).
- Hardware (equipment necessary to show software).
- Staging (the showing of the software) which will be covered by a separate Agreement.

B.) The software budget for this presentation is not to exceed **[$AMOUNT]** not including any additions, changes, or post-production work that may be required.

Appendix C   Standard Production Agreement: AMI, continued

(NOTE: A BUDGET BREAKDOWN CAN BE INCLUDED AT YOUR DISCRETION AS FOLLOWS):

C.)   The software budgetary allocations are:

- Creative/supervision: $[AMOUNT]
- Script: $[AMOUNT]
- Design/visual choreography: $[AMOUNT]
- Soundtrack preparation: $[AMOUNT]
- Original photography/graphics: $[AMOUNT]
- Art preparation/typography: $[AMOUNT]
- Rephotography/masking: $[AMOUNT]
- Editing of visuals: $[AMOUNT]
- Assembly of show/mounting & trays: $[AMOUNT]
- Programming: $[AMOUNT]
- Administrative: $[AMOUNT]
- [OTHER]. $[AMOUNT]
- Contingency [AMOUNT %]: $[AMOUNT]

D.)   The hardware budget for this presentation is [$AMOUNT] including: [LIST ALL HARD-WARE AND PURCHASE AMOUNT AND/OR RENTAL PERIOD AND RATES].

E.)   You recognize that time is of the essence with regard to payment as set forth in the [PRO-DUCTION]/Payment Schedule (below). In the event payment is not made within five days of the dates specified in the Production Schedule, [PRODUCER'S NAME] may, at their discretion, stop work on this project. Additional costs of production incurred by such delays will be the responsibility of [CLIENT'S NAME] and will be payable within 15 days of presentation of invoice(s).

6.) PAYMENT SCHEDULE:

- [CLIENT'S NAME] will pay on signing of this Agreement 1/3 of the total software price ([$AMOUNT]), and 1/2 of the hardware price ([$AMOUNT]).
- 1/3 of the total software price on approval of soundtrack ([$AMOUNT]).
- Final 1/3 of total software price in cash or certified check on final approval of software prior to release of software to you ([$AMOUNT]).
- Final 1/2 of hardware payment ([$AMOUNT]) and all hardware shipping costs within 15 days of delivery.

7.) TRAVEL EXPENSES:

A.)   [CLIENT'S NAME] shall prepay all transportation, travel, and hotel expenses for all [PRO-DUCER'S NAME] personnel required, the number of which will be supplied by us prior to departure.

B.)   These travel costs are currently contemplated to include [LIST ALL PERSONNEL WHO WILL WORK ON LOCATION] and a [CLIENT'S NAME] representative accomplishing work at the locations outlined below.

C.)   Any other costs of travel shall be paid within ten (10) days of billing.

8.) LOCATIONS AND DATES CONTEMPLATED:

   [LIST ALL LOCATIONS AND PRODUCTION DATES FOR EACH LOCATION.]

(NOTE: A FULL PRODUCTION SCHEDULE CAN BE INSERTED HERE IF DEEMED NECESSARY.)

9.) ADDITIONS:

Any and all further services or materials requested by you over and above those set forth in this Agreement [PROPOSAL] will be billed separately and paid within 15 days of presentation of invoice(s).

Appendix C   Standard Production Agreement: AMI, continued

10.) APPROVALS:

A.)   You designate the following people who may give approval where called for herein:

_____   _____
[NAME]   [NAME]

_____   _____
[TITLE OF PERSON]   [TITLE OF PERSON]

B.)   Written approvals are needed for script, soundtrack, [OTHER] and final approval of the show per the following schedule (we will provide appropriate approval forms as needed).

(NOTE: SEE ATTACHED APPROVAL FORM.)

- We submit first draft of script: [DATE]
- You comment on revisions necessary for acceptance by: [DATE]
- We submit final script for final approval: [DATE]
- You give final approval of script by: [DATE]
- We submit soundtrack for approval: [DATE]
- You approve soundtrack by: [DATE]
- We submit [OTHER] for approval: [DATE]
- You approve [OTHER] by: [DATE]
- We submit final show for final approval at our studios   [DATE]
  [OR LIST OTHER LOCATION]:

(NOTE: THE ABOVE APPROVAL SCHEDULE CAN BE MADE MORE DETAILED IF DEEMED NECESSARY — HOWEVER IT IS RECOMMENDED THAT IT BE KEPT AS SIMPLE AS POSSIBLE.)

C.)   You realize that a delay on approvals may seriously jeopardize the project. Therefore, each day of delay in approval of the script and soundtrack will result in extra charges of [$AMOUNT] per day, payable immediately.

D.)   Should the delay in approval of script and soundtrack be more than [NUMBER] days, then the Agreement is terminated and the total sums paid by you shall be considered liquidated damages.

E.)   If final approval of [NAME OF SHOW] is delayed more than [NUMBER] days, then the Agreement is terminated and you are liable for and will pay the balance due for the total production budget upon presentation of invoice.

11.) LIABILITIES:

A.)   We will not be liable for delays in production caused by acts of force majeure or the actions or performance of any products or of any unions, guilds, companies, agencies/agents, talent, or of any other causes that are beyond our control.

B.)   In any event we shall only be liable for our sole gross negligence with regard to injury to any person or property in the performance of this Agreement.

12.) POSTPONEMENTS:

In the event of postponements caused or created by you, you will be responsible and liable for any additional costs, expenses, or charges incurred as a result of such postponements. If postponement is more than [NUMBER] days, we have the right to treat this Agreement as cancelled.

13.) CANCELLATIONS:

In the event of cancellation caused or created by you within [NUMBER] days of signing of this Agreement, you shall be responsible for and will pay 50% of the total amount agreed upon, less whatever amount has been paid. In the event of cancellation more than [SAME NUMBER] days after the signing of this Agreement, you shall be responsible for and will pay the entire amount agreed upon herein as though the entire Agreement had been completed, less any amounts paid to date.

Appendix C   Standard Production Agreement: AMI, continued

14.) CREDITS:

You grant us the right to include production credits in the show as is normal in motion picture production and approved within the guidelines of the Association for Multi-Image.

15.) DEMONSTRATIONS AND COMPETITIONS:

You grant us the right to screen [NAME OF SHOW] to prospective customers of [PRODUCER'S NAME] as a demonstration of our techniques and capabilities, as well as to enter and screen the show in various multi-image or film competitions and festivals, with the exception of the following portions:

[LIST PORTIONS THAT INVOLVE INFORMATION THAT IS CONSIDERED CONFIDENTIAL OR PROPRIETARY BY THE CLIENT.]

16.) GENERAL TERMS:

A.) The waiver by either party or any breach of this Agreement shall not prevent the subsequent enforcement of the Agreement and shall not be deemed to be a waiver of any subsequent breach.

B.) The terms and conditions of this Agreement constitute the entire agreement between [PRODUCER'S NAME] and [CLIENT'S NAME] and replace any previous communications or agreements whether oral or in writing.

C.) If any provision contained in this Agreement is or becomes unenforceable or invalid it shall nevertheless not make the Agreement as a whole unenforceable or invalid and shall be changed to give effect as far as possible in the original provision.

D.) No variation, waiver or modification of any of the terms of this Agreement shall be valid unless supported by a written memorandum signed by both [PRODUCER'S NAME] and [CLIENT'S NAME].

E.) Any notice required to be given hereunder shall be deemed to be duly serviced if sent by any commercial courier or mail service that provides proof of delivery, addressed to the last known registered office or principal place of business of either of the parties hereto. Every notice shall be deemed to have been delivered at the address to which it was sent.

F.) The construction, validity, and performance of this Agreement shall be governed by the laws of [NAME OF STATE].

17.) ARBITRATION:

Any and all disputes arising out of this Agreement, its performance or validity, shall be arbitrated in [CITY, STATE] pursuant to the rules of the American Arbitration Association, and the laws of [NAME OF STATE]. Judgment in the award may be entered in the highest Federal or State Court having jurisdiction.

18.) NOTICE OF TIME LIMITATION:

If not signed by both parties and delivered to us within [NUMBER] days of the issue date, this Agreement becomes null and void.

[PRODUCER'S NAME]

By: _____
[TITLE OF PERSON SIGNING]

Date: _____
[CLIENT'S NAME]

By: _____
[TITLE OF PERSON SIGNING]

Date: _____

Appendix D: Script for "SAFE in the City"

Script Sheet

Visual Concepts

Titles, 6 slides

Script/Audio

(Music Up,

and Under ...)

NARRATOR: San Francisco is a beautiful city.

We pride ourselves in our friendliness,

our individuality, our outlook,

and value the privacy of our homes.

So when this vision of ourselves and our community is

disrupted -- when a burglar breaks into our homes,

or a neighbor is mugged --

we react with pain and outrage.

Something should be done about it!

Well, something is being done.

All over the city people are organizing --

on their blocks, in their homes --

to prevent breakins,

to keep violence off their streets.

They are forming Neighborhood Alert groups.

They are making their homes SAFE.

They are showing their concern for each other.

More than twelve hundred Block Clubs in San Francisco

are now participating in a city-wide neighborhood

alert program, and the program is working!

(Music change pace, and under)

Who are these people?

Why are they succeeding?

Appendix D   Script for "SAFE in the City," continued

| Date _____ | **Script Sheet** | Page __2__ of __5__ |
| Title _SAFE In The City_ | Writer _P. Mezey_ | Draft No. 1·2·3·Final |

Visual Concepts	Script /Audio
	Through SAFE, <u>S</u>afety <u>A</u>wareness <u>for</u> <u>E</u>veryone, a community-based organization working closely with the police department, people in the neighborhoods are getting together and drawing up their own master plan -- with the help of the SAFE staff -- to keep their streets and homes secure from burglary, vandalism, and crimes of violence. In one neighborhood, following a joint effort by SAFE and the community, crime dropped 30%. (Music change, and under) JACKIE: When one of our neighbors, who was pregnant, got mugged, we called SAFE and they helped us organize a meeting in one of our homes. We wanted to know what we could do to prevent this and other neighborhood crimes from happening again. About 15 neighbors came to our first meeting. We discussed home security, personal security, and other crime prevention measures. We met three times with the representative from SAFE. A police officer was also invited to talk with us. This week we had a block party and garage sale. I feel a lot safer now that I know my neighbors care. We are watching out for each other. (Music change pace, under)

Appendix D   Script for "SAFE in the City," continued

Date _____	**Script Sheet**	Page __3__ of __5__
Title _SAFE In The City_	Writer _P. Mezey_	Draft No. 1·2·3·Final

Visual Concepts	Script/Audio
	SAFE COORDINATOR: SAFE, <u>Safety Awareness for Everyone</u>, started as a joint venture of the police department and the citizens of San Francisco in 1976. The original intention was to enhance the relationship between citizens and police ... to encourage citizens to report crimes... and to teach them crime prevention techniques. When the original funding was expanded by community development monies, the project became city-wide.

SAFE COORDINATOR: SAFE, <u>Safety Awareness for
Everyone</u>, started as a joint venture of the police
department and the citizens of San Francisco in 1976.
The original intention was to enhance the
relationship between citizens and police ...
to encourage citizens to report crimes...
and to teach them crime prevention techniques. When
the original funding was expanded by community
development monies, the project became city-wide.

In 1980, with federal funds expended, concerned
citizens got together and were determined they were
not going to let this program die, so with volunteers
and staff we quickly formulated the beginning of a
non-profit structure, soon to be known as San
Francisco SAFE, Inc.

Block Club organizing is our major focus. It's
called Neighborhood Watch. We also run three other
safety programs: for our elder citizens, for school
children, and for small businesses.

Our Neighborhood Watch program helps people organize
their own block clubs to discuss issues and concerns
that may be unique to their street. It is through
these meetings that they can discover the resources

Appendix D   Script for "SAFE in the City," continued

Date _____	**Script Sheet**	Page __4__ of __5__
Title _SAFE In The City_	Writer __P. Mezey__	Draft No. 1·2·3·Final

Visual Concepts	Script/Audio
	that are within their own block, as well as outside resources that are available to them.
	At these meetings our crime specialists demonstrate techniques that will insure Personal Security; introduce Identification Tools with which neighbors can engrave or photograph their personal property; and survey and make recommendations for the improvement of Home Security.
	(Music change pace, under)
	We believe that children as well as adults have the basic human right to be safe. Along with this right goes the responsibility for making intelligent choices, and taking the necessary steps to insure and preserve personal safety and well being. Through our Children's Safety Program, children are encouraged to problem solve and think critically, and to recognize and value their own intuition and survival instincts.
	(Music change slightly, under)
	We also have a Senior Safety Program.
	Our older citizens are one of our most valuable resources. Our trained staff makes community presentations in churches, neighborhood centers, and homes. We show our older citizens ways in which they

Appendix D Script for "SAFE in the City," continued

Date _____	**Script Sheet**	Page __5__ of __5__
Title _SAFE In The City_	Writer _P. Mezey_	Draft No. 1·2·3·Final

Visual Concepts   **Script/Audio**

can insure their personal safety -- on the street and
in their homes.

(Music change slightly, and under)

In the area of Merchant Security, our staff, working
with the San Francisco Police Department, conducts
seminars on crime prevention, alarm systems,
shop-lifting and burglary. We also provide
information on security products, evaluation
procedures and earthquake preparedness.

(New music up, and under)

NARRATOR: In the past four years, San Francisco SAFE
has done an outstanding job in making citizens aware of
the need for alertness and cooperation.
There are now 1200 Block Clubs in SAFE.
You can start your own block club today by calling
SAFE. Phone 673-SAFE, and a staff member will
discuss your problem and help you set up your first
neighborhood meeting. Our police count on the people
of the neighborhoods --the residents and merchants --
for help in the never-ending battle against crime.

San Francisco is a beautiful city.
By caring, by working together,
WE can build a SAFER city.

Appendix E: Script for "A Gift Among Friends"

<table>
<tr><td>Date _____</td><td colspan="2">**Script Sheet**</td><td>Page <u>1</u> of <u>8</u></td></tr>
<tr><td>Title <u>Gift Among Friends</u></td><td colspan="2">Writer <u>J. Harrison</u></td><td>Draft No. 1·2·3·Final</td></tr>
</table>

Visual Concepts	Script/Audio
	The waiting is the hardest part.
	SFX: PHONE RINGS
	And every phone call makes your heartbeat even faster. (chuckles) They say that's not too good for a guy with a bumticker.
	You wonder if this is the call you've been waiting for.
	FRANK: (Excitedly) Hello! (Then suppressed) Oh, hi. No. Nothing yet.....
	NARRATOR: Frank MacCrae has been living next to a telephone and a beeper for over three months. It's costing him about two thousand a month to live just 10 minutes from Stanford Hospital. The townspeople in Ohio where he comes from took up a collection. Without their help...without a new heart...Frank MacCrae will die within the next six months. He won't even see his oldest child graduate from high school.

Appendix E Script for "A Gift Among Friends," continued

Date _____   **Script Sheet**   Page __2__ of __8__

Title _Gift Among Friends_   Writer __J. Harrison__   Draft No. 1·2·3·Final

Visual Concepts   Script /Audio

There are a lot of other people, like Frank, who
are waiting. George Brody is waiting. And so is
Janet Gerkin.

George is a fisherman who lost his vision in a
chemical explosion. With a corneal transplant he
will see again.

George says being blind isn't so bad. Your
hearing gets a lot sharper. But it's not a
substitute...not really. And the time moves
slowly.

Jane Gerkin has been undergoing dialysis
treatments three times a week. It's been over
two years since her kidneys stopped functioning.
The process is emotionally and physically
wearing. One kidney transplant was unsuccessful.
She's waiting for another, but the right donor
has yet to be found.

Sometimes Janet will admit that all her hopes
make her a little guilty. Because her chance of
a normal life depends on another person's tragedy.

Appendix E   Script for "A Gift Among Friends," continued

Date _____	**Script Sheet**	Page __3__ of __8__
Title _Gift Among Friends_	Writer ___J. Harrison___	Draft No. 1·2·3·Final

Visual Concepts	Script/Audio
	Transplant surgery is possible when people are willing to work together in a time of crisis.
	The donation calls for awareness, understanding and support by those who play the most critical roles.
	The process can begin months or years earlier when the choice to be a donor is made and a card is filled out. Although a donor card is not necessary, it makes the donation process easier.
	There are several things that must be taken care of as soon as possible. First, the family must be informed of the accident.
	The family arrives at the hospital.
	Here in the waiting room the nurse explains the situation. The patient is slipping away.
	It looks hopeless.

Appendix E   Script for "A Gift Among Friends," continued

Date _____	**Script Sheet**	Page __4__ of __8__
Title _Gift Among Friends_	Writer __J. Harrison__	Draft No. 1·2·3·Final

Visual Concepts

Script /Audio

NURSE: You can see the pain in their eyes. The helplessness. The...the wish that they could do something...anything.

NARRATOR: There IS something the family can do. But it's considered only after the hospital has made every effort to save the patient. Only then is the issue of donation raised.

In time of shock and grief the family may not be thinking of donation. So it is usually the staff who must bring it up.

Sometimes it's simply a matter of reminding the family of a commitment made by their loved one at some moment in the past. At other times the issue has to be raised the first time.

NURSE: It's always such a delicate moment. In the beginning I was afraid to ask. Afraid of intruding. I didn't even know HOW to ask. And then the first time I did ask, the family was really thankful that their son could make this incredible gift.

Appendix E   Script for "A Gift Among Friends," continued

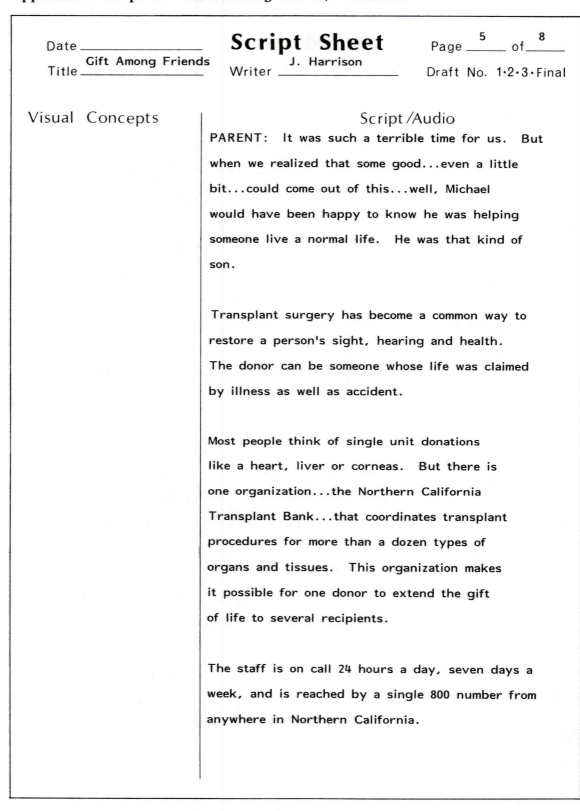

Date _____   **Script Sheet**   Page ⁵____ of ⁸____

Title __Gift Among Friends__   Writer ____J. Harrison____   Draft No. 1·2·3·Final

Visual Concepts   Script/Audio

PARENT: It was such a terrible time for us. But when we realized that some good...even a little bit...could come out of this...well, Michael would have been happy to know he was helping someone live a normal life. He was that kind of son.

Transplant surgery has become a common way to restore a person's sight, hearing and health. The donor can be someone whose life was claimed by illness as well as accident.

Most people think of single unit donations like a heart, liver or corneas. But there is one organization...the Northern California Transplant Bank...that coordinates transplant procedures for more than a dozen types of organs and tissues. This organization makes it possible for one donor to extend the gift of life to several recipients.

The staff is on call 24 hours a day, seven days a week, and is reached by a single 800 number from anywhere in Northern California.

Appendix E   Script for "A Gift Among Friends," continued

Date _____	**Script Sheet**	Page __6__ of __8__
Title _Gift Among Friends_	Writer ___J. Harrison___	Draft No. 1·2·3·Final

Visual Concepts

Script/Audio

For the recipients the news comes quickly. And in the case of Frank MacCrae there isn't a moment to spare.

FRANK: Hello (Excitedly) It is? Right now? Oh my God! Where's my bag?

NARRATOR: While Frank is on his way to the hospital, the surgical teams that attend to the donor and the recipient must be coordinated, especially since they are often in different cities.

A new heart must be transplanted within several hours. Other organs, such a kidneys, can be stored for up to 60 hours before transplantation. Tissue, such as the tiny middle ear bones used to restore hearing, can be kept for up to five years. But the demand is so great that the tissues are used almost immediately after they are processed.

In the days that follow, normal funeral

Appendix E   Script for "A Gift Among Friends," continued

Date _____ **Script Sheet**   Page __7__ of__8__

Title _Gift Among Friends_   Writer ___J. Harrison___   Draft No. 1·2·3·Final

Visual Concepts	Script/Audio
	arrangements are conducted for the donor. There is no sign of the contributions he made. But the family knows and is proud.
	Frank MacCrae, four months after surgery, is rediscovering life. Life the way it used to be.
	Although it's the same world, it somehow looks totally different. Just to be able to walk with the dog and climb the stairs without feeling faint.
	You can find George Brody back on his fishing boat. He still loves watching the gulls...and the freighters as they churn slowly through the Golden Gate.
	And Janet? Janet is still waiting. Two patients received kidney transplants, but Janet wasn't one of them. She didn't match up.
	For every Frank and George who are liberated, there are 10 like Janet who continue to wait.

Appendix E   Script for "A Gift Among Friends," continued

Date _____	**Script Sheet**	Page __8__ of __8__
Title _Gift Among Friends_	Writer ___J. Harrison___	Draft No. 1·2·3·Final

Visual Concepts

Script/Audio

Some will wait for years.

For others, time will simply run out.

The real tragedy is that each day hundreds of

potential donors in California are lost as a

resource. They are lost because those involved

haven't heard about the Transplant Bank and don't

know what to do.

Today, more than ever, it's important for

families to talk ahead of time about donation

to facilitate the process, should the need ever

arise.

Potential donors need to know that they can

choose to donate only what they wish.

To be able to reach out is one of the greatest

gifts. The gift of life is a gift among friends.

Appendix F: Evaluating a Production: MIS

Multi-Image Showcase
PO. Box 622 San Francisco, California 94101 415/826-1744

EVALUATION FORM

SHOW TITLE _____

PRODUCER_____ DATE_____

Score From 1 (Poor) to 10 (Excellent)

☐	**OVERALL SCORE**	How effective was the overall show?
☐	CONCEPT/THEME	How successful is the show in developing a strong central idea?
☐	STRUCTURE/SCRIPT	How well does the show's framework provide a progression toward resolution of the theme?
☐	VISUAL DESIGN	How well do the visual elements work together to create a strong visual style?
☐	IMAGE QUALITY	How would you rate the technical quality of the images?
☐	AUDIO DESIGN	How successful is the selection and arrangement of the audio components (music, narrative and sound effects)?
☐	AUDIO QUALITY	How do you rate the technical quality of the soundtrack, e.g. mixing and clarity?
☐	EDITING	How concise is the final selection and sequencing of the show elements?
☐	DISSOLVE TECHNIQUE	How effective was the use of overlapping ("third") images and dissolve rates and pacing?
☐	IMAGE/SOUND RELATIONSHIP	How effectively do the audio and visual elements synchronize with and support each other?

COMMENTS_____

_____

_____

_____

Bibliography

Beaumont-Craggs, Ray. *Slide-Tape and Dual Projection.* Boston: Focal Press (Butterworth Publishers), 1975.

Bunnin, Brad, and Peter Beren. *Author Law and Strategies: A Legal Guide for the Working Writer.* Berkeley, CA: Nolo Press, 1985.

Burke, Ken, ed. *An Anthology of Multi-Image.* Abington, PA: Association for Multi-Image, 1980.

Duncalf, Brian. *The Focal Guide to Slide-Tape.* Boston: Focal Press (Butterworth Publishers), 1978.

Eastman Kodak Company. *Planning and Producing Slide Programs.* Publication S-30.

Gordon, Roger. *The Art of Multi-Image.* Washington, DC: Association for Educational Communications & Technology, 1978.

International Communications Industries Association (ICIA). *The Equipment Directory of Audio-Visual, Computer, and Video Products.* 34th ed. Fairfax, VA: ICIA (formerly NAVA), 1988.

Kemp, Jerrold E., and Deane K. Dayton. *Planning & Producing Instructional Media.* 5th ed. New York: Harper & Row, 1985.

Kenny, F. Michael, and Raymond F. Schmidt. *Images, Images, Images.* 3d ed. Rochester, NY: Eastman Kodak Company, 1983.

Lewell, John. *Multivision.* Boston: Focal Press (Butterworth Publishers), 1980.

Matrazzo, Donna. *The Corporate Scriptwriting Book.* Portland, OR: Communicom Publishing Co., 1985.

Nisbett, Alec. *The Technique of the Sound Studio.* Boston: Focal Press (Butterworth Publishers), 1979.

Q, Mike and Pat. *The Manual of Slide Duplicating.* Garden City, NY: AMPHOTO, 1978.

Sunier, John. *Slide/Sound and Filmstrip Production.* Boston: Focal Press (Butterworth Publishers), 1981.

Swain, Dwight. *Scripting for Video and Audiovisual Media.* Boston: Focal Press (Butterworth Publishers), 1981.

Young, Jeffrey S. *Inside MacPaint.* Belleview, WA: Microsoft Press, 1985.

Magazines

Association for Multi-Image International (AMI) Newsletter, Tampa, FL.

AV Communications, Media Horizons Inc. New York.

AV Video (formerly *AV Directions*), Montage Publishing Inc., Torrance, CA.

Multi-Image Showcase Newsletter, Box 622, San Francisco, CA.

NCC AMI Newsletter, (Northern California Chapter), 1033 Battery Street, San Francisco, CA.

Photomethods, Lakewood Publications Inc., Minneapolis, MN.

Technical Photography, PTN Publishing Corp. Woodbury, NY.

Index

Numbers in boldface indicate illustrations.